Girl from the Gulches

Mary Ronan at the time of her marriage, 1873

Girl from the Gulches

THE STORY OF MARY RONAN

As told to MARGARET RONAN

Edited by ELLEN BAUMLER

MONTANA HISTORICAL SOCIETY PRESS

Helena

Cover design by Diane Hall, The Art Dept., Helena, Montana
Book design by Arrow Graphics, Missoula, Montana
Typeset in Janson

PRINTED IN CANADA

Generous support from the Charles Redd Center for Western Studies
helped to fund publication of this book.

Distributed by the Globe Pequot Press, 246 Goose Lane,
Guilford, Connecticut 06437, (800) 243-0495

ISBN 978-0-917298-97-4

13 14 15 16 17 18 19 20   10 09 08 07 06 05 04

LIBRARY OF CONGRESS CATALOGING-IN-PUBLICATION DATA

Ronan, Mary, 1852–1940.
  Girl from the gulches: the story of Mary Ronan as told to Margaret
Ronan; edited by Ellen Baumler.
      p. cm.
Rev. ed. of: Frontier woman. c1973.
Includes index.

   1. Ronan, Mary, 1852–1940. 2. Women pioneers—Montana—Biography.
3. Pioneers—Montana—Biography. 4. Frontier and pioneer life—Montana.
5. Indians of North America—Montana—History—19th century.
6. Montana—Social life and customs—19th century. 7. Montana—Biography.
8. California, Southern—Biography. I. Ronan, Margaret, 1883–1935.
II. Baumler, Ellen. III. Ronan, Mary, 1852–1940. Frontier woman. IV. Title.
F731.R575 2003
978.6'02'092—dc21   2003001967
                                                               CIP

Contents

ILLUSTRATIONS

ACKNOWLEDGMENTS

A number of women played significant roles in this project. Vivian A. Paladin (1918–2002), mentor and friend, was the longtime editor of *Montana The Magazine of Western History.* Her lifelong dedication paved the way for all of us women who strive to put Montana's memories within common reach. Martha Kohl, book editor at the Montana Historical Society Press, immediately recognized Mary Ronan's important contribution to the study of women in the West and shared my enthusiasm from the very beginning. Not only that, but she stringently supported this project and convinced others to support it. My daughter, Katie, typed most of the original manuscript. Her work was nearly flawless and her contribution enormous. Mary Clearman Blew and Dee Garceau kindly read the manuscript and offered invaluable comments.

Carly Delsigne and Bergetta Hubbard contributed their editing skills, fine tuning the language and the annotations. Annie Hanshew secured the illustrations. Kitty Herrin and Diane Hall designed the interior and cover, respectively.

Not all assistance came from women, however. I am indebted to Professor Harry Fritz, chair of the University of Montana's Department of History, and to the Charles Redd Center for Western Studies, which helped fund publication of *Girl from the Gulches.*

Finally, I am especially grateful to Mary G. Hayes, Mary Ronan's namesake and great granddaughter, and other members of the Ronan family. Their support of this publication ensures the safekeeping of Mary's grand legacy.

INTRODUCTION

A covered wagon on a dim road, the promise of a long journey, and the wonder of what lay ahead filled the shadowy spaces of Mary Ronan's earliest memories. By the time she was a married woman in her twenties, Mary Sheehan Ronan was a well-seasoned pioneer, having crossed most of the country and retraced her steps back across a third of it. Born Mary Catherine Fitzgibbon Sheehan in 1852 to Irish Catholic immigrants James and Ellen Sheehan, her story is unusual for its range of experience, its feminine perspective, and the distances it spans during an era that witnessed monumental changes in the western United States.

There were three major sequences of western gold rushes in the mid-nineteenth century—to California from 1849 through the 1850s, to Colorado between 1859 and 1862, and finally to Montana from 1862 to 1866. Mary Ronan and her family traveled with the peak waves of immigrants to the goldfields of both Colorado and Montana, caught up by the lure of gold and promises of the West. The "girl from the gulches" grew to young womanhood in the rough-and-tumble western gold camps that formed the backdrop of much of her childhood. Her descriptions of the early Montana gold camps at Virginia City and Helena are perhaps the most detailed and certainly among the best extant.

The lesser-known parts of Mary Ronan's story, however, reach beyond the Montana gold camps to the railroad camp of Corinne, Utah, as the Union Pacific neared completion, and to the ruins of the Spanish mission of San Juan Capistrano in southern California, where the Sheehan family homesteaded in 1869. There, Mary made friends within the Mexican community, learned to speak Spanish, was a guest at the *rancheros* of the wealthy Hispanic-American elite, and received her education from the Catholic Sisters of St. Vincent de Paul in the village of Los Angeles. Once back in Montana as wife of a newspaperman (and later Flathead Indian agent), Mary witnessed firsthand the consequences of westward migration and the iniquities of the government toward Native Americans.

Like thousands of other westward pioneers in the nineteenth century, the Sheehans were ordinary people living through extraordinary times. Mary described the places they pitched their tent, the cabins they made into homes, and the people they met with passion, depth, feeling, and enthusiasm. The exhilaration of a forbidden sled ride, the creaking of the hangman's rope, her father giving the last of their water to his dying mule—these things she remembered with vivid clarity, and they make her reminiscence a joy to read.

Mary's story begins with her first recollections of her mother, Ellen Sheehan, who died when Mary was very young. Her father, James, shouldered the responsibility of single parenthood and on the heels of a second tragedy assumed guardianship of his brother's three orphaned teenagers as well. James's financial struggles and his lack of roots determined the family's nomadic cross-country wanderings, and his itinerant employment kept the family moving and sometimes required months of separation from the children.

The Sheehans' westward trek took them from Kentucky, where Mary was born, to Indiana, Illinois, and Iowa, and then, on the brink of the Civil War, to the plantation of slave-owning relatives at St. Joseph, Missouri. Leaving Mary and her cousins in St. Joseph, James remarried and headed west to the stark mining camps near Denver, Colorado, where he opened a small store in the boomtown of Nevada City. There he and his new wife Anne awaited the arrival of a baby daughter, Kate. James returned to St. Joseph for Mary with the outbreak of the Civil War in 1861. Less than two years after Mary's arrival in Colorado, James took up freighting, and the Sheehans pushed on to Bannack in what would become Montana Territory. Mary remembered the journey as a pleasant one: "I can picture the golden sunsets gliding behind distant mountain peaks and flooding the valleys with magic light. Joyous eager childhood and the rhythm of going, going, going combine to make a backdrop and a theme song for that long trek into the land of gold."

Gold discovered the previous year on Grasshopper Creek brought the first sizable population to the remote Montana wilderness east of the Continental Divide. Although its fame rapidly spread, Bannack was little more than a collection of cabins, shacks, and tents teeming with hopeful miners and camp followers looking to turn a fast profit. The Sheehans arrived in the boisterous gold camp around June 1, 1863, on the eve of the great stampede to Alder Gulch. A week earlier, on May 26, along the alder-choked banks of a clear stream some sixty miles east of Bannack, a party of miners had made a very lucky strike. Word of the discovery soon leaked out, and the stampede to Alder Gulch began, with James taking the first wagonload of freight to the new camp. The Sheehans soon followed the trampled ground in the wake of several hundred miners to the overnight boomtown of Virginia City. To her father's amusement, Mary whittled a stick to scrawl her name in the dirt and stake an imaginary claim. "Even children caught that fever," she recalled, looking back on her family's arrival at Alder Gulch.

In the months following the stampede, Virginia City rose to such significance in the settlement of the frontier that it has been compared to Colonial America's Williamsburg.[1]

Mary's place in this tumultuous frontier settlement was that of a schoolgirl and a keen observer. She knew the road agents hanged by the vigilantes (one of them took meals with her family during the brief period that her stepmother ran a boardinghouse). She attended one of Montana's first schools, run by Thomas Dimsdale, who published an account of the violence in Montana's first book, *The Vigilantes of Montana*. Mary danced with her secessionist-minded classmates at the news of Lincoln's assassination (much to the dismay of her father), and she got close enough to the town's fancy ladies to smell their cigarettes. She helped dress the makeshift altar for the first Catholic Mass in the territory, cleaned gold dust from the miners' sluice boxes, and sold freshly picked wildflowers and "table greens" to boardinghouses until her father forbid the practice.

A major gold strike, this one 120 miles north of Virginia City in July 1864, opened new opportunity for the Sheehans. Placer mining along Alder Gulch had become less profitable by 1865, and like many of their neighbors that year, the Sheehans moved to the new boomtown of Helena along Last Chance Gulch. Helena was bursting with activity and new adventures, but the new camp was also an extension of Virginia City. Much of the population was the same, allowing some friendships to continue despite the transitory nature of mining camp communities. The Sheehans' social life was grounded in the growing Democratic Irish community and the Catholic Church. Mary, for example, makes little mention of prominent radical Republicans such as Wilbur Fisk Sanders.

Ironically, Mary's world became more constrained in cosmopolitan Helena than it had been in Virginia City; her parents'

concerns about social propriety grew as Mary moved from girlhood to womanhood, the gold camp matured, and the town became more socially minded. Nevertheless, Mary's father's business
often took him away from home, and her stepmother Anne still
allowed her relative freedom in his absence: Mary writes of sleighing parties, oyster suppers, horseback riding, and her courtship
with Peter Ronan, a friend of her father's and the editor of Helena's
Rocky Mountain Gazette.

In 1869 the Sheehan family left Helena, a move prompted by
James's financial trouble and his disapproval of sixteen-year-old
Mary's engagement to the much older Peter Ronan. Mary's engagement—and her heart—broken, the family headed south to
Corinne, Utah, where the Union Pacific neared completion. At
Corinne, Mary endured the gruff, rude railroaders as the Sheehan
women served boarders in a tent and contributed income to the
family's coffers. They soon packed up for California, but the experience at Corinne was a turning point, after which James in-
creasingly relied on Mary for help, allowing her to perform tasks
more commonly undertaken by men. Like other women who came
with their families to the western frontier, the Sheehan women
had not actively sought liberation from established women's roles,
but they adapted to new situations and the needs of their family
as they arose. Like other frontier daughters, Mary took on more
nontraditional tasks than did her stepmother.[2] On the journey to
California, she drove the heavy freight wagon for her father; once
there she helped him build their house, hauling mortar in the
wagon, transferring it into buckets, and hoisting it up to him on
the scaffolding.

On the Sheehans' homestead near the Spanish mission ruins
of San Juan Capistrano, Mary settled into a very different life
than she had led in the gold rush towns of Montana. James filed
on a tract of 160 acres on which he planted hay, corn, potatoes,

and grape vines, as well as walnut, peach, apricot, and pear trees. Mary found herself moving between the world of physically demanding work on the homestead and the elegant *rancheros* of the Spanish elite, where she attended fiestas in carefully ironed white dresses. Mary's entrée into community life was the Catholic Church, but although local Mexican families welcomed her into their homes, they resented the arrival of her family. When the United States acquired California in 1850 after the war with Mexico, ownership records and land titles were vague and contradictory. Confusion over land ownership led to years of squatting and legal battles. Although Mary was aware of her family's status as squatters on untitled land, she did not fully comprehend the plight of her Mexican neighbors. The arrival of squatters like the Sheehans foreshadowed lengthy, costly court cases for the Mexican population and ultimately the loss of their land.

Mary left the homestead in 1871 to study with the Sisters of St. Vincent de Paul in Los Angeles. Her father desperately needed money, and the plan was for Mary to eventually earn enough from teaching to help the household. Although she enjoyed school, "I knew that I was not capable" of teaching, she remembered. In retrospect it seems that Mary knew then that she did not want to teach school. And so in a self-fulfilling prophecy, she graduated with flying colors but did not pass the teacher's examination in "mental arithmetic." Nor did she ever try again. Instead, after seriously considering joining the convent, she decided to marry her Montana suitor, Peter Ronan.

Mary's love story with Peter Ronan began in Virginia City and threads its way throughout much of the narrative. Even before their first meeting, Mary and Peter were on paths that would eventually converge. In fact, Peter's trek west mirrored that of Mary's long before the two met at a sluice box in Alder Gulch. When the Sheehans' St. Joseph, Missouri, relatives lost their slaves at the start of the Civil War, Peter Ronan, at almost the same time, was less than fifty miles away in Leavenworth, Kansas, editing a Democratic newspaper. Peter's Southern sympathies landed him in the Fort Leavenworth guardhouse where the Sisters of Charity brought him his meals and did his laundry. Mother Vincent, then the mother superior of the Leavenworth-based order, especially took him under her wing. Their friendship likely helped bring the Sisters of Charity to Montana, for according to Mary, Peter asked the Catholic priests to invite the sisters to Helena. In 1869 the first Sisters of Charity arrived and founded St. John's Hospital and St. Vincent's Academy, the first of their many institutions in Montana.

While Mary attended school in Los Angeles, she initiated correspondence with Peter, who was still in Helena editing the *Gazette*. Their courtship resumed through letters. The decision of whether to accept Peter's proposal of marriage was a difficult one: choosing a husband was the most important decision of a young girl's life, and in this case, marriage would mean leaving her family far behind. Nevertheless, the two married in the little chapel at San Juan Capistrano early in 1873.

The couple returned to Helena where Mary established a home for her husband and gave birth to the first of their nine children (only one of whom—Louise, a twin—died in infancy in 1885). Peter's *Rocky Mountain Gazette* flourished until fire destroyed his uninsured equipment. After a brief period mining at Blackfoot City, Peter accepted a government appointment to fill out an unexpired term as Indian agent to the tribes of the Flathead Reservation in 1877. He remained in that position until 1893.

Peter Ronan was an unusual Indian agent. Generally appointed by political favor, many agents were unscrupulous and neglectful of their duties, and few remained in office long. Eight of Peter Ronan's predecessors between 1864 and 1877 were either suspended or terminated; one died in office, and one resigned.[3] Ronan's sixteen years of office set him apart, as did his honesty and genuine concern for the Salish, Kalispel, Kootenai, and Pend d'Oreille Indians who lived on the reservation. During his term as agent, he saw the reservation through several turning points, including the Nez Perce War, the building of the transcontinental railroad, and the removal of Chief Charlo and members of his band from their Bitterroot Valley home to the Flathead Reservation. A sincere believer in the United States' civilizing mission (a mission whose racist assumptions are today widely recognized), Peter worked conscientiously on behalf of the reservation Indians to promote among them the practice of agriculture, to encourage their education, and to instill in them the value of religion.

Mary enjoyed life on the reservation, although she found that from the time she assumed the "mask of the smiling hostess" as wife of the Flathead agent, she never again had the luxury of being alone in her own house. Eight children, others the Ronans took in, guests, and officials of all kinds kept her table nearly always full at mealtimes and her household crowded in between. That she would not have had it any other way is abundantly clear in the charming portraits of her children and Indian neighbors and servants, and in the steady loyalty and devotion to her husband that her reminiscence reflects. Mary and Peter experienced life on the reservation through a "prejudicial veil" of unself-conscious ethnocentrism and casual racism common among whites of their time, even as they genuinely desired to improve the lives of Peter's "charges."[4] Mary's reminiscence clearly reveals both this ethnocentrism (note her use of such terms as "squaw," "children of the forest," and "noble red man") and her belief that the Indians under her husband's protection were good people who had been wronged and deserved better. Her account provides a fascinating perspective on the events of her day and of the daily life of the wife of an Indian agent. Mary's descriptions, however, should not be read as an accurate portrayal of tribal life, nor are her viewpoints and opinions in any way objective.

Peter's sudden death from a heart attack in 1893 at the age of fifty-five left Mary with financial difficulties and legal entanglements, presumably over Peter's numerous mining claims. But Joseph Carter, Mary's son-in-law, was appointed Peter's replacement, and as long as he remained in that position, Mary and her younger children made their home at the agency. In 1898 Joseph moved to California, and Mary took the four youngest children to Missoula. The oldest child still at home was Katherine, sixteen; Margaret was next at thirteen. The youngest two were Isabel, ten, and Peter, seven. Mary bought a house on West Pine Street, free and clear. She must have had some financial resources having sold her father's California property in 1899. In fact, the 1900 census records show her occupation as "capitalist," a claim that seems to indirectly declare her independence.

Mary's circumstances may not have been so steady by 1903. Correspondence from that period indicates that Mary sold many items the Ronans collected during their years at the agency. In a letter dated March 14, 1903, to Montana Historical Society librarian Laura Howey, Mary wrote that she had a number of other Indian items "that the state may have for seventy-five dollars. Were I differently situated, I should gladly donate [them]." Even so, some of Mary's eight children attended college, and two of her four daughters—Margaret and Isabel—chose to pursue careers instead of marriage, remaining at home with their mother.

In 1929 Mary began dictating her reminiscence to Margaret, an English and journalism teacher at Missoula County High School and a graduate student in English at the State University of Montana (now the University of Montana). It was Margaret who transcribed and organized her mother's thoughts and encouraged her through the project. In 1932 Margaret submitted the well-researched thesis, under the title *Memoirs of a Frontiers Woman*, to the English Department in partial fulfillment of the requirements for her master of arts.

Margaret continued her duties as teacher and assistant principal of Missoula County High School where she had taught for nearly twenty-five years. Margaret's life, however, was troubled. In January 1935 she suffered a nervous breakdown and obtained a leave of absence. On May 24 of that year, Margaret drowned in the Missoula River. Her death was most likely a suicide. The community mourned the teacher who, for a quarter of a century, encouraged aspiring journalists and then did the same for their children. Warren Davis, editor of the *Missoulian*, wrote, "No woman could have been more generally loved than was Margaret Ronan."[5]

Mary Ronan died in 1940, outliving four of her eight children. Her memoir, lovingly prepared as Margaret's thesis, lay gathering dust in the University of Montana library for nearly forty years. In 1973, at the age of ninety, former University of Montana English professor H. G. Merriam, who had served as chairman of Margaret's thesis committee in the 1930s, prepared an edition of the manuscript published under the title *Frontier Woman: The Story of Mary Ronan as told to Margaret Ronan*. It had limited distribution. In a very brief preface, Merriam praised Mary Ronan's account for its historical accuracy and the diversity of places, people, and events it discussed.

Merriam's edition omitted what he termed "items of personal family interest," including the love letters that passed between Mary in California and Peter in Montana. Presumably these omissions were in deference to close family members still living in 1972. A mentor of numerous well-known Montana authors including A. B. Guthrie and Dorothy Johnson, Merriam himself had a long, prolific career as an editor and author. Among the many titles to his credit are *Way Out West* (University of Oklahoma Press, 1969),

Montana Adventure: The Life of Frank B. Linderman (University of Nebraska Press, 1968) and *Recollections of Charley Russell* (University of Oklahoma Press, 1963). *Frontier Woman* was a readable work that unfortunately lacked promotion and availability.

Girl from the Gulches offers a more complete version of Margaret Ronan's original manuscript. Most of the material left out of the Merriam edition has here been restored, although some of the more lengthy correspondence, pedantic quotes, and material Mary included to bolster Peter's reputation in his role as Indian agent have been either eliminated or shortened. The threads of the love story, especially, are fully included in this edition, as I think Mary surely would have wished.

Following Merriam's example, wording has been changed only for clarification. Some of the scattered events have been rearranged by subject matter and/or by chronology for ease of transition. I have added a few more chapter divisions, but I have also restored Margaret's original three-book format. The footnotes written by either Merriam or myself are marked "Ed."; I have tried not to burden the reader with too many of them. Other footnotes are those of Mary Ronan, so designated, or undesignated, those of her daughter, Margaret.

Girl from the Gulches

The Story of Mary Ronan

FOREWORD

For years people urged my mother to write the recollections of her varied and unusual experiences. When leisure came at last, it was not the leisure of ease in which to carry out long cherished plans, but that which is enforced by weariness from much work and by pain and illness.

"I am so tired of being a pioneer!" she sighed from the depths of her being one day after a particularly tedious session with one of the long procession of interviewers by whom she is continually besieged.

She had always been gracious, eager, interested, and anxious to help anyone who came to get a story—seasoned reporter, budding student of journalism, or freak—that her declaration of fatigue alarmed me. Then and there I promised to do what I had long intended: write my mother's memories, make transcripts of historically interesting letters, articles, and papers that she had long treasured, file all together in a library, and thereto refer the next and all succeeding interviewers. Out of this promise grew these chapters.

My mother and I spent the summer of 1929 delightfully collaborating. Each morning she undertook an "assignment" in reminiscence on a topic. Earliest memories of childhood, of father, mother, of this place and that, of this event or that. Each morning she talked up the topic agreed upon by us the day before and she also wandered into such unforeseen bypaths as the first process of deliberate remembering happened to open. I jotted notes; sometimes I interrupted with questions; sometimes I listened to oftheard stories, a sort of folklore of our family, that I knew word for word as my mother would tell them. In the afternoons, while she rested and mused upon her next "assignment," or stimulated her memory by reading old letters or by looking at old pictures, I transcribed upon the typewriter, as nearly as possible word for word, the recollections of the morning.

My mother was always eager to read what I had typed and to make sure that I had quoted her exactly, without understanding or overstating, to know how her own words spoke back from the paper. So eager was she, in fact, that sometimes she stood over me as I typed. Sometimes I would find her sitting at the typewriter scanning the unfinished page that I had left in the machine. To many pages she added in her own handwriting other memories suddenly wrenched from oblivion. We made no attempt at first to weld the mess of material our method yielded into such form that it would be read connectedly or progressively. That attempt came later and meant rigorous excluding, since so many events and acquaintances of a lifetime form into a mere agglomeration.

In order to check accuracy of my mother's statements, during such leisure as I had in the busy years following the summer of 1929, I read Northwest history, reminiscences and diaries of pioneers, old letters, and newspapers. I can truly say that I never found her memory in error. I read also with the purpose of seeing if I could find an account of the everyday experiences and real point of view of a woman who grew from girlhood among frontier conditions. Such a story I did not find; such a story I have endeavored quite sincerely to set down, as I have said, word for word as my mother told it to me, interpreting only now and then.

It was our plan that my father, too, should tell his own story. Because many years have now passed since he journeyed into the valleys of silence, this story was to have been gathered from personal glimpses given here and there in articles he wrote, in his reports to the Department of the Interior, in penciled paragraphs we found among his private papers, in his letters, and in interviews he granted various newspapers. When we assembled this material, we found that the story was not forthcoming, for as a newspaperman and as a government official, Peter Ronan wrote objectively of the stirring events in which he was active. He was modest in interviews and even his private letters are reticent, so his story has been woven into my mother's own.

Verbatim though this account is, I am conscious that I have not been able to capture my mother's dramatic quality: the cadences of her soft voice; the kindling lights of her blue eyes; the changing expressions of her sweet, sensitive, mobile face; the nuances of her personality. These things have always charmed everyone and still do.

When I think of my mother's picturesqueness, of the aura of romance surrounding her, which not even the petty events of everyday can dispel; when I think of her intelligence, her sweetness, her refinement, her delicacy; and when I recall these as the distinguishing qualities of other pioneer women who were her friends, I appreciate that no desire set off a rhetorical display, but genuine sincerity inspired the tribute paid by Colonel Wilbur F. Sanders in Helena on July 6, 1902, at the formal acceptance by the commonwealth of the capitol, to the pioneer women:

> What adequate words shall be spoken of those brave and accomplished women who first journeyed into these unknown fastnesses with love and loyalty and courage immeasurable. They beautified the rudest homes, and in all our labors were veritable helpmeets. Whether fighting savages, swimming rivers, crossing trackless wastes by night or day, they were examples of fortitude and devotion worthy of all praise. Taking up cheerfully the all too neglected burdens which refined society and tamed our wilderness, they achieved for the state a magnificent

contest and for themselves the immortality of fame. They hold a secure place in popular esteem as the builders of a great commonwealth, whose foundations they laid in prudence not recklessness, in liberty not obstinance, amid militant struggles and with inspiring hopes.[1]

Truly there were thousands of women of another sort who had, also, a great part, an equally hard, no doubt more bitter part, in the settling of this frontier. Gaunt, grim, shrill, weather-beaten women with rough skin, unkempt hair and coarse hands, clad in soiled, crumpled calico or gingham dresses and sunbonnets, shod in shapeless dusty boots—not picturesque, not romantic according to the usual connotation of these words—interesting, no doubt, certainly dauntless, devoted, loyal, deserving too of having their stories told. Women such as these scarcely enter my mother's story. If they do, it is as if they have been led gently in by one who had pitied them, who has brushed from them the grime of the trail, who had softened the lights of harsh reality and has afforded them a gracious aspect, shed from the wonder of the strangeness or the beauty in which life appeared to her in all vicissitudes.

BOOK ONE

Into the Land of Gold

Did a prairie schooner pass this way
In the dusty haze of a summer day,
Rolling and dipping over the swells
As it followed the winding grade?

—Elliott C. Lincoln
"Wheel Tracks," *Northwest Verse*

Mary Ronan with her father, James Sheehan

Early Recollections

My first experience traveling in a covered wagon and camping out at night came to me when I was so young, and the daily journeying was so much a matter of course, that I have only a vague recollection. I had traveled with my father and mother from Kentucky to Indiana, from Indiana to Illinois. I then journeyed with my widowed father from Illinois to Iowa and on to Missouri. The journey alone with him from Missouri to Colorado is a little clearer, and clearer still come those long treks from Colorado to Montana, from Utah across the desert to southern California. Clearest of all is the memory of the journey back from California to Montana with my husband by boat and train and stagecoach.

In my earliest memories, I see a covered wagon halted on a dim road. It winds out of sight on a wide prairie undulating endlessly toward a vast, shadowy background of looming mountains. Just ahead of the wagon a little girl ventures along the road, gazing across the expanse of country. I can recall my wonder at the bigness of the world and what the long journey might promise me.

My father, James Sheehan, was a sixteen-year-old Irish emigrant when he came from County Cork in Ireland. His wanderings in search of livelihood led him to Louisville, Kentucky, where he met and married my mother, Ellen Fitzgibbon, an Irish girl not long from Limerick. At Louisville in July 1852 (my father was not one to recall exact days of the month), I was born and christened Mary Catherine Fitzgibbon Sheehan, but family and friends called me simply Mollie Sheehan, and by that name many of my old time friends still call me. A little boy, Gerald, was born while my parents lived in Louisville. I have a vague memory of being on a boat on a river and of a man who tried to coax me to trade my brother for a doll. I presume my father was on the way to Indiana with us where he had a contract to do railroad construction. How the poor, young Irish emigrant accumulated enough to equip himself for such work I do not know. My father was always reticent, and I took him for granted as most young people do their parents. When I longed to ask the details of his life story, he had followed my mother forth beyond my questionings.

I remember playing with my little brother Gerald. His eyes were dark blue; his hair was light and curly. From Ireland my father brought his brother, a widower, and that brother's three children, Patrick, Mary, and Ellen Sheehan, to live with us. My uncle could not work because of heart trouble. One day he carried Gerald out to watch the men at work with their teams of oxen and their carts. He sat the little boy on a stump around which green grass was growing, and left him there for a moment while he stepped a few paces away to speak to Patrick, who was working among my father's men. A yoke of oxen, grazing, nosed nearer and nearer to the stump, knocked the baby off and trampled him to death in an instant. I have faint memories of sorrowing and mourning. Gerald must have been buried there in Indiana, and there, too, my uncle lies. I used to hear my relatives say that he died suddenly from the shock of this tragic occurrence.

My father's work took him to Illinois. My mother gave birth to a baby girl who lived for only two weeks. I have heard my father tell that in order to take the little body to a cemetery for burial, he had to wade a swollen stream. Neighbors advised him not to take the risk, but he did, carrying the tiny coffin on his shoulder. In the night while he was away the "shanty" in which we were temporarily living burned to the ground. Being carried from the burning house into the cool darkness is a recollection that comes back even now with a little thrill reflected from the terror of long ago. My mother was carried out from her sick bed; she caught a cold and in less than a week she died. I was taken in someone's arms to her bedside to kiss her goodbye. I can dimly remember my father crying and crying. Though I did not know what it was all about, my Aunt Margaret, my mother's sister, whom the neighbors called Mrs. Coffee, came from Kentucky. I was awakened and there she sat, a shadowy woman in the doorway of our cabin. This dim memory is all I recall of any contact with my mother's people.

My father took my cousins Patrick, Mary, and Ellen with us to Ottumwa, Iowa. We lived with a family named Lauder in a house that had a big fireplace. That impressed me and so did the wide bed in which I slept with my father. How I loved Jane Lauder, the daughter. She went away, and I cried and cried. For the first time I experienced winter and cold. I used to stand by the window and watch for my father to come through the dusk from work. When spring came and the weather grew warm I would go walking with my father on Sundays. I would run ahead and gather flowers to give to him. I wore white pantalets that I was told were made from the fine linen sheets my mother had brought with her from Ireland. Other underwear and nightdresses, too, I had made from that same linen.

I have nothing left of my mother. The women of the Lauder household talked with Mary and Ellen about a chest of linens belonging to my mother. My father had been keeping it for me but it had been stolen. Years afterwards my stepmother used to wear some brooches that I thought beautiful. They had belonged to my mother, she told me in her reticent way, and would be mine some day. However, they were not, and I have never known what became of them. As late as 1869, in our household in San Juan Capistrano, there was in use a fine woolen comforter that my mother had brought from Ireland. In Last Chance Gulch, in the early days, I had a green parasol that had been my mother's. One day when I was riding horseback around Mount Helena, I took the parasol with me and lost it off the horn of the saddle. I was sorry and searched diligently but did not find it. These things and a lock of her soft brown hair, which I still treasure, were the only mementos I ever had of my young mother, and I have told much of them because they meant much to me. Often through long years I have dwelt in fancy on these bits of things, trying through them to divine the kind of woman my mother was, to call back to mind her face, for I never had a picture of her.

A Catholic priest started a school in Ottumwa. The Lauders, who were not Catholics, took me regularly. While we lived with the Lauders, my cousin Patrick was married and dropped out of my life forever. The second winter of our stay in Iowa was so cold that there was no work in my father's line. He left Mary and Ellen with the Lauders and took me with him into the country to care for his horses and mules, his investment capital. We lived with an Irish family. The cooking was done over a fireplace in the big farmhouse kitchen. The lady of the house marked her accounts of my father's bill for board and lodging on the bricks above the fireplace with charred wood. Those strange marks, cryptic and portentous, fascinated me.

That winter I went to a little country school. The children used to crowd around the big stove. I would sit shivering on the edge of the group, my feet curled under me. I suppose that I was too small and too timid to assert a right to share the warmth. One day I came home with frozen feet. My father was wrathful and made a terrible scene. Another time I went on an expedition with my schoolmates to a cemetery said to be haunted. When the cry went up, "The ghost! The ghost!" I fled, terrified, firmly believing that I had seen the ghost. In the evenings I remember that the Irish neighbors danced first at one house and then at another. As there was nothing else to be done with me, my father took me with him. No sort of musical instrument was in evidence, not even a fiddle. The men made music, or at least rhythmic sound for the jigs and quadrilles, by putting paper over the teeth of coarse combs. In this manner they blew forth "The Irish Washerwoman," "The Rocky Road to Dublin," and other old favorites.

At last the ominous marks on the bricks above the fireplace were erased. Mary and Ellen rejoined us and we set forth in the covered wagon, this time for St. Joseph, Missouri, where either a new road-building contract or freighting took my father. Our new home was with my father's cousin, John Sheehan, who had been settled in the South for some time and owned a plantation and a number of slaves. He lived with his family of eight children in a large white house.[1]

After we had been at St. Joseph for some time, my father married Anne Cleary, a young lady whom I had seen but once before the marriage. He went to Colorado with his bride, freighting provisions for frontier settlements. Because I so loved my father I was lonely in my Cousin John's household. I wept bitterly when the children read or told stories in which the cruel stepmother caused evil and suffering. Mammy Caroline, the old Negress who took care of us children, consoled me. When I was told that my father was coming to take me to Colorado, I felt that of all the household I would be the saddest to part from Mammy Caroline, and that parting came in an unexpected way.

Those were the dark days at the beginning of the Civil War. One morning we woke to find all the Negro servants gone. All the horses, too, were gone from the barns. I heard members of Cousin John's family say, for they were in sympathy with the cause of the South, that Union soldiers had come in the night, stolen the horses, and driven the darkies away. One terrifying night we children were aroused from bed and dressed in readiness to flee; I heard whispering that the soldiers would surely come and turn us out and burn the house. Before any tragedy happened, my father returned. That was in the autumn of 1861. During the year and more that he had been gone, he had established a little store in Nevada, Colorado, and there he had left my stepmother in charge while he came back to St. Joseph for me.[2]

Overland to Colorado

My father and I made the journey from St. Joseph, Missouri, to Denver, Colorado, alone. We were six weeks on the way. I remember no hardships, only joy at being with my dear father again in the covered wagon on the road with the world all before us.

I was nine years old and I felt great satisfaction in being helpful. If we camped for the night by a stream, I jumped down from the wagon at once and ran to get a bucket of water. Then I picked up sticks to start the fire, or buffalo chips when we traveled through buffalo country. It was most exciting to help put the nosebags on the mules. My father always drove a six-mule team with a jerk-line.[3] He said that mules were stronger than horses and got over the ground faster for longer distances.

Most of the time as we jogged and jolted along I sat beside him on the high seat of the wagon and played with my kitten, or listened to him sing. He had a good voice and knew many Irish, Scotch, and southern melodies and Civil War songs that were beginning to sweep the country even to its farthest outposts. He taught me "The Irish Immigrant," "Old Folks at Home," "Nellie Grey," "Swanee River," "I am Captain Jenks of the Horse Marines," and other songs. To the tune of "Gentle Annie," my father had composed words in honor of his gentle little wife, Anne Cleary. These, also, he taught me. How gay we were when we made our voices ring out together:

Gramachree, ma cruiskeen
Slanta Gael, mavourneen!
Gramachree ma cruiskeen lawn, lawn, lawn!
Gramachree me cruiskeen
Slanta Gael, mavourneen!
Gramachree me cruiskeen lawn, lawn, lawn!
Arrah, ma colleen bawn, bawn, bawn,
Arrah, ma colleen bawn.[4]

Often while we were singing the kitten would spring from my arms to ride upon the back of one of the mules. "Perhaps the kitten does not understand our songs," I might say. "Perhaps she wants to get a better view," my father might answer, for the prairie country must then have worn the warmth of autumnal browns and the glory of scarlet and gold.

I crawled into the back of the wagon for a nap on the heap of bedding when I grew tired, but this was not often, for besides songs my father had stories in his repertory of entertainment. I liked best a new one about a dear little baby sister that I would find in our new home. She was born in Empire City, Colorado, on July 30, 1861, and christened Katherine Empire, "Katherine" for Pa's dear old mother back in Ireland and "Empire" because Kate was the first child born in Empire City. The enthusiastic citizens saw in her birth the portent of permanency for their settlements, so they deeded to her several town lots. The bestowal of her middle name was a return of courtesy on the part of her parents. Before the town or the child was many weeks old, the boom had burst. Whatever became of those lots I do not know for once he had moved away from a place, my father never returned. My sister never investigated the registers of that old town.[5]

When we came to our journey's end in Denver, for some reason my father left me for a month with a German man and wife while he went on to Central City.[6] I remember well how lonely I

The Sheehans lived only briefly in the gold-rush town of Empire, Colorado, shown here in the late 1860s. In 1861 Mary's sister Katherine Empire was the first baby born in the town.
DENVER PUBLIC LIBRARY, WESTERN HISTORY COLLECTION, X-8181

was in the days immediately following and how I sighed and wept to be traveling again with my father. However, my German land-lady was kind to me. I sometimes thought her a trifle severe when she made me learn to hem, practicing on her husband's shirttails. When the allotted portion had been laboriously stitched, I was al-lowed to go outdoors and scamper with the dog. My German hosts also took me to my first play. How thrilled I was, how complete the illusion. How puzzling it was to understand that what seemed so real was "a play!"[7]

I remember nothing of the trip from Denver to the new home in Nevada City on Clear Creek in Gilpin County, Colorado. I do remember the joy of meeting my stepmother and the thrill when she kissed me and held out the plump little red-haired baby sister for me to kiss. Red hair was something new and interesting in our family. All the Sheehans, my stepmother too, had brown hair, blue eyes, and dark brows and lashes.

My father had not told me what to call his wife. This worried me, yet I was too shy to ask. I treasured one memory too dear to call Anne Cleary "Mother." It never occurred to me that I might call her "Anne." So impressive a personage, my father's wife! After more than seventy years I look back and try to realize that she was then just a girl. We grew to love each other. The problem of what to call her was solved by hearing other little girls call their mothers "Ma," and that name corresponded well with "Pa," the approved way of the period for addressing one's father.

I used to play in the tailings from Pat Casey's quartz mill, delighted with the shining bits of iron pyrite. Casey's night hands—the crew that worked the night shift—were much talked of in early days. I liked to whisper over and over again the phrase, "Pat Casey's night hands." It had a mysterious ring. When I peered through the windows of the shack where the night hands were fed, nothing strange or frightful was to be seen. Long tables were set quite in the ordinary way with tin cups and plates and many, many salt and pepper shakers and bottles and bottles of condiments.

I walked from Nevada to the school in Central City every day. The girls taught me the waltz and other round dances, as those engaged in by two couples were called. They were very daring and pious people looked askance at them. My father's freighting expeditions took him away from home often and for long periods of time. For company Ma began to take me to dances with her. When she left me at home, she always brought me, in her handkerchief, bits of frosting from the cakes served at the hearty midnight suppers. One old Irish woman scorned the sweets and kept saying that when her turn came to entertain the neighbors she would serve "thim refrishmints that wuz refrishmints." She did. I know for I went to the party. In the middle of the night the guests sat down to corned beef, cabbage, bread, jam, and coffee. For weeks after the ladies who came to see my stepmother talked and laughed about that supper. I secretly thought that the cabbage had tasted good, but I said nothing for fear they would laugh at me. My father was much displeased when he came home and found that his young wife and little daughter had been going to dances without his escort and protection. We went no more.

Mine was a loving but stern father of the Irish type who believes that a man is the master of his home and makes his belief the practice of his household. Children must mind. I never thought of disobeying him. I feared, respected, and loved him. He had a high regard for learning. He sent me to every little school that was started at any place in which we established our residence, however brief. As I grew older, he talked and talked of sending me back to "the states" to be educated. Always, though, there were obstacles: the expense, the distance, the difficulties of the journey. If ever my dear father had a little leisure, he read. Whenever he could, he bought books. Even during our residence in Alder Gulch, so wild, so isolated from civilization, we had Shakespeare's plays, some of Scott's romances, and Moore's and Byron's poems.

Our big yellow dog, Dange, always went with my father on his trips to Denver to guard the wagons. One night my father was camped alone in a little tent just out of Denver when Dange failed to give alarm. Marauders awakened him. As he sat up in his bed one of them toppled over the tent and grappled with him. My father seized his Bowie knife and jabbed furiously and at random through the canvas. The marauder loosed his grip and fleeing steps sounded. When my father disentangled himself from the canvas of the fallen tent and crawled out, no one was to be seen. In the breaking light of morning he made his way to the police to notify them about what had happened. They returned with him to the place of his encampment. The trampled grass was spattered with blood; drops of blood showed on the canvas of the tent. In his offhand account of this incident, my father explained his escape by saying, "It was always my habit to be quick."

I learned much during that year at Nevada City. My father taught me to ride Charley, his fine-spirited horse. Ours was a far-off, wild western settlement and I was just ten years old, but there were proprieties to be observed. I must sit sideways on the man's saddle. For a long time I did not dare go faster than a walk. One day Pa "accidentally" struck Charley with the bridle rein. The horse broke into a gallop. After that I loved to ride fast.

Ma taught me to recite pieces. I enjoyed the jingle of the voices, but the meaning did not concern me particularly. At any rate, I had my own way of saying and understanding some of the lines. This passage meant to me just what it did to my older listeners, but the lines, "If I should chance to fall below/Demosthenes or Cicero," I understood this way: "If I should chance to fall below/ The moss, the knees, or Sis Ero."

Once when I was left at home to take care of the baby, I dressed in one of Ma's silk dresses and, playing lady, trailed it through the mud as I carried plump little Kate about to visit the neighbors. When my stepmother saw her bedraggled dress, she said severely, "Mollie, you shall never play lady again." I was plunged into the depths of mortification and utterly surprised for I had never seen my stepmother angry.

DENVER DAYS

In the fall of 1862 we moved to the straggling town of Denver and lived on F Street next door to a store kept by P. S. Pfouts, whose acquaintance we continued later in Alder Gulch. My father must have met with financial reverses. We lived in a house that seemed to have been built for a store or saloon. Ellen came out from St. Joseph and joined us. She did domestic work for one of our neighbors. Mary had been married in St. Joseph where she continued always to make her home.[8]

Christmas time came with Pa away from home. In a certain store window I saw doll's dishes for which I yearned. I do not recall that we ever talked about Santa Claus, but someplace I had got the idea of hanging up my stocking on Christmas Eve. When I talked about doing so to see if an angel would come and leave those doll's dishes or something, Ma laughed and said that I was talking nonsense. I did slip out of bed in the night and hang up my stocking. It was empty on Christmas morning, and I was a sad little girl.

At school my *Readers* and those of the other children in grades above and below me absorbed my attention. I looked through them for the poetry, all of which I read and reread. Pages and pages I learned by heart and still remember. Memorizing was a practice with me throughout my school days. I cannot state exactly which ones I learned during the Denver school days, yet some I remember definitely and clearly that I did learn at this time for the gentle sound of the words: "Down in a green and shady bed / A modest violet grew."[9]

Moralizing lines and lines weighted with admonition appealed to me. Often in the midst of the hard tasks of childhood my will to do was renewed by gritting my teeth and repeating,

'Tis a lesson you should heed
Try, try again;
If at first you don't succeed,
Try, try again.[10]

Sad stories about separation and death were fascinating to me. Because we had lived near the town of Black Hawk, I became interested in learning by heart the speech of Chief Black Hawk when he was taken prisoner. Sympathizing with Indians was not usual among the families of emigrants. Now when I recall my intensity in reciting that speech, it seems as if I had almost a premonition of the experience of living among the Indians and of sorrowing for their wrongs and dispossession that was awaiting me in the far years to come.[11]

Every Friday afternoon at school we spoke pieces. In this I reveled. I recited with flourish of pathos and luxuriance of gesture in the approved manner of the period. I loved my teacher at the Denver school. It was she who taught me to curtsy to my elders and to the audiences at the Friday afternoon performances. On one gala day I was given permission to invite her home to dinner. The joy of having her was almost extinguished by the worry about how I should introduce her to my stepmother. I was anxious to be correct. It seemed a delicate matter to submit to the counsel of Ma and Pa. I could not say, "This is my mother," for it was not true, and I did not want to say, "This is my stepmother."

Teacher might feel sorry for me, and neither she nor anyone else needed to feel so. Ma was not a bit like Cinderella's stepmother or the others in the tales we children talked about so solemnly. "Meet my father's wife." Dreadful! Unconscious of my worries, Ma dispelled them quite simply by greeting the guest cordially at the door of our humble home, waiting for no ceremonius introduction to the learned lady.

I attended instructions given by a priest who was preparing a class for first Holy Communion. Early in the morning of the important day, I dressed myself with care in my white frock and veil. As I went through the kitchen on my way to join the other children, I stuck my finger in and tasted the thick cream that had gathered on a pan of milk on the table. Then I remembered! I ran to Ma's bed and asked her if I had broken my fast. She said that I had, that I must not touch food or drink from twelve o'clock the night before until after I had received Holy Communion. I was ashamed that I had forgotten. I suffered deeply sitting alone on the bench and seeing all the children of the catechism class going to the altar rail without me. On the following morning, in my white frock and veil, carrying a candle in my hand, I marched alone down the long blocks of F Street to Mass and my first Holy Communion.

My father had come home and said that we were soon to set forth again in our wagons to the rich, newly discovered gold diggings in Bannack, Montana.[12] The priest who had prepared me for first Holy Communion gave me a penance to say every day on the journey: the Lord's Prayer, Hail Mary, and Glory Be to the Father five times each. Now I think that he did this to provide a little girl with a means of passing time while the wagons creaked monotonously mile after mile, hour after hour, and with the deeper purpose of fixing the habit of daily prayer. He must have known that in a far-off frontier not much would be found to minister to the spirit. I was a lively, healthy child, never at a loss for something interesting to see or do, so that sometimes I would let my prayers go for days at a time and become so dreadfully in arrears that I thought I would never get them said. I always felt the obligation that had been put upon me. I was glad to reach Bannack chiefly because I was released from saying my penance.

River crossings, such as the one shown here, were the most dangerous part of any overland trip.
NEBRASKA STATE HISTORICAL SOCIETY PHOTOGRAPH COLLECTION

THE LONG TREK

In April 1863, we set out for Montana. A few nights before, Ma hung a big washing on the lines so that she might have everything clean at least at the beginning of the long trek. In the morning she found that thieves had stripped the lines.

My father always had two wagons drawn by six-mule teams, one loaded very heavily and driven by a hired man. My father drove the other wagon in which the family rode. Supplies covered the bottom of this wagon. Over the supplies, Pa spread mattresses, blankets, and comforters; there we slept at night. Sometimes during the daytime Ma, Ellen, or I would be glad enough to crawl back for a nap with Kate. Fastened on the back of the wagon were a sheet-iron stove, a little rocking chair for my stepmother, and a mess box containing the food we needed day to day. When we stopped for a couple of days or more, the stove was set up and we cooked and washed. While the bread was baking and the clothes were drying, Ma rocked in her little chair and mended. In the evenings as we traveled right along, we cooked supper over a campfire. If we were out of bread, biscuits or shanter's bannock was baked in a Dutch oven.[13]

It was my duty in the mornings to help gather up the food and pack the mess kit. Wood, water, and grass were necessary for a good camping site. We watched for the three essentials as soon as afternoon shadows began to lengthen. My father took a chance on finding wood or buffalo chips and water, but he always carried some grain for the horses and mules. They were our faithful servants and a surer means of livelihood than the elusive gold in the mines.

I do not remember that we left Denver with other people but from time to time other emigrants joined us. No one in our family kept a diary, so I do not know what route we followed. Much of the way must have been the route traced by John Owen in the journal of his trip in the fall of 1864.[14] Up Green River Valley, through the Wind River Canyon, the ford on the Big Horn, and Bridger's route west of the Big Horn Mountains are phrases that come back to me with the familiarity of an old refrain.

Bridger's Cutoff is the most familiar of all. The grown-ups looked forward to reaching Bridger's Cutoff where a large emigrant train was to form. We waited there several days. I dimly remember a blockhouse-like structure, and nothing else of the place. Around the campfires at night I heard excited talk about the rich placer diggings in Montana and the increased hostilities of the Indians. When my father cut my thick brown hair, I suppose so that it could more easily be kept clean and kempt, I heard it remarked that Jim Sheehan "wasn't goin' to have no Injuns git his little girl's scalp." This did not frighten me nor impress me as gruesome; it was all part of the day's talk and jesting.

Our train of twenty-five or thirty wagons set out from Bridger's Cutoff about the first of May. A man named Clark was elected captain. Everyone in our train drove horses or mules except Nelson Story who, with his beautiful sixteen-year-old bride, had joined us there. Mr. Story drove oxen. Though they were slow, he had decided that rather than wait for an ox train he would try to keep up with Captain Clark. He did. His wagon was always the last in camp in the evenings, but it always drew into its place in the circle before darkness fell. As the years passed and I witnessed Mr. Story's financial success, I came to see its explanation. His indomitable spirit led him to join our train and keep his oxen traveling with the horses and mules no matter what the effort.

I remember Mr. Story so vividly because I watched for him with childish eagerness each evening hoping that he would reach camp early enough to give me a ride on one of the little donkeys he had in his outfit. When I did get a ride, whether on bareback or on a man's saddle, I always sat primly sideways. Never in all my riding days did I ride "cross-saddle" ("astride" was a coarse expression). How my father used to laugh when I would beg him to buy me a donkey from Mr. Story.[15]

Another person who joined our train at Bridger's Cutoff was Jack Gallagher, afterwards known as a desperado, who forfeited his life at the hands of the vigilance committee in Virginia City on January 14, 1864.[16] I remember him standing about the campfires in the evening. He was tall, dark, and striking looking. He often spoke to me in a pleasant, quiet voice, and praised me for reading so well. I knew by heart pages from the little books I had with me. One was a story similar to the Little Eva portion of *Uncle Tom's Cabin.* I would sit by the campfire in the dim light, a book on my lap, say the words by heart and enjoy the adulation that I would receive. One of life's little ironies is a memory of Jack Gallagher—headed swiftly to destruction—praising the little girl whose special book for the journey was Reverend Preston's *The Life of Mary Magdalene or The Path to Penitence.*[17] On the flyleaf Pa wrote, "Mary C. Sheehan from her father Denver, Colo. March 1863." He bought it just before we set out. I did not understand nor care for it then. What child of ten would? But I grew to love and cherish the little book.

Men on horseback rode beside the wagon train, reconnoitered, and guarded the rear. The guards were especially vigilant in Indian country. Word was brought to camp one day that the train ahead of ours had come upon some murdered bodies. We passed by a mound of fresh earth with a board marker on which a penciled message stated that an unidentified body had been found and buried. In one narrow canyon the mounted guard was more watchful than usual. Ma, Ellen, and I were warned to keep out of sight. The wagons drew into a great circle at night and guards patrolled outside it to protect the sleepers and stock, picketed and grazing a little way from camp. One night Indians did steal a few fine horses. That is the only mishap to our train that I recall. I often heard it said that ours was an unusually fortunate or well-directed journey, made in almost record time.

The accounts of hardship, of suffering, of fear one reads in the diaries actually written from day to day by emigrants of the sixties left little impression on me. The monotonous miles of jolting, weariness, illness, cold, heat, acrid dust, alkali water, mosquitoes, cactuses, rattlesnakes, perilous ascents and descents on scarcely broken roads, terrifying fordings of great rivers, dread of lurking Indians, apprehension that the parting from loved ones back home was for life, and forebodings that new surroundings might hold worse not better fortunes are not what I remember. I can picture in my mind gorgeous sunsets gliding behind distant mountain peaks and flooding great valleys with magic light. Joyous eager childhood and the rhythm of going, going, going combine to make a backdrop and a theme song for that long trek into the land of gold.

We arrived at Bannack, a mile above sea level near the Continental Divide, about the first of June, 1863. From a hundred flumes the tailings were dumped in piles with just a slather of water and the arrastra's huge wheel turned.[18] Bearded, suntanned miners in gum boots and faded red flannel shirts with six-guns in holsters on their hips sweated in the heat of early summer. Although the Grasshopper Creek diggings were nearly worked out, hope charged the air with excitement when some of them passed on a story. A party of horsemen had just come to Bannack from "somewheres east," leading a horse loaded with gold. They were bartering for a grubstake. They were trying to keep their secret from all but a few "pardners," but someone let it leak out. The discovery men were watching for a chance to slip away, but a crowd waited at every turn, camping around them. When they did start, three or four hundred men on foot and on horseback went right along with them.[19]

My father pitched a tent for our family on the outskirts of Bannack on Grasshopper Creek where the water near the bank was richly mantled with tender green cress. He provided us with food, loaded his wagon with supplies, and set out to follow the trampled path of the stampeders over that eighty rugged miles between Bannack and Alder Gulch. My father made his way, broke his own road, and drove the first wagonload of supplies into Alder Gulch.

More memorable to me than witnessing this historic stampede was a black puppy someone had given me and playing with a little girl named Annie McCabe. After a few days my father returned to Bannack, pulled up our tent stakes, and loaded our belongings. Soon we were creaking in the warm sunshine amid a hovering cloud of alkali dust over endless tobacco brown ground, through long stretches of parched, gray-green sagebrush. It was more pleasant going through Beaverhead Valley and along the river bottom. In the backwater, when we camped, we could hear the slap of beavers' tails and the sudden splash of muskrats.

At a queer closing in the valley near the huge rounded Beaverhead Rock, the landmark which guided my father and countless other travelers long before him, we crossed over to another river, now called the Ruby or the Passamari.[20] We forded and traveled over a great flat bench surrounded by distant mountain ranges, fold upon fold of them. We dropped into a smaller valley, green with great cottonwoods growing along the little river, guarded by near and friendly wooded mountains. A long pull up the benchland brought us to a large creek, beautifully clear, running over stones made gay with red jasper, mica, and rose quartz. It was hidden by a thick growth of alder bushes whose clean red bark flashed among the dark green leaves.

The mules kept stopping to rest. At one of these stops I asked to ride in the back of the empty wagon driven by the hired man so that I could play with my puppy. On a steep slope the wagon tipped over. My father saw the accident and jumped from the wagon he was driving. He came running and picked me up. I was neither bruised nor scratched nor even frightened. My only concern was that the puppy, which I had continued all the while to hold in my arms, had been hurt.

At last the mule teams panted into a little valley, green and homey, snuggled among the hills. We camped where a large stream wound intricately among the high wooded hills from under the rim of a great bald crater to join a tiny crossline creek that crept from among the grassy rolling hills toward the east. I jumped down from the wagon in haste and excitement (for even children caught that fever), searched for a stick, whittled a place for my name, scrawled "Mollie Sheehan," pounded the stick into the ground, and announced that I had staked my claim. Father looked on and laughed.

Alder Gulch

Hundreds of tents, brush wickiups, log cabins, and even houses of stone quarried from the hills were springing up daily in the windings of Alder Gulch and Daylight Gulch, in the hollows of the hills, and along the ramblings of Alder Creek and the Stinkingwater. Soon over a stretch of fifteen miles a cluster of towns had assumed the importance of names: Junction, Adobetown, Nevada, Virginia City, Pine Grove, Highland, and Summit. In a few weeks the population numbered into the thousands.[21] Every foot of earth in the gulches was being literally turned upside down. Rough-clad men with long hair and flowing beards swarmed everywhere. Some were digging for bedrock and some were bent over barrow loads of the pay dirt that they wheeled to the sluice boxes. Others shoveled the dirt. Up and down the narrow streets bull trains and sixteen- or twenty-horse teams labored, pulling three and four wagons lashed together, and there were long strings of packhorses, mules, and donkeys. Loafers lolled at the doors or slouched in and out of saloons and gambling and hurdy-gurdy houses too numerous to estimate. Frequently the sounds of brawling, insults, and oaths echoed through the gulch. Bowie knives flashed and pistols cracked. When my stepmother sent me down the street on errands, she often said, "Now run, Mollie, but don't be afraid." I was never spoken to in any but a

*Virginia City, Montana, grew quickly from the tent camp Mary first
encountered to the booming metropolis pictured here in 1866.*
MONTANA HISTORICAL SOCIETY PHOTOGRAPH ARCHIVES

kindly way by any of those men. What Dimsdale said of the regard
which was accorded respectable women and girls was, indeed, true.[22]

I took our surroundings for granted as was the way of little
girls. Nevada, Central City, and Denver in Colorado and Virginia
City were very much alike. Here, as in those other towns, was a
certain class of women whom I have heard called "fancy ladies"
because of their gaudy dress, so different from that of the ladies
who were our friends. The fancy ladies were easily recognizable
on the streets by their painted cheeks and the way they flaunted
their gaudy clothes. They were always to be seen either walking
up or down the streets, clattering along on horseback, or riding
in hacks. Sometimes one appeared through a window, lounging
in a dressing gown and puffing on a cigarette. These women were
so in evidence that I felt no curiosity about them. I knew that

besides being so evident upon the streets, they went to hurdy-gurdy houses and to saloons and that they were not "good women." I did not analyze why that was.

After a while I made the acquaintance of Carrie Crane, Lizzie Keaton, and some other little girls, but not many, for there were very few in Virginia City as long as I lived there.[23] We spent our leisure time playing in the back streets or learning the haunts and the names of the wildflowers and their times for blossoming. There were tall buttercups and blue flags in the valley. Up Alder Gulch snow and timber lilies bloomed; wild roses and syringa grew in sweet profusion; flowering currant bushes invited canaries to alight and twitter. There were great patches of moss flowers with a scent and blossom like Sweet William. And such forget-me-nots! Larger and bluer and glossier than any other I have ever seen. On the tumbled hills among and over which the town straggled, the prim-roses made pink splotches in early spring. There the yellow bells nodded and the bitterroots unfolded close to the ground with their perplexity of rosy petals. In watered draws among the hills, blue, yellow, and white violets bloomed. In a place we thought was our secret, by the creek in Daylight Gulch, was a patch of white violets tinted with pink. We gathered wild gooseberries in the gulch and serviceberries and chokecherries on its steep sides. Robins, meadowlarks, bluebirds, black birds, camp robbers, blue jays, crows, and magpies lured us away from where men were ravishing the gulch.

A walk that was never denied us because it branched away from the diggings led up Daylight Gulch to a spruce grove called Gum Patch in a wooded canyon. We learned to distinguish the fir and nut pine and juniper and the dwarf cedar with the blueberries. Striped badgers were everywhere among the hills and so were their holes, which menaced a horse's way. Gophers amused us, whistling, flipping their tails, and whisking down their holes. It was fun to startle the cottontails and to watch them dart into the under-brush, or to climb up the mountainside and make the rock chucks scurry away along the sunny walls. Sometimes a deer flashed a white signal of danger and we glimpsed him leaping to cover. On rare occasions we were permitted to go so far out on the benchland that we used to see, or think that we saw, an antelope in the distance, or a lone buffalo, or a wraith of an Indian smoke signal. Under the blue, blue sky in the clear air of that high valley, nearly seven thousand feet above sea level, we could see a hundred miles.

My family lived in a big log cabin on Wallace Street, the main thoroughfare running up Daylight Gulch.[24] Because my father was a freighter, the Sheehans were well provisioned and always set as good a table as was possible to set in a remote mining town. My stepmother's and Ellen's dried apple and dried peach pies were rare delicacies much in demand, and so it came about that we began to take in boarders. Among these were the "discovery men," as Bill Fairweather, Henry Edgar, Barney Orr, and the others were called. Among the men who dropped in now and again to a meal was our companion on the journey to Montana, Jack Gallagher. He was always courteous and soft-spoken to us, and yet within the year we came to know that he was one of the most hardened of all the road agents. Another of this gang who came often enough so that I remember him distinctly was George Ives. My attention was directed to him because of the long blue soldier's overcoat he wore. I went on to notice that he stood head and shoulders above most of the men who gathered around our table. Unlike the others, Gallagher was smooth-shaven and he was blonde and handsome. Henry Plummer was only a name to me, but after his execution I heard him discussed at home; when he had last come to Virginia City, how picturesque in appearance, how gentle in manner. Who could have guessed the unutterable depth of his deceit and depravity?[25]

Long before the vigilantes organized, my father had evidently made his own observations and drawn his own conclusions about the character of some of the patrons of our boardinghouse. He soon closed the doors of our cabin to Virginia City's public and moved the family into a little two-room cabin off Wallace, the main street.

Grasping desperately and by any means for gold—brawling, robbing, shooting and hanging—was not all of life in the mining camp. Into our midst came the man of God. Father Joseph Giorda, S.J., whom I came to know so well in later years, was a sweet-faced Italian gentleman. He had made the long drive from St. Peter's Mission and had only two days to carry spiritual consolation to the far-flung frontier.[26] When he asked wherein he might say Mass, two young Irishmen, placer-miner partners Peter Ronan and John Caplice, offered a cabin they were having built. Miners from neighboring claims helped to level the dirt floor and put the cabin in such order that it could be used the next morning. My stepmother was asked to dress the improvised altar. Together she and I covered the rough-hewn boards with sheets and arranged the candles. Mr. Ronan often told me that it was there that day with my stepmother that he first noticed me, busy and serious. He thought, "What an old-fashioned little girl Mollie Sheehan is."

That first Mass in Virginia City on the Feast of All Saints, November 1, 1863, was a memorable event.[27] It was a simple, reverent congregation that knelt on the dirt floor within the four walls of new-hewn logs on that crisp morning. The majority were bearded miners in worn work clothes. Many received the Holy Eucharist from the consecrated hands of Father Giorda. I was distracted from spiritual to human contemplations by the tinkling sound of large tin cups that passed from one man to another. I saw each pour a trickle of gold dust from his buckskin pouch. Then the gold dust from all the cups was poured into a new yellow buckskin purse and Peter Ronan, whom the miners had chosen to make the presentation to the priest, laid it upon the altar.

When Father Giorda went to the stable where he had left his team and asked for his bill, he was told that it was forty dollars for the two days. He turned to Mr. Ronan, saying that he had not enough money to pay so excessive a price. Mr. Ronan inquired if he knew how much he had in the buckskin purse. Unworldly and unconcerned with money, Father Giorda had not thought of weighing its contents. Together he and Mr. Ronan did so and found that the purse contained several hundred dollars in gold dust.

Almost every evening the miners cleaned their sluice boxes with a tin contrivance called a scraper. Much fine gold was left in the cracks of the boxes and around the edges. Often after the miners had gone into their cabins for supper, Carrie Crane and I would take our little blowers and the hair brushes, which we kept for the purpose, and gather up the fine gold. We took it home, dried it in the oven and blew the black sand from it. Sometimes we would find that our gold dust weighed to the amount of a dollar or more. I had a little gutta-percha inkwell, which had traveled with us in the covered wagon from Denver. I kept my gold dust in it and carried it when I went to the store to buy rock candy. Carrie and I thought that this sweet was kept especially for the accommodation of little girl shoppers. The phrase "rock and rye" was a familiar one to us but not meaningful.[28] We found little on which to spend our gold dust. Sometimes the storekeeper had stick candy, candy beans, or ginger snaps. Twenty-five cents was the least that was ever accepted across the counter. The amount of the purchase in gold dust would be measured out with blowers on scales. Once I bought my father a present of a shirt, which cost $2.50 in gold dust, the only kind of money that I ever saw in Virginia City.

A man would have entered another miner's sluice box at the risk of being shot on sight, but it amused the miners to have us

little girls clean up after them. We were given so much encouragement that we actually thought we honored the men whose
sluice boxes we chose to clean. One evening I busied myself about
the property of Peter Ronan. I was wearing my new "shaker," a
straw poke-bonnet my stepmother had just made. It was trimmed
with bright pink chambray. For fear that I might rub against the
sides of the sluice boxes and soil the bonnet, I laid it on the cross
piece of a box while I stooped to brush and blow. Mr. Ronan, not
noticing me, lifted a gate above and let muddy water run through
his boxes. It splashed on the adored pink chambray "valance."
Many times afterwards I heard Mr. Ronan tell in his inimitable
way how the angry little girl suddenly stood up straight, then
scrambled from the sluice box, crying out indignantly, "I'll never,
never, never again, Mister, take gold from your sluice boxes!" How
his dark eyes flashed, how gaily he laughed as he apologized and
begged me to reconsider. This is my first memory of Peter Ronan.
Child as I was, vexed and embarrassed, even then I felt his great
personal charm and a harmony between us.

My father objected to my going about where men would speak
to me. He did not approve of the expeditions to the sluice boxes
and finally forbade them. From some of my Alder Gulch gold a
jeweler in Virginia City wrought me a ring. A few years later in
Last Chance Gulch I put it on Mr. Ronan's finger, saying, "Keep
it till I ask you for it."

On Christmas Day, 1863, the first marriage to be contracted
in Virginia City took place between Ellen Sheehan, then seventeen
years of age, and William Tiernan, who owned what was called the
"upper discovery claim." Bill was black bearded, tall, rangy like the
type so familiar in Wild West romances. Ellen was little and trim as
a brown wren. Henry Edgar was the best man. I remember no
other detail, I suppose, because the wedding was not made an occasion since there was no priest in the vicinity nor would there be,

perhaps, for months. Only the civil ceremony could be observed. My father disapproved of the marriage without a priest to officiate and Ellen grieved because of his disapproval.

Ellen and Bill went to live in a little cabin up Alder Gulch at the discovery claim. Ellen took the discovery men to board and kept their tollgate to the road leading up the narrow gulch. Added to her other duties, she became a banker in a certain sense. The miners trusted her. Many who had no safe place to keep their gold dust and nuggets left their buckskin purses with her for days at a time. She would hide their purses in the mattress. She has often told how lumpy and uncomfortable her bed would get as the "bank deposits" grew, and how doubly relieved she was when the "savings accounts" were drawn out and sent by stagecoach to Salt Lake City.

First one person and then another in Virginia City would start a little school. Professor Thomas J. Dimsdale (every man who taught school was called "professor") is the one I remember most distinctly. He was an Englishman, small, delicate looking, and gentle. I liked him. It seemed to me that he knew everything. In his school all was harmonious and pleasant. While his few pupils buzzed and whispered over their variously assorted readers, arithmetics, and copy books, the professor sat at a makeshift desk near the little window of the log schoolhouse writing, writing during the intervals between recitations and at recess, always writing. When, during 1864, *The Vigilantes of Montana* was being published at the *Montana Post*, I thought it must have been the composition of those articles which had so engrossed him.[29]

We children took advantage of Professor Dimsdale's preoccupation. Carrie Crane and I would frequently ask to be excused. We would run down the slope, for the schoolhouse was just below what the tourists now call Boot Hill Cemetery, into a corral at the bottom of Daylight Gulch. We would spend a few thrillful moments sliding down the straw stacks. We thought our absences daringly prolonged; probably they were not. At any rate, we were never chastised. Lettie Sloss is the only other teacher of this period whose name I recall, for we never had the same one a second term and the terms of school were brief and uncertain periods.

Coming from school one winter day, January 14, 1864, I cut across the bottom of the gulch, climbed the steep hill, and passed close behind a large cabin being built. People were gathered in front on Wallace Street. The air was charged with excitement. I looked. The horror of what I saw is photographed on my memory. The bodies of five men with ropes around their necks hung limp from a roof beam. I trembled so that I could scarcely run toward home. The realization flashed on me that two forms were familiar. One was Jack Gallagher, the other was Club Foot George, who used to notice me and speak in a kind way. His deformity had arrested my attention and made me pity him. I did not know that he and Jack were bad men. The three men that hung with them were Frank Parish, Haze Lyons, and Boone Helm. After some time the bodies were taken down and buried on top of the bleak, windswept hill overlooking the scene of their last turbulent days.[30]

One frosty morning a few weeks later when I opened the back door of our cabin, I saw in the gulch below a crowd of men gathered around a scaffold. There stood a young man with a rope around his neck. He shook hands with several of the men, then he pulled a black cap over his face. I knew the portent. I rushed into the house and slammed the door, but I could not shut out then, nor ever, from my memory that awful creaking sound of the hangman's rope.[31]

One day when my stepmother sent me to the meat market with the usual injunction, "Now run, Mollie, and don't be afraid," I was alarmed by a clatter of horses' hooves and the crack of pistol shots. A man galloping his horse recklessly down the street was firing a six-shooter in the air and whooping wildly. Suddenly he reared his horse back on its haunches, turned it sharply, and forced it through the swinging door of a saloon. I sidled into the first open doorway that I dared enter.

"That's Slade," said the storekeeper, "one of his sprees, shootin' up the town, scarin' women and children. That smart alec orter be strung up."

He led me out the back door and warned me to run home quickly and to stay in the house out of range of any stray bullets. "He'll git his needins yit," he threatened.

One day in early spring not long after this incident, we children were delayed at school because of a milling crowd of men gathered in Daylight Gulch, directly across the homeward path of most of us, around a corral called the "Elephant's Pen." Many of the men were armed. From the steep hillside path I could look down into their midst. I recognized Slade, dressed in fringed buckskin, hatless, with a man on either side of him. They forced him to walk under the corral gate. His arms were pinioned, the elbows were bent so as to bring his hands up to his breast. He kept moving his hands back and forth, palms upward, and opening and closing them as he cried, "For God's sake, let me see my dear wife! For God's sake, let me see my dear wife! For God's sake, let me see my dear wife!" Three times distinctly I heard him say this in a piercing, anguished voice.

The stir among the men increased. Voices rose louder, more angry, more excited, gesturing arms pointed to the long road winding down the hill from the east. Down that long hill road a woman was racing on horseback. Someone shouted, "There she comes!" A man in a black hat standing beside Slade made an abrupt, vigorous movement. I turned and sought the refuge of home.

Soon excited neighbors came in to say that the woman galloping so swiftly down the hill was, indeed, Mrs. Slade on her

Kentucky thoroughbred, Billy Bay. When she was recognized, the men of the vigilance committee made haste to do their dreadful duty for fear her presence would arouse so much sympathy among bystanders that the hanging would be stayed. They dwelt grimly on the details of how the man in the black hat had hastily adjusted the rope when the warning was given of her approach. He had kicked the box from under Slade so that he swung with a broken neck from the cross piece atop the corral gate. Many good citizens, among them my own people, criticized this act of summary vengeance because Slade had actually committed no crime in Montana. All admitted that he was a braggart and a brawler and had risked manslaughter on many a rowdy spree when he put on a show by shooting up the town. When he was sober he was said to be a good workman and a likable fellow.[32]

Slade's body was taken from the scaffold, used ordinarily for hanging beeves, and delivered to his wife in the old Virginia Hotel. My heart ached for Mrs. Slade. I slipped away from home, determined to go and tell her how sorry I was for her. I found her sobbing and moaning, bowed over a stark form shrouded in a blanket. I stood beside her for a moment trembling and choking, then I slipped away unnoticed, or so I have always thought.

Though he was on the road so much, freighting to and from Salt Lake City or Fort Benton, my father was never robbed by the road agents. He always carried his gold in buckskin bags attached to a belt that he wore under his clothing. We lived through days and nights of anguished uncertainty whenever he went on his long lonely expeditions for supplies. One anxious time in the fall of 1863 when the road agents' reign of terror was at its height, my father had so much gold dust to carry out of Virginia City that it was too heavy to conceal in his accustomed way. He was warned that the road agents had him "spotted," but if his business was to continue, he had to make the trip. He decided to try a ruse. He put the buckskin purses filled with gold into the old carpetbag in which he carried his clothes. He tossed it into the bottom of the wagon and threw his bedding and camping equipment on top. He hired a driver for this wagon and sending him on with instructions on where to camp, he told his driver that he would overtake him later. The driver did not suspect that he carried the treasure. Late at night my father sped away on horseback alone, armed, and determined to dispute his rights. He overtook his driver without being challenged. Later he learned through the confessions of Dutch John Wagner, I think to my father's friend Neil Howie, that he had not outwitted the highwaymen. He had been allowed to pass in safety through the good grace of George Ives who demanded that

Freight wagons pulled by mules are pictured here on the corner of Van Buren and Wallace streets in Virginia City, Montana, circa 1865. The Sheehans lived for a time in a log cabin on Wallace; as a freighter, James Sheehan transported goods to Virginia City from Salt Lake City using mule teams such as these.
MONTANA PICTURE GALLERY PHOTOGRAPHERS, MONTANA HISTORICAL SOCIETY PHOTOGRAPH ARCHIVES

this should be because of "Jim Sheehan's nice wife and two little girls living in the gulch."[33]

In the spring of 1864 when the work of the viligantes had been accomplished, life became quieter, happier, more orderly and ordinary. Carrie and I and our schoolmates could roam farther and more freely over the hills, gullies, and benchlands. I often stopped at the home of one of our near neighbors with flowers for John Creighton, a young man who was confined to the house with a broken leg.[34] Boardinghouse and hotel keepers began to offer us little girls twenty-five cents in gold dust for a big bouquet of wildflowers with which to deck their tables, most of them laid with red-checked cloths, half-inch thick earthenware or tin cups and plates, and cheap assorted knives, forks, and spoons. Among the thousands of people who thronged Virginia City were some who would pay for the pretty little touches that give a semblance of gracious living.

Naturally no fresh vegetables were to be had during that first spring. We girls knew that lamb's-quarters, what we called "goosefoots," were edible when young and tender; they were an even tastier pot-herb than spinach. Lamb's-quarters grew riotously in the ground turned by the miners the previous summer and fall. From gathering these for the table at home we extended our activity to selling them at $1.50 in gold dust for a gallon bucket crammed full.

My career as a marketer of fresh flowers and "greens" lasted only until my father learned what I was doing. Indignantly and right off quick he put a stop to it, saying that he would not have a daughter of his running about the streets and into hotels and public places. My gentle little stepmother never questioned my flitting about as free as a bird.

Excitement ran high in the summer of 1864 when Cornelius and David O'Keefe arrived from Hell Gate with a wagonload of potatoes.[35] I rushed home with the news of their precious cargo, and my stepmother went in great haste to be in time to purchase some. As a result she made the acquaintance of the genial, witty, rollicking Cornelius O'Keefe. Later, for the magnificence of his manner in dispensing the simplest hospitality, General Thomas Francis Meagher gave O'Keefe the sobriquet of "Baron." My stepmother introduced him to Hannah Lester, and she and the Baron were married. Together they drove back across the territory to his log cabin home on the ranch at the mouth of the remote, rugged, rocky Coriacan defile now known as O'Keefe Canyon, through which wound the road to the Flathead Indian Reservation.

Hannah was romantic, venturesome, and lonely. The story of her coming to Montana, as my stepmother told it to me, was that a younger sister of Hannah's, also a lover of adventure, had agreed with some friends to make one of their party on the long journey to the promising new country. The Lester family protested against their youngest going so far from home. Hannah took her sister's place and so came to Virginia City. Accustomed as she was to refinements, intellectual pursuits, and quoting as well as writing poetry, Hannah found the crudeness of a frontier settlement almost unbearable. She was told that Cornelius O'Keefe had a wonderful ranch in a beautiful, long-settled agricultural district. When her suitor described his holdings in his glowing, Irish way, Hannah's vivid imagination flashed the picture of a manor house and an estate similar to those she had known in England and Scotland, and she accepted him as her deliverer. There she lived the rest of her life in great simplicity, sometimes enduring great hardships.

On one of my father's sojourns at home he moved the family from the little cabin off Wallace Street, whose particular location probably accounts for my being a witness to the terrible scenes of the days of vigilante justice. We went to live in a little frame house on the hillside across Daylight Gulch on Cover Street away from the main thoroughfare. One room was used for storing supplies. In it were many bags of flour that my father freighted to Last Chance Gulch and sold at a hundred dollars for a hundred pound sack. As I remember my poor, dear father, himself so honest, so trusting that he was always being imposed upon and losing money on his investments, I think he must have been lucky rather than shrewd in getting out of Alder Gulch with his flour before it was confiscated.

The citizens arose in wrath at the price of flour and threatened to raid those who were hoarding. A committee was formed to search all known sources of supply and to secure an equitable distribution. My stepmother emptied a barrel of beans, half filled it with flour and put beans on top. When the members of the investigating committee searched our house, they did not discover the deception. They found only the amount of flour agreed upon for each family.[36]

Near neighbors of ours while we lived on Wallace Street were Granville Stuart and his Indian wife. They had a little baby that the mother used to put in a hammock made Indian fashion with a blanket folded over suspended ropes. I liked to swing the baby and so was a frequent visitor. One day the incongruity of the situation struck me, young as I was. Mr. Stuart was handsome, and looking like a scholar and an aristocrat, he sat writing at a combination desk and bookcase. The Indian wife in moccasined feet was padding about doing her simplified housekeeping. Impulsively I stepped close to his chair and said, "Mr. Stuart, why did you marry an Indian woman?" He turned, smiled, put his hand caressingly on my shoulder and said sweetly, "You see, Mollie, I'm such an odd fellow. If I married a white woman she might be quarreling with me."[37]

This incident I could never, never forget, because when I related it to my stepmother she impressed upon my mind that it was rude of me to ask personal questions, terribly rude if the question might hurt one's feelings. I was deeply mortified, for I wished to appear gently bred and to have manners like those of Hannah Lester and Mrs. W. F. Sanders. Mrs. Sanders lived in a little frame house, whitewashed with green shutters on the windows. I thought it beautiful. It was cozier than any other house I had encountered since we had left the cousins in Missouri. Mrs. Sanders had a board floor in her house and pieces of furniture and bits of carpet that she had brought from "the states." She once told me that she had sold almost all of her Brussels carpet in two and three yard strips to saloonkeepers who had besieged and besought her for it. They used it to dress their bars.[38]

We had some Jewish neighbors named Goldberg. Once they concluded their celebration of the feast of the Passover by serving supper at sundown to all Jewish people in Virginia City. Mrs. Goldberg asked me to help her serve her guests. I was more impressed by the hostess's large, flat feet than by any other detail of that supper. I wanted to share my amusement with my step-mother. When I was going home Mrs. Goldberg gave me a generous basket filled with the good things she had prepared to take home to the family. I watched my chance to slip in also one of her astonishing slippers to show my stepmother. The next morning I took the basket back and returned the slipper to its accustomed place. I always thought our kindly, odd friend Mrs. Goldberg was unconscious of our little fun at her expense.

My stepmother took Kate and me with her to spend a day with a friend named Mrs. McGrath who lived in Nevada City, a mile down the gulch. Her home was next door to her husband's place of business, no doubt a saloon, for Mrs. McGrath referred to it as "the place." While the ladies chatted we children went to play in the backyard. Beyond the high board fence that shut off "the place" from the residence, we heard shouts, cheers, murmurs, thuds, grunts, and heavy breathing. We found a broken board, pried the crack wider apart, and peeked through. Two men, all but stripped on a platform circled round with rope, were brutally and furiously pommeling each other. Crowds of men surged about in seething excitement. We two little girls were glimpsing one of the historic fights between Con Orem and Hugh O'Neill. [39]

On St. Patrick's Day, whether 1864 or 1865 I cannot be certain, my parents took me to a dance. Candles in sconces stuck into the log walls of the cabin flickered softly over that long-ago festivity, leaving more shadows than lighted places. Out of the dimness of that far away memory, two forms emerge. A fiddler at one end of the crowded little cabin sat with knees crossed, tapping his foot to accentuate the rhythm of the quadrille, varsovienne, schottische, polka, minuet, waltz, jig, or whatever his nimble fingers were tearing or picking from the fiddle strings. Wreathing gracefully through every dance with first one and then another shadowy partner was a slender, beautiful, interesting woman in a tightwaisted black dress. Her black hair was smoothed back from her eager face and coiled softly low on her neck. A bit of spray broken from a cedar branch was tucked under the coil at one side and lying against the glossy black hair just above one delicate ear. She was "Mrs. Lyons," that was all I knew of her then and all that I have ever known. Though I was but twelve years old, or scarcely that, women and girls were so few that young men sought me for dances. While this flattered me, it made me more uncomfortable than happy, for I felt very young and very, very shy. I enjoyed sitting quietly watching "Mrs. Lyons."

News, only a little belated, of the assassination of Abraham Lincoln came in by Pony Express. The little girls who were my particular friends and playmates were all the children of Southern parents. They had reawakened in me all the prejudices that were mine because of my Kentucky birth and because of association with my Missouri cousins. It pains me to recall what we did when we were told of Lincoln's death. The news reached Virginia City in April 1865. It was noon. We girls were in the schoolhouse eating our lunches, which we sometimes carried to school with us. The Southern girls, by far the majority, picked up their ankle-length skirts to their knees and jigged and hippity-hopped around and around the room. They cheered for the downfall of that great, good, simple man whom they had been taught to regard as the archenemy of the South. They believed him the first and last cause of any and every misfortune that had befallen their parents and driven them to seek new fortunes amid the hardships of a far western frontier. When my playmates called, "Come on, Mollie, come on join the dance; you're from Kentucky; you're a Southerner!" I did join half-heartedly, with a guilty feeling. At home that evening I told what we had done. My father was shocked.

"I am ashamed of you, Mollie," he said, "I am a Democrat, but I am first, last, and always for the Union and for Lincoln."

My last recollection of Virginia City is of a day atingle with motion, color, and music. People thronged the street in wagons or on horseback, or jostled each other on the boardwalks and footpaths to view the proud parade of July Fourth, 1865.[40] There was I, none more proud, riding with thirty-six other little white-clad girls in a "triumphal car" or "float" (a dead-ax wagon—a wagon without springs—bedecked with evergreen and bunting and drawn by eight mules). The tallest and fairest of us, her long blonde hair flowing over her shoulders and dressed in the traditional Grecian tunic corded in at the waist, stood in the center—Columbia! We sat in groups at her feet, the States of the Union, forming the prettiest "tableau vivant." On a blue scarf crossing the left shoulder and tied under the right arm, were the letters of the state each of us represented.

And therein, for me, was one of the two drops of bitter in the ointment. My scarf flashed the name Missouri! I thought it essential to an adequate celebration of Virginia City's first Fourth of July that I should represent Kentucky, the state of my birth. The other bitter drop was the worry lest, after all, my hair (which I had worn done up for a night in the sufferance of rags) was too kinky and bushy. And so the memory of Alder Gulch breaks off, and again we were on the road with all our household possessions loaded in the wagons, trekking the hundred and twenty-five miles to a new home in Last Chance Gulch.

LAST CHANCE GULCH

John Cowan and his party from Colorado discovered Last Chance Gulch, July 21, 1864.[41] They had prospected in vain for a long time and were about to give up when someone in the party suggested that they take a "last chance" there in the gulch. Pay dirt was struck, and thus the name given. The town was christened in September 1864, at a meeting called to organize the mining district. Suggestions of Pumpkinville, Squash Town, Tomahawk, Tomah, and so on, given with guffaws, threatened to split opinion and break down the dignity of the occasion. The chairman, John Somerville, according to local story, stood up and stated peremptorily that he belonged to the best country in the world and had lived in the best county, Scott, in that state, and the best town, Helena, in that county. "By the eternal," he said, "this town shall bear that name."[42]

A Deer Lodge correspondent for the *Rocky Mountain Gazette*, December 26, 1866, had this to say about conditions in the gulches:

> women, many of them young and good-looking, go about dressed up in men's clothes, wear short hair and have the swaggering gait of a gambler and a drunkard. Every camp abounds more or less with prostitutes; the coaches and hotels are full of them. In fact, the country abounds in sin and iniquity. Many young men just landed in the country with a few greenbacks

in their pockets hang around these dens of vice until winter comes upon them and catches them out of money, hence they have a terrible time through the cold, bleak winter in this latitude.

A. K. McClure, who came to Last Chance Gulch on August 24, 1867, wrote:

Helena has all the vim, recklessness, extravagance and jolly progress of a new camp. It is but little over two years old, but it boasts of a population of 7,500 and of more solid men, more capital, more handsome and well-filled stores, more fast boys and frail women, more substance and pretense, more virtue and vice, more preachers and groggeries, and more go-aheaditiveness generally than any other city in the mountain regions. It has gradually swelled beyond the narrow, crooked gulch to the tablelands, and many beautiful cottages adorn its suburbs.[43]

Amid these surroundings and unconscious of their danger, I grew to young womanhood.

How I loved Helena! I loved its setting, high in the hills of the valley of the Prickly Pear. I loved its narrow, crooked Main Street that followed the course of Last Chance Gulch a little way and broke off abruptly in a wilderness. I loved the cross streets that led up and down steep hills and ended suddenly against other steeper hillsides, in prospect holes, or in piles of tailings. It did not matter that the thoroughfares were trampled deep with dust or churned oozy with mud by long strings of mules, oxen, or horses drawing heavy wagons. I had known life only in towns that were thus, and for that reason I was unaware of the ugliness of the hastily constructed frame and log buildings with false fronts and rickety porches. I paid no attention to the inconvenient board-walks at different levels and only occasionally continuous. I continued, as in Virginia City, to be neither curious about Helena's vices nor interested in their blatant demonstrations. The dry, light sparkling air of the place invigorated me and gave zest to living.

My father came into Last Chance Gulch in the spring of 1865 with flour and other supplies. The boom was waxing. He started a store that he put in charge of a man named Barker and procured a cabin on Clore Street. By late summer my stepmother, Kate, and I had settled there. I date our arrival in Helena by an outstanding and exotic incident. A pack train of camels was herded into the gulch.[44] My father took me to see them unloaded. I was given a strange wobbly ride on one of the strange creatures. The wonder of it was never to be forgotten.

I vividly remember our cabin home. I thought it quite cozy and comfortable. There was one large room which, according to my standards seemed very large, with a dirt floor covered with rawhides stretched over the ground and fastened down with wooden pegs. Later my father added a little lean-to kitchen with a board floor. This we covered with braided rag rugs my stepmother and I made. We hung calico partitions so as to divide the cabin into a sitting room, a bedroom for my father and stepmother, and a smaller bedroom for Kate and me. The sitting room was furnished with one rocking chair and several straight-back chairs. One was made from a barrel and covered with bright calico. A long mirror hung on one wall and there were one or two pictures. White muslin curtains were tied back from the three windows. Commanding the scene, more dominating even than the heating stove, was the "stand" covered with a bright-colored throw. Our kerosene lamp was in the center and grouped around it were books. We always had a prayer book and a little testament, selected plays of Shakespeare, and collected poems of Moore, Byron, and Scott.

We were no sooner settled than my father followed another stampede into Blackfoot, and in Blackfoot City he started another little store which he left in charge of hired help. He returned to Helena, where in the winter of 1865 or 1866 he built and stocked an icehouse, the first one in the city. In the spring of 1867, when

*The Sheehans lived just up the block from the Pioneer Cabin in Helena,
a typical dwelling from the mid-1860s that still stands today.*
MONTANA HISTORICAL SOCIETY PHOTOGRAPH ARCHIVES

the boats came up the Missouri to Fort Benton, he sent his wagons
and mules in charge of a man named Moore to freight supplies
back to Helena. Moore did not return at the appointed time. Some
other freighters or some passengers coming in from Fort Benton
asked my father why he had sold some of his mules and wagons.

53

He went hastily on horseback to Fort Benton and found that Moore had sold some of his property to people in that vicinity and had gone down the river on the returning boat. After days of delay, my father followed on the next down-river boat. He did not find any trace of Moore, nor was he ever apprehended. My father was able to recover some of the stolen property, but financial difficulty beset him.

After he returned from his expedition in search of Moore, my father made preparations to go to Utah on a road-building contract with the Union Pacific Railroad. My stepmother remained in Helena with us children during the year and a half that my father was gone. He made money on this contract, but how much I do not know. When he returned to Helena, he found that Barker had sold out the entire supply of provisions in the little store and the icehouse but had no money to pay over. He found a similar state of affairs at the store in Blackfoot City. And so his venture in both places was concluded.

Meanwhile the busy stir of school occupied my life. For a short time the beloved Lettie Sloss was my teacher again in a little log schoolhouse clinging to the steep side of the gulch. The distinguishing memory of this school is that on Friday afternoons we had lessons in embroidering and that Miss Sloss directed my making of some pin cushions. An Irishman named Thomas A. Campbell, son of Alexander Campbell, the founder of the Christian Church was, I think, my next teacher.[45] I used to go see his wife. She told me that she spoke Gaelic. We were always planning that she would teach me the language, but we were also always postponing beginning, and so I never even had my first lesson.

Going to school I used to pass the office of the weekly *Rocky Mountain Gazette*, of which Peter Ronan was coeditor and owner with Major E. S. Wilkinson. Of course my father was a subscriber. I must have read the paper diligently, for when my little dog was stolen I stopped one morning to ask Mr. Ronan if he could not help me find the dog by advertising for it in his paper. He always noticed me and spoke politely to me. Either I had chosen to overlook or had, for the time being, forgotten the Alder Gulch episode of the sluice box. The next issue of the *Gazette* carried among the locals a paragraph demanding that whoever had taken a certain little dog from a certain house on Clore Street should restore it at once to a young lady owner or expect to feel the heavy hand of justice. With what pride I read the paragraph and displayed it to my friends and acquaintances. The dog was never found, but that paper I treasured for nearly forty years.

Another day as I was passing his office, Mr. Ronan called, "Here's something for you, Mollie." It was a little "holy picture" of Pharoah's daughter discovering the infant hidden in the bulrushes. Pictures and picture books were rare in those days. I was delighted with the gift, and treasured that picture. I used it to illustrate the story of Moses for each of my own little ones again and again.

Hangman's Tree stood in Dry Gulch near the head of Wood Street, going south. One morning when we children came up from Last Chance Gulch to the crest of the hill, we saw the limp form of a man hanging with a rope around his neck from a branch of the tree. There the body continued to hang for three days as a warning to lawbreakers. During the days of this gruesome display and for a long time afterward we children were in a state of extreme nervous tension. All the distressing details were viewed and reviewed. The boys kept running down to the tree at recess and between sessions. There was talk of how the "bad man" had been aroused from sleep by the avengers, made to dress hurriedly, and taken out and hanged in the dead of night. No doubt the story was enlarged to include circumstances having to do with three recorded executions on Hangman's Tree: Jake Silvie, John Keene, and James Daniels.[46] I hated the talk. It made me shiver. I did not want to know by what name he had gone in life—that dreadful, pitiful object, with bruised head, disarrayed vest and trousers, with boots so stiff, so worn, so wrinkled, so strangely the most poignant of all the gruesome details. I tried to forget, but I have never forgotten. I have heard the story told, but for its truth I will not vouch, that one over-zealous Sunday school teacher marched her class to the foot of the tree for a close-up view of this horrible example of the results of a wayward life, hoping by means of an object lesson to frighten her young charges into paths of righteousness.

As early as the summer of 1867 a circus came to Helena, heralded for weeks in advance. Horses were the only animals. Daring bareback riders, equestriennes, acrobats, tightrope walkers, and clowns performed. In chorus the company sang and a big darkie with a fine mellow voice rolled out the words of a foolish song:

> I feel, I feel, I feel so queer
> I can't tell what to do!
> My heart beats fast as she goes by
> In dark dress trimmed in blue.

So many interesting, worthwhile, beautiful things have slipped from my mind. Why should this insipid melody and these more insipid words remain so distinct?

Professor Stone and his brother opened a private school in August 1867, on Academy Hill not far above the first little Catholic Church where the Cathedral of the Sacred Heart was later built.[47] At one end of the long room Professor Stone taught us older children. At the opposite end his brother taught the primary grades. We sat in prim rows on long, rough benches. This was the largest and most interesting school I had ever attended. Professor Stone began a Latin class and I was a member. This gave me a feeling of great importance; I felt I was standing on the edge of real intellectual achievement! Most stimulating was the lesson each day in

Webster's school dictionary, with strange sounding words to spell and define. Before school closed each afternoon the older students would pronounce words; we would each in turn rise, repeat the word, spell it, and sit down. Sallie Davenport always spelled down the school.[48] One day Professor Stone's brother was conducting this drill. It was Raleigh Wilkinson's turn. Raleigh was the son of E. S. Wilkinson, Peter Ronan's partner in the *Rocky Mountain Gazette*. He misspelled the word.

"Try it again, Raleigh," said Mr. Stone.

"I don't think I can spell it," Raleigh replied.

"Well, try it," insisted Mr. Stone.

"I told you I don't think I can spell it," growled Raleigh.

Mr. Stone, himself young, large, and athletic looking, flushed angrily and repeated his command. "Well, try it, I tell you." Raleigh repeated his refusal. For several times more command and refusal were bandied back and forth in rising crescendo until a tempestuous climax came in an exchange of blows. Suddenly up jumped all the big boys and precipitated a melee. We girls fled from the schoolhouse to our homes. This free-for-all fight was the occasion of much talk among the patrons of the school for many days.

Professor Stone encouraged dramatic reading. One of my boy schoolmates and I practiced a dialogue, without any coaching, which we gave at a public "entertainment" in the schoolroom. Our stage was the little platform where the teacher had his desk. I was a Roman matron encouraging her husband:

"Have the walls ear? I wish they had and tongues, too, to bear witness to my oath and tell it to all Rome."

"Would you destroy?" my opposite intoned.

Fervently I picked up my cue, "Were I a thunderbolt! Rome's ship is rotten! Has she not cast you out?" The applause thrilled me and fired my ambition to be an actress. Professor Stone added fuel to the flame by complimenting me warmly.

I learned the part of Lady Anne in *Richard III*. I practiced at home in the little sitting room before the mirror, trying a variety of interpretations from mincing to flamboyant. My stepmother, who often admonished me for my vanity, became now positively alarmed for the salvation of my soul and forbade me to go on with the practices or to present at school what was to have been my "big performance."

My choice of parts and ideas about interpretation I got from attending the theatre. I saw the Langrishes in the Lady of Lyons. Couldock and his daughter, Eliza, played at the People's Theatre on Wood Street in the autumn of 1867. I was deeply impressed by them. Among what I suppose were the current dramas of the period, included in the repertoire of the Couldocks, I recall most distinctly *One Touch of Nature*. The plot had to do with the separation of a father and daughter, their trials and tribulations, and their final restoration to each other. Having a real father and daughter play these parts added "one touch of nature" so thrilling that I was set daydreaming.[49] I could see in the Couldocks an analogy to my father and me. I fancied the Sheehans, father and daughter, as actors. Better still, when my father was at home for any length of time we would sing all our old songs together, as grand opera stars! Needless to say I had never seen but had only heard of grand opera.

I did not go to the theatre often, but it was a great treat and long-to-be-remembered occasion when I did go. For me the play was the thing. Escorts who took me have remained but dimly in my memory. I should like to say that my parents thought it part of my education to attend the theatre, but I do not know that this was true. Perhaps I went because to attend the productions of classic drama was the thing to do.

On another occasion, my father took me to hear General Thomas Francis Meagher deliver his famous lecture on the Irish

Brigade; it stirred me and kindled my imagination.[50] The setting was that same shabby, tawdry little theatre on Wood Street. Either backstage or in a little cabin near the theatre, my father introduced me to General Meagher before the lecture. He was a gallant, most exciting person. He had the Irish gifts of beautiful speech, of laughter and tears. Ideas flowed from him picturesquely and dramatically. He often quoted poetry with richness of tone and accentuation of rhythm. I remember clearly, after the lapse of sixty-five years, how in the course of that lecture he quoted lines from "The Irish Emigrant." I thrilled to that. I knew the lines and sang them.

An event in our own family about this time was the birth of a baby boy. I do not remember the exact date because, as I have said before, birth dates were not kept in my father's family. We were all happy to have a son, but my father was especially delighted. I was allowed to name my little brother. I called him James for my father and Francis so that [he] might have the same middle name as General Meagher. According to signs and superstitions of the old country connected with the baby's birth, great things were predicted for him. Most significant of all these signs and wonders was the fact that he was born with a "veil" over his face. This bit of tissue my poor, dear little stepmother had mounted in some way and treasured all her life.[51]

Norma Ewing was my chum at Professor Stone's school. Her father, General R. C. Ewing, was a Kentucky gentleman and Confederate soldier. He was the first clerk and recorder of Lewis and Clark County, and Norma used to help out in his office. All the girls were clever. Ella, the eldest, had gone to school in the "states." When Professor Stone was called away from school on business or was ill, Ella would teach—even his Latin class. Birdie, another older sister of Norma's, was the society belle of those days in Helena. She was petite, gay, and coquettish with tiny tripping feet and modish clothes. Her trousseau, when she married John McCormick, was a wonder and delight to all of us girls. None of us had ever seen anything so stylish or so elaborate as her Dolly Varden dresses.[52]

Florence Lamme used to come to school looking so pretty. She had beautiful dark red hair that her mother spent much time and care in arranging in the elaborate fashion of the period. Dr. A. Lamme soon moved to Bozeman with his family. Julia Lowry was a Southern girl. I thought her mother unusually refined and her home lovely. After a short time that friendship, too, was broken off, for Julia's father took his family back to St. Louis. Friendship, like everything else in a mining camp, was in a constant state of flux and change.

Raleigh Wilkinson, of whom I have already spoken, was among the boys at Professor Stone's school. Several tall young men from the mines and ranches attended in the wintertime. My first beau was Massena Bullard.[53] We called him Mattie. He was lame. It was said that his leg had been broken when he was immersed for baptism. The overture to this friendship came in his offer one day to carry my books home from school. I surrendered the books but was too shy to walk with Mattie, so I marched down one steep side of Broadway and he down the other, keeping directly opposite me. Later we braved the teasing of our friends and walked home together on the same side of the street, Mattie burdened with our combined stacks of books. Boy and girl natures don't change, not so much as language does. To have spoken of Massena Bullard as a "fellow" would have invited reproach and worse. Whatever fringe meaning of the word "fellow" had for my father I do not know, but it was a word he would not permit me to use.

Massena Bullard's family lived on a farm in the Little Prickly Pear Valley. Sometimes his mother invited me to visit. But the first time I ever went with an escort was on a sleigh ride with Mattie. When I looked out the window and saw him coming, shyness possessed me. I ran into my room behind the calico partition. My father was standing in front of the mirror clipping his beard. He let his amusement be quite evident, yet he did succeed in reassuring me. Mattie and I had but started when—oh ignominy!—the sleigh tipped over into a ditch. My father came running to the rescue, helped to right the sleigh, brushed the snow from my cloak, and sent us jingling on our way. The horse was bedecked and bedight with sleigh bells and more sleigh bells. Mattie outdid himself to overcome the inauspicious beginning of our drive and make his horse pass every other one on the road. This incident I long tried to forget but could not because of my parents' jesting and teasing.

Sleighing parties and oyster suppers afterwards at the St. Louis Hotel or at someone's home were social diversions of the winter season. As usual in mining camps the male population greatly outnumbered the female. Girls blossomed quickly into young ladies, passed from the companionship of school boys, and began to be escorted about by men of mature years.

To one of these sleighing parties I went with Mr. Ronan. Coming down Broadway, the driver, to add thrills to thrills, purposefully and very skillfully tipped over the sleigh. Neil Howie, also an acquaintance, was my escort on another occasion.[54] We drove about singing such old songs as "Kathleen Mavournee," "Only a Lock of Her Hair," "We Met 'Twas in a Crowd," "Her Bright Smile Haunts Me Still," and "Then You'll Remember Me." This time we went to the home of one of the girls for supper. As we drew near the house, we sang and shouted as loud as we could. After supper we played drop the handkerchief. Soon we tired of that and gathered in a circle and sang more old songs without accompaniment.

Not only school boys but also men, some of them verging on middle age, made merry from morning to night coasting down the steep hills of Helena. Down Broadway into Main was a favorite speedway. They vied with each other in the manufacture of sleds. Many of them were gaily painted and, after the manner of ships, displayed names. One was "The Bird" because it flew. Sometimes they were named for Helena's belles. This sort of compliment was extended, but the fun of coasting was denied to even little schoolgirls. Coasting was not ladylike. Only "tomboys," a term of deep reproach, did so. When the hilarity of the boys did tempt my girl companions and me to try the fun of sliding down hill, we retired to side streets far from the main thoroughfare.

One Christmas Eve, a group of us young people had brought evergreens to the church and had spent the afternoon decorating. When we started home, Charlie Curtis said, taking hold of a branch of one of the fir trees, "Get on, Mollie, and I'll coast you down Broadway!" I stepped on the thick branches. A young man on each side took me by the hand to steady me, Charlie pulled the tree down the steep incline, and home we went, gay, laughing, and shouting. For me, it was a breathtaking adventure!

During the pleasant weather from April sometimes through the month of November, we girls took long walks. We climbed Mount Helena. We trudged the miles of ups and downs to the hot springs, where the Broadwater Hotel was later built, to gather wild gooseberries. Fresh fruits and vegetables were only a little less rare than they had been in Alder Gulch. A little shack had been built over the springs and they were beginning to be somewhat of a resort.[55] Buggy and horseback riding were other summer pastimes. Alone, on my father's horse and always seated sideways on his saddle, I explored the hills and wooded canyons within easy riding distance from Last Chance Gulch. When young men took us girls riding they hired saddle horses, equipped with side saddles, at the livery stable. I remember one ride with Mr. Whitlach and many with Mr. Ronan.[56]

An Irish tailor made me a black alpaca riding habit. He took my measurements and made it without ever trying it on. It fit me perfectly. It was tight and small waisted with a long flowing skirt. I wore white cuffs and collar with this suit and a little black hat. I can never forget this tailor's sign. It was suspended in some way across the middle of the narrow street. Approaching from either direction one read in large letters:

THE TAILOR
E PLURIBUS UNUM
ERIN GO BRAGH!

Among the ancient Romans, the assuming of the toga meant a young man's entrance upon manhood. So, in Helena in the sixties, did the wearing of a long dress have a somewhat similar significance for girls. I wore my first long dress to a private dancing party to which Mr. Ronan took me. This combination of events made the details of that dress memorable. The material was poplin with wide stripes of alternating red and brown. The low neck was square cut and the sleeves puffed out at the shoulders, fitted close down the arm, and were fastened around the wrist. The basque fit close and the skirt billowed out in ample folds to stiffly touch the floor. My family and friends remarked how tall and womanly I looked. I was five feet five and three-quarter inches, and slender, and I took thought to stand erect. My friend Lizzie Ryan and I had taken particular pains in dressing our hair alike for this occasion. It was rolled high on top of the head and held back with a fillet of white net so fastened that the loose ends of the net fluttered about the shoulders. We were conscious of creating an effect.

Lizzie Ryan's was a sad little story. An uncle, Jim Ryan, who was her guardian, brought her to Alder Gulch to live with his cousin, Mrs. Henneberry. Lizzie was lonely and dissatisfied. On a short acquaintance, without the knowledge of her relatives, she married a young man who was said to be utterly worthless, a gambler, and so unsuccessful a one that his father had to support him. Immediately after the marriage the groom took the stagecoach for Helena to inform his father of the step he had taken. In spite of the protests of her guardian, Lizzie followed on the next coach. The young man's father and Lizzie's uncle set at once about having the marriage annulled. The young man went to California. Branded as a good-for-nothing by his own father, he nevertheless was successful, married again, and established a home in California. After a few years Lizzie married a printer named Morrison. She died while still young. I have the impression that the whole of her short life was unhappy. She admired Mr. Ronan. But of course she did, for he was everyone's favorite.

Peter Ronan was a handsome, dashing-looking young man of medium height and well proportioned. I have never since seen, not even in the son and daughter that resemble him, such flashing and expressive dark eyes. He had a straight, high-bridged nose, and delicate nostrils, and slender, shapely hands and feet. All his features suggested well bred and sensitive forebears. His hair was dark brown at the roots, shaded into the tawny of the sunburned miner and wayfarer. His mustache was dark auburn. I recall him at this period in a suit of brown broadcloth with cape (called a "talma") to match. Usually he wore a broad-brimmed tan hat and high-heeled boots. I cannot paint the picture. Still less can I do justice to his rich and radiant personality. He was full of gaiety, of fun, of mimicking. Every day some encounter yielded him another humorous story. He laughed much and he loved much. He was openhearted, openhanded, even too generous. Things of the mind appealed to him. There were spiritual depths to his nature for which I have no words.

Our love story, if so I am to speak, commenced quite simple. Mother Vincent, of the Sisters of Charity of Leavenworth, Kansas, who had indeed been a mother to Mr. Ronan before he came to Montana during the troublous days in Leavenworth, wrote to him asking about the prospect of starting a school in Helena. Mr. Ronan brought the letter to my father to read, thinking that it might interest him on account of his two little girls, Kate and me.[57] I answered Mr. Ronan's knock and admitted him to our little home on Clore Street. Often afterwards he told me that I wore such "a pretty little tunic." His attention was attracted first by that and then to the fact that I was no longer only an amusing little school-girl. From that evening Mr. Ronan was a frequent visitor in our home. He read poetry to me. We went about together to social affairs. He was my avowed lover.

When I was sixteen we were engaged, with the approval of my stepmother. Mr. Ronan gave me an engagement ring set with a cluster of three diamonds. As a double plighting of our troth, I took from my finger the ring wrought for me from the gold of the placer diggings of Alder Gulch and slipped it onto his little finger. All this came about during the time that my poor, dear father was working under contract with the Union Pacific Railroad, and during an interval between my brief periods of attending school.

My father owned a little frame house near our cabin that was standing unrented. Some of our neighbors suggested that I make use of it to open a school for their young children. I did. Tuition for each pupil was $1.25 a week. Fourteen or fifteen tots attended. Among them was a lovely little boy about seven years old, the child of J. Jules Germain, proprietor of the International Hotel. Mr. Germain was separated from his wife. She and their little boy were living at the St. Louis Hotel. One morning, after my school had been in session for several weeks, when I rang the bell for the children to come in from recess, little Jules Germain did not march in with the other children. I looked out but did not see him. The children said that he had run down the street to the hotel to see his mother, as he sometimes did.

The noon hour passed. Mrs. Germain came asking for her child. She had not seen him since he left for school in the morning. She feared his father had taken him away. We questioned the children. They said that they had not seen Jules since they had played with him at recess. The mother went to the father. He had not seen the little boy. A search began. Near a prospect hole, half filled with water, a little distance from the school, a child found the little boy's cap. The hole was dragged and true enough, the little dead body was brought up. The funeral took place in the parlor of the St. Louis Hotel, and there I marched my little scholars, two by two. We stood in a group around the little casket and sang: "I want to be an angel and with the angels stand, / A crown upon my forehead and a harp within my hand." As I look back on it now I realize that the part my scholars and I took in the sad occasion was heartrending. I choked so that I could scarcely get through the song. I could hear the sobbing of the heartbroken mother and father and of their friends and mine. Over the dead body of their son, Germain and his wife were united. After this tragedy I did not have the heart to go on with my little school.

Of that which touches us most profoundly we can say the least, and so I have said nothing of the influence that religion had come more and more to have upon me. Tied up inextricably with the story of the establishment of the Catholic Church in Helena is not only my story and my family's, but also that of Peter Ronan. The old *Gazette* office on Ewing Street became the dwelling place of Helena's first parish priests. Then it sheltered the Sisters of Charity and later housed their boys' school. My family was present at the celebration of the first Mass on November 1, 1866, in the first little Catholic Church on the hill. One of our dearest friends and

Mr. Ronan's, John M. Sweeney, supervised the building, built partly with his own skillful hands. My dear father's name is signed to the historic document, the petition addressed to Father U. Grassi asking for the appointment of two priests to the Helena mission.[58]

I knew them well—Fathers Francis X. Kuppens, A. J. Vanzina, C. Imoda—better still Father Leo Van Gorp and best of all dear, dear, gentle little Father Jerome D'Aste. Each in turn was my confessor, my confidant, my adviser on concerns temporal as well as spiritual. Besides soul solace these men, reared amid an old-world culture, brought some of that worldliness, culture, and courtliness into our frontier settlement, where various and banal provincialisms, crudeness, and lawlessness combined to form our social background. Through their influence my soul and its needs became a major concern. Perhaps, in fact I am very sure that, this religious influence accounts for my growing up so oblivious of the viciousness that I realize now was flaunted on the streets of every mining camp in which I lived.

When I was attending Professor Stone's school I used to go to Father Grassi for help with difficult lessons, with my Latin and my compositions. Through Father D'Aste's interest I sang in the first Catholic choir in Helena. At one Christmas Mass I sang as a solo one verse of the "Adeste Fidelis." I remember a few of the members of that choir: Charlie Curtis had a fine baritone voice; Lizzie Ryan; a Mr. Smedley; three Germans; a woman and two men with splendid rich voices. A man named Clark played the organ and directed the choir. He was a quiet, gentle, ordinary appearing man who earned his living playing in saloons. He offered to teach me to play the organ. He was a married man. I was to go to his home for the lessons. To this plan my stepmother, who only occasionally opposed me in anything, absolutely objected.

Major and Mrs. Martin Maginnis were dear and close friends of mine all their lives. They were both intellectual, cultured, clever, and distinctly different. The Major was witty and scintillating; Mrs. Maginnis was astonishingly frank, a kindly but keen observer upon life who expressed those observations with a dash of cynicism that was spicy rather than bitter. I thought their three-room home charming. Its interesting and unusual pictures and books, every detail of its furnishing, reflected the rare personalities of the owners. Many evenings I spent there in that delightful atmosphere. When I came alone the Major always ceremoniously escorted me home, down the hill to the bottom of the gulch. On Sunday evenings, although Mrs. Maginnis was not then a Catholic, she and the Major would go with me to vespers. I loved to sing in the choir and never willingly missed.

Hattie and Julia, the beautiful daughters of Charles Rumley, were friends of those yesterdays. Mr. and Mrs. Hugh Galen, their little daughter Nellie (Mrs. Thomas Carter), Mr. and Mrs. H. N. Holter, Mr. and Mrs. John Ming, Mr. and Mrs. H. N. Parchen, John Curtis, T. H. Kleinschmidt, Richard Lockey, A. J. and D. W. Fisk—their names, their faces, little incidents—all rush to mind. When I come upon the names of people in reading accounts of early days in Helena, I am surprised to find, young girl that I was, how wide were my acquaintances. C. W. Cannon once told me that when he first came to Last Chance Gulch my father gave him a couple bags of flour with which he started a bake shop. W. A. Clark, to select a name very widely known, often waited on me when he was engaged in the mercantile business in Helena. He was slender, sprightly, gave his customers prompt and courteous attention always. With such disconnected bits of memories I could fill volumes.[59]

My father returned from Utah in March 1869. What a storm of wrath broke. His little girl marry! Indeed not! She was too young! She was to go to school and learn something. I was commanded to return the engagement ring to Mr. Ronan and all his other gifts. There was nothing else for me to do. I never questioned my father's authority. I never argued. I always obeyed.

Among these gifts was a precious copy of "The Lady of the Lake," the first poem that Mr. Ronan had read aloud to me, from that very volume. There was also a scrapbook, the scrapbook which I still have after more than sixty years, the old scrapbook which has yielded me so many reminders and much material for these wanderings through my yesterdays. When we became engaged, we planned to keep it together—the newspaperman's idea—clipping things we fancied such as sketches Mr. Ronan wrote, newspaper accounts of social affairs we attended together. Nothing had been entered when my father issued the stern command to break the engagement and to return the gifts. Before I gave back the scrapbook, I wrote in pencil on the inside of the cover:

To Peter Ronan—

Other skies may bend above you,
Other hearts may seek thy shrine,
But none other ere will love thee
With the constancy of mine.

> Your friend,
> Mollie Sheehan

I read the lines over and over again. I felt that I was being disloyal to my father and not entirely obedient. I erased the lines; the words showed faintly through the blur.

My father and Mr. Ronan had been friends since they had met on the stampede into Alder Gulch. The whole situation was unhappy and embarrassing. Considering everything, the closing of my father's stores in Helena and Blackfoot City, the fact that my stepmother had always wanted to go to California, and the fact that San Diego was said to be booming, it seemed the time for us to load the wagons and push on.

Among the things that I had given or loaned to Mr. Ronan, which he now returned to me, was a volume of Tom Moore's complete works, given to me by a good neighbor and friend, Andy O'Connell. He was a great admirer of Thomas Francis Meagher. After the General's tragic death, Mr. O'Connell came into possession of some of his hero's personal belongings. He wanted me to have one of the precious relics and so he had presented me with this volume, inscribed in Thomas Francis Meagher's handwriting with his own name. After Mr. Ronan had given it back to me, I found that he had marked passages with which to convey messages from him to me whenever I turned those pages, and they did. When my children had read that volume to tatters, years after their father's death, I saved one particular page and clipped from it the poem, "When Cold in the Earth." His pencilings made in that time long past speak now with exquisite sadness.

Shortly before we left Helena, on St. Patrick's Day, April 17, 1869, with my parents I attended a costume ball. I wore a white Swiss dress, with rows and rows of paper shamrocks glued on for trimming. On a wide green satin ribbon, arranged over the left shoulder and fastened at the waist on the right, were a gilded harp and shamrock. I wore a gilded crown on my head. Under this array was a heavy heart. With my father's permission, Mr. Ronan danced once with me. He still wore my little gold ring!

Our little house on Clore Street was emptied. We spent our last night in Helena at the St. Louis Hotel. Very early in the morning the family drove off in the covered wagon down the steep slope toward the valley. It had been arranged for me to overtake them in the afternoon. The gypsy instinct had slipped away with the things of childhood. I was heavyhearted at leaving the place, the friend, the one above all others that I loved. As I went back through the narrow hall of the hotel, after having seen my family off, I met Mr. Ronan. He said, "Goodbye, Mollie, and here is your ring." As he held it out in the palm of his hand, the finality of this parting crushed me. "Keep it till I ask for it and goodbye," I barely whispered, and turned quickly into my room.

In the afternoon John M. Sweeney came for me, driving a spirited team hitched to a light buggy. As we neared the little church on the hill, he said, "Mollie, let us go in and say a little prayer for your safe journey and that all may turn out well and happily for you." He tied his team to the hitching post and we went into the church and knelt down, side by side, and prayed silently, simply, earnestly. John Sweeney was the best man I have ever known. A success financially, a man among men, he was deeply religious. He never lost the simplicity and faith of childhood.

We overtook my family in the valley where camp for the night had been made. Because I was taken up with my heartbreak, or because of memory's strange tricks, I recall no other incident of this journey. We stopped to visit Ellen and Bill Tiernan at their ranch in the Ruby Valley, about twenty miles from Virginia City. Ellen was expecting a baby and needed my stepmother's help. Carrie Crane, the Alder Gulch schoolgirl chum, was living on a ranch on Wisconsin Creek, a few miles away. We renewed our friendship. While we waited for the coming of the baby, I helped with the sewing for the event and with the housework. Bill Tiernan took me horseback riding. Carrie's friends invited me about to country dances. After a few weeks, the baby was born. We called her Elizabeth and I was her godmother. As a farewell for me Carrie Crane gave a quilting bee. Then the Sheehans were again trekking westward over tableland and hill and mountain pass and desert.[60]

BOOK TWO

Youth and Romance

And yet souls go adventuring down
The old, old ways which all have gone,
To find them all mysterious still;
Oh Life, we'll live you with a will.

—Donald Burnie
"Mystery," *Tesceminicum*

Peter Ronan

PETER RONAN

Peter Ronan was thirty years of age when we became engaged. In those thirty years he had done and dared and endured more than many men have in twice that time. Naturally the close ties that knot kin to kin had been, not exactly broken, but stretched wide, as often happens even today when great distances and varied interests intervene. He had traveled far, very far, from the little village of Antigonish, Nova Scotia, where he was born on June 1, 1838, the sixth child in a family of eight with a litany of sweet old names—Mary, Thomas, James, Margaret, John, Peter, Theresa, Louise.

Matthew Ronan, the father of this family, had come from County Wexford, Ireland, to Nova Scotia, and there had married Margaret Carter from County Limerick, Ireland, on February 13, 1825. He was far down life's western slope even when I came to know of him, retired and the beloved pensioner of devoted sons and daughters. He had a farm in Nova Scotia. What trade or business he followed when he came into the States, I do not know, but Peter epitomized his father as a fine gentleman and a practical Christian.

Peter Ronan had story after story to tell of his mother's mildness and sweetness. The severest punishment she ever administered to any of her big, healthy brood was to whip the spirited culprits with her apron strings and then point to the switch hanging upon the kitchen wall and threaten to use it "next time." There is no formal record of Peter's boyhood spent in the little, unknown, quaint village of Antigonish, nor of his early life.

Young Peter attended school until he was thirteen years of age, learning from the village master, an old soldier, who emphasized one lesson above all others that are found in books. The boy that was to succeed in life must fight at the drop of a hat. Before Peter was fourteen years of age his family moved from Nova Scotia to Rhode Island. He entered the job printing department of the *Pawtucket Gazette-Chronicle* as an apprentice. He learned his trade so well that at seventeen years of age he was foreman of the book and job printing office of M. B. Young, Providence, Rhode Island. Meanwhile his father, mother, and sisters had taken up permanent residence in Malden, Massachusetts. So he came to Boston to work at his trade for a short time. In 1859 he went to Dubuque, Iowa, as a compositor on the *Dubuque Evening Times*.

In February 1860, with six other young men, Peter Ronan set out on a voyage of adventure to the unexplored country of Pike's Peak. He spent two years mining in the mountains of Colorado, and then he recrossed the great plains to Leavenworth, Kansas. He became associated with W. H. Adams, who a few years before had printed the first newspaper in Kansas, the first issue of which he struck off on a Washington handpress under a tree on the townsite of Leavenworth. This spot continued to be the "press room" until a board shanty could be built. In 1862 Adams was engaged in publishing the *Daily Enquirer*, and in it Peter Ronan purchased a third interest.

The venture was drawn into the Civil War and hurled to disaster. The *Daily Enquirer* was the only Democratic newspaper in the State of Kansas.[1] Dennison D. Taylor, the political editor, had formerly been a member of the *Kentucky Statesman*. General James Gillpatrick Blunt caused the suppression of the paper because of its partisan articles. The three proprietors were arrested and thrown into the military guardhouse. It was at this time that Peter Ronan first made the acquaintance of Mother Vincent of the Sisters of Charity of Leavenworth, Kansas. With a few other Sisters, she came to the guardhouse and brought the prisoners food and administered to their comfort in every way that she could. She noticed that the young pressman needed a clean shirt. She brought him one. She took his soiled clothes away and laundered and mended them. Whatever it was possible for her to do, in the name of sweet Charity, she did. She was for Peter Ronan like a star in the darkness that guided him home.[2]

After some days he was released and permitted to publish the paper. Finally the senior members of the firm, W. H. Adams and Taylor, were also released and resumed their work. The sullen feeling against them continued to ferment until at last the explosion came. The office of the *Daily Enquirer* was attacked by a mob. The printing press and equipment were unlawfully demolished. And so the junior member of the firm turned again westward, almost penniless. With hundreds of other fortune seekers, he joined the gold rush of 1862, heading for Florence, Idaho Territory. On the way he chanced to fall in with some old Colorado acquaintances and turned off with them to the camp at Bannack, Montana, then also in Idaho Territory. Thus he was among the first followers of that stampede who staked their claims at Alder Gulch on that early June morning in 1863.[3]

The claim proved to be a good one, and so Peter Ronan sent for his brother Jim to come and share with him in the "clean up." Jim, who was married and had a family to support, had been injured and maimed in a railroad accident. Jim made enough from the Alder Gulch claims to return to Dubuque and establish himself in business. By 1865 the claims of the Ronans must have been worked out, for they sold the property.[4]

The *Montana Democrat* of Virginia City, the second newspaper published in the territory, was established by Major John P. Bruce in November of 1865.[5] Peter Ronan was foreman, local editor, and part owner. Within a year, he entered into partnership with E. S. and C. H. Wilkinson and established the *Rocky Mountain Gazette* at Helena. He made a trip east to visit his family in Malden and to purchase equipment for the new venture. On the way he stopped at Leavenworth and instituted a lawsuit, suing the city for the destruction of the plant of the *Daily Enquirer*. He won the suit and received his share of the damages.

The *Rocky Mountain Gazette* first came off the press on August 11, 1866, announcing that it was to be published weekly by Wilkinson, Maguire, and Ronan in the building formerly occupied by the Helena Academy on Academy Hill. As swift changes were characteristic of the mining camps, H. N. Maguire retired from the partnership after the third issue on August 25, 1866. Major Martin Maginnis then became a member of the firm and the paper began to be issued tri-weekly. Commencing March 30, 1868, the *Rocky Mountain Gazette* was issued daily. In 1870, a press operated by steam power was installed, and on August 22 of that year was issued the first paper in the territory to be printed by steam. Another innovation was the lighting of the whole plant by gas manufactured on the lot behind the building.

It was a tremendous undertaking for the pioneer journalist to obtain supplies and keep them readily available. He had the challenge of establishing communication with the world—even the world immediately outside the gulch—when storms obstructed the roads. Mail was uncertain even in the best of weather. A telegraph line from Salt Lake City to Virginia City was completed November 2, 1866, announced in the *Gazette* on November 3. It was carried into Helena a few weeks later. This contact with the great world was precarious. The lines were often weighted down with winter snows, or the telegraph poles toppled over in summer tempests. They were maintained at great expense. Typographers, pressmen, reporters, help of any kind could scarcely be found and could seldom be kept. Maguire's resignation from the partnership soon after the venture began is one example. Concerning the real drama of the publishing of the *Rocky Mountain Gazette*, I have scarcely a realization since I was only a schoolgirl when Peter Ronan did his own editing, set his own type, and was always ready to do his own fighting on the rough and troublous frontier.

Generosity, sympathy, wit, resourcefulness, imagination, high-hearted temperament, hopeful, heroic—these were the qualities of the pioneer journalist, the journalist that I knew the best. I loved him, and because I did my mind, my heart, my whole being turned back to Helena with such yearning that the journey, in 1869 when I was in my seventeenth year, to Sheridan, Montana, and to Corinne, Utah, is almost a blank.

BOUND FOR SAN DIEGO

The city of Corinne on the Bear River a few miles north of the north end of the Great Salt Lake was booming in the summer of 1869. It was the supply and employment center for a great deal of the construction work during the closing months of the building of the Union Pacific Railroad. Houses, mere shacks, rented at a premium; town lots were selling at fabulous prices; everybody was speculating. Sanguine fortune seekers were predicting that the burg was surely going to be the "Chicago of the Rocky Mountains."[6]

My father, whose investments at Helena and at Blackfoot City had failed, saw a chance to make some money. He halted our journey, pitched our tent, unpacked our wagon, and contracted to do some teaming. Because we were in need of ready money, my stepmother and I began to serve meals to boarders amid the inconveniences of tent living—dirt, flies, and heat—and the hum and hustle of that construction camp.

This episode was a nightmare to me. The railroad camp and its workers had none of the romance, the picturesqueness, or the golden promise of the mountain mining camps and chivalrous miners. It sometimes seemed to me that all the rough-toughs in the West had swaggered into Corinne. I was seventeen, tall, dignified, and somewhat mature as a result of my associations and experiences during the last two years in Helena. Most of our boarders were men. A few of them were patronizing in their manner toward me. Many of them were crudely and rudely flirtatious. My pride was deeply wounded. I hated waiting on the table. I begged my stepmother to let me stay out of sight back of the canvas partition and do the cooking and dishwashing.

All was not drudgery and humiliation. Through an old Alder Gulch acquaintance, John Creighton, I met his cousin Harry Creighton, an attractive, well-bred young man. Through Harry I met other pleasant young people with whom I enjoyed parties and picnics and one strange, new, almost shocking experience—a midget show in which the performers were Mr. and Mrs. Tom Thumb, General Warren, and Minnie Warren. I was touched by the brave pathos of the tiny general, trim and dapper in his little uniform and splendid insignia, prancing up and down the rough boards of the rude shack, singing gaily, "I am Captain Jenks of the Horse Marines; / I feed my horse on corn and beans."

Another new and wonderful experience was my first ride on a railroad train. My father took me on a two-day pleasure trip to Salt Lake City. Its substantial buildings and wide streets were indeed a revelation to the girl from the gulches. As tourists do today, so my father and I visited the Tabernacle, which was then under construction. We saw Brigham Young sitting among a group of men on the porch of our hotel. Among the people whom I observed, there was one woman who charmed me with her beauty and dash. I was told that she was an actress and I became all the more interested in her. Several times she caught my eyes fixed on her, frankly admiring her. Each time she bowed and smiled. I longed to accept the implied invitation to approach her and speak to her, but shyness prevented me.

As I came out of the hotel and was about to enter the horse-drawn bus that was to take my father and me to the railway station for the return trip to Corinne, this lovely lady was sitting on the porch. She arose, most attractively attired, descended the steps with queenly grace and advanced to me. She put a book into my hands, delivering a little well-pronounced speech, saying that she hoped I would accept Owen Meredith's *Lucile* from her and that I would enjoy reading it. Some men seated on the porch of the hotel, among them Brigham Young, were the audience for this well-timed, well-staged, well-costumed bit of acting. Even in my simplicity I was aware that such it was. Because I did not know what else to do, I fell into my part and kept the book. And I did enjoy reading it. To me, it was an altogether new sort of book.[7] On the way back to Corinne I was torn between the pleasure of reading it and the pleasure of merely sitting and gazing out the window of the train, enjoying this new, swift, wonderful means of locomotion.

By autumn the railroad construction was practically completed. Corinne's bubble of prosperity had burst and its floating population began to drift away. The time had come for us to launch our prairie schooner on the road westward. My father collected the money that was owed him, converted it into greenbacks and deposited his roll in his buckskin purse attached to a belt he wore under his clothing. He loaded all our property into a covered wagon and continued our journey toward San Diego, California.

I suppose that in coming from Montana to Utah we had followed the old stage route, as we now did, traveling through Utah and Nevada, and directing our course to connect with the Santa Fe Trail into California. Some young men who were looking for a location to establish a stagecoach line traveled along with us in their stagecoaches and on their saddle horses. They let me ride one especially fine-spirited animal, but most of the time I was on the high seat of our wagon, taking turns with my father in driving our six-mule team.

The journey traveling south through Utah was deluxe compared to that north to Montana six years before. Usually we made camp for the night near the ranch house of some Mormon settler from whom we bought milk, butter, fresh meat, vegetables, and sometimes even fruit. Many of these ranch homes were neat and thrifty looking. Plural wives were quite in evidence and there were many, many children. Observations of this kind I set down in the diary I kept on this trip. The diary was not packed among my things when I was married at San Juan Capistrano, and so it was lost.

We crossed the Virgin River that flows into Lake Mead from the north and recrossed it and crossed it again. Before we started across the Mojave Desert, we rested for a day in a beautiful camping place. Here we filled our water kegs. We commenced the trip across the desert in the evening in order to make as much progress as possible in the cool of the night while the mules were fresh. When my father grew sleepy he called me and I took my turn driving. I remember the brooding darkness, how the mystery of night and loneliness and the unknown pressed down upon me. The stars were unfriendly, small, cold and withdrawn. I looked toward the sky while the trusty mules took their own way through the sand. I thought of the events of my life, of my dear father, of the standards he set up for me, the books he directed me to read. Then I thought of the strange and crude new places that he was always moving toward. I summed my reflections up in a phrase I whispered to myself. Later I wrote it down in my diary. I have often used it since, "What a strange bundle of consistent inconsistencies we all are."

Sometime during the following morning we stopped to rest and water the mules. Then in a few hours we had to urge the poor beasts on so as to make camp at a watering place to which we had been directed. We found the little oasis with its few struggling trees and bit of trampled grass. There were two springs where the water gurgled up sluggishly and meandered around great dry boulders. One spring was posted with a warning sign that the water was polluted, and that man and beast drank in peril of deadly illness. We camped through an afternoon and night. Our mules and the horses of our fellow wayfarers were kept tied for safety and were allowed to drink only a small amount of water for fear that the pollution might have spread to both springs. We risked no campfires that night on account of the precious trees and grass. By dawn we were on our way again.

In the afternoon as the mules, with heads drooping and tongues lolling, trudged over the sweltering, glaring sand, one of them dropped weakly to his knees and rolled over on his side. My father poured the water that was left on the mule's parched tongue and down his throat. He undid the harness, managed to get the suffering creature to stagger to his feet and to the side of the road. My father then adjusted the harness in some way, gave me the line, and told me to drive on and try to keep the stagecoaches in sight.

It was terrible leaving my father alone there on the desert sand trying to give relief to the poor, worn-out beast. I kept looking back and looking back. After what seemed an endless time, I saw him coming along in the gathering dusk, carrying the dead mule's halter over his arm. He walked with the heart-stabbing, weary droop of the laboring man at the close of a long day.

At the first place beyond the desert where we came to clear water, green trees, and grass, we camped for several days to rest and refresh ourselves as well as our jaded, faithful mules. When we reached Los Nietos, a rancho not far from Los Angeles, my father got a little house for us. For days we rested, then we set about washing and mending and making ourselves again as clean and neat and respectable looking as possible. The mules and my father had little time to rest for there was an opportunity to earn money plowing. Meanwhile, the young men had gone with their stagecoaches to San Diego.

My first acquaintance with Los Angeles was on horseback. Most of the population traveled on horseback about the unpaved streets, knee deep with dust in hot weather and seas of mud during the rainy season. My father and I rode from Los Nietos one Sunday to attend Mass at the church of Our Lady of the Angels, opposite the Plaza on the west side of Main Street, near the corner of what is now Sunset Boulevard. Strangers though we were, we had no trouble in finding our way since Los Angeles was then a little desert town of less than 6,000 inhabitants.[8] It was predominantly Mexican in population, spirit, culture, and architecture. Frame cottages here and there were surrounded by picket fences. A few of the more pretentious buildings, such as the Bella Union, the United States Hotel, and the Stearns Block were two-story structures with flat roofs. There were alternating porches upstairs and down across the front, sometimes on two sides and even across the back with alternating windows and doors running their entire lengths. There were open courts at the backs, especially on the larger Mexican houses. Now and then a pepper tree, a sycamore, or a palm showed above the roof, motionless in the still air.

On our return to Los Nietos in the late afternoon, we took the wrong turn at the crossroads and were lost. We stopped at a little mustard-colored house, such as the Mexicans used to build, to inquire our way. We were advised to wait until morning before going back to the crossroads and on to Los Nietos by an entirely different road. Then we had our first experience of wholehearted Mexican hospitality. The residents urged us to spend the night, ushered us into the little house, and provided each of us with a clean, comfortable bed. In the morning they sent us on our way, but first we had a breakfast of coffee, frijoles, and tortillas.

After two weeks at Los Nietos, we set out for San Diego. When we reached San Juan Capistrano, we met the young men who had been our fellow travelers returning in their stagecoaches. They said that the story of the boom in San Diego was fictitious, that the place was full of idle men with no prospect of work, and that we had better return with them to Los Angeles. My father had not seen any opportunity there. The purse on his belt had become alarmingly thin and so he made his decision quickly.

"We might as well stay right here and see what I can do while I still have a few greenbacks left," he said.

That is how we came to make our home on a little hill just outside the old Mexican pueblo off the King's Highway. We settled a few hundred yards from the romantic ruins of San Juan Capistrano where we could see the rolling fogs of the ocean and hear the roaring waves break against the mighty shorecliffs.[9]

The Sheehans lived near and attended church in a chapel within the ruins of the Mission San Juan Capistrano, shown here in a late 1800s photograph. The Spanish founded the mission in 1766; the Great Stone Church, constructed between 1796 and 1806, was destroyed in an earthquake in 1812.

SAN JUAN CAPISTRANO HISTORICAL SOCIETY

Casa Blanca, San Juan Capistrano

In San Juan Capistrano, the hotelkeeper was an Irishman married to a Mexican woman. He told my father that it would be possible to file on government land that had been put on the market by the United States Land Commission in an effort to adjust Mexican land titles that had been in confusion since the surrender of California.[10] The hotelkeeper introduced my father to Richard Egan, known throughout the community as Don Dick, the *alcalde*. The *alcalde* was a mayor with judicial power. Although he was then only twenty-seven years of age, and he had lived for little more than two years in San Juan, he was the chief citizen of the place, everything to everyone. He had taken up a tract of government land and was familiar with all the legal intricacies connected with doing so. Under his direction and advice, my father found and filed on a tract of 160 acres for which he paid the United States government at the rate of $2.25 an acre.

The land seemed promising, a creek flowed through it, and otherwise the location was desirable. It adjoined the mission olive orchard where the old vats for pressing the olives were still in use. I remember one beautifully branching, gray-green olive tree just off our land. It blew over and my father set it back up, caring for it with genuine sentiment in the vain hope that the veteran might take root and flourish again. In a little cup of those softly swelling

87

hills, *lomas* the Mexicans called them, beside the arroyo, my father pitched our big army tent. He partitioned it with canvas into two rooms, and my stepmother and I set up our household things and established home. It must have been late in November, but in the wild and gentle climate of that sequestered, beautiful valley opening onto the Pacific Ocean, one spent most of the time out of doors. In that climate one could live even during the winter months with a minimum of shelter.

My father immediately set about getting some of the land under cultivation. I helped him plant corn and potatoes. In a season he had a splendid crop. Next he hired a carpenter to erect the frame for an adobe house, which he planned to finish himself during odd moments snatched from wrestling with soil, seeds, and weeds, and nourishing plants, vines, and trees. For as soon and as fast as possible he had planted grape vines and walnut, peach, apricot, and pear trees.

Besides toil and sweat, all this had meant an outlay of capital until scarcely a dollar remained of the $600 roll of greenbacks my father had had when he pitched our tent in San Juan Capistrano. Mules, a wagon, and $600 was all my father had left after working so hard along the frontiers of Kentucky, Indiana, Illinois, Iowa, Missouri, Colorado, Montana, and Utah. At the age of forty-six he had reached his last frontier in California, on the very shores of the westward flowing sea where lay the shadowy line between civilization and the setting sun.

The little house was so long in being finished with the few hours my overworked father could find between supper time and dark to work on it that my stepmother and I began to get anxious, for warm days were coming. My father said that as soon as he got enough money ahead to hire someone to drive the wagon and haul mortar, he would finish laying the bricks himself. By spending all his time at it, he could finish the house in a couple of weeks.

I insisted that I could do the driving and hauling just as well as any hired help. My father permitted me to try. He mixed and loaded the mortar, and I hauled it, put it into buckets, and hoisted it up to the scaffolding to him. True enough, the work was soon done.

It was a square, one-story house with four rooms. The first floor was partitioned into a fair-sized living room and small bed-room. There was a stairway on the outside of the house to the attic, which was floored and partitioned into two bedrooms. The kitchen was in a small cabin a few steps from the back porch. Both buildings had a coat of whitewash and in accordance with their customs, the Mexicans bestowed a name upon our little house. Casa Blanca it was called even though it was just the typi-cal little pioneer house. It had no wide verandas, and no shadowy inner court invited the luxury of an afternoon *siesta*.

We could not yield to the inertia of a drowsy Mexican pueblo for we had too much to do and to accomplish. But we were not too busy to enjoy from our hillside the gray wraiths of ships sailing past in the distance, ocean sunsets, and the greater riot of color when a California spring swept over the hills. Nor were we too busy to answer the invitation of the bells swinging in the *campanario*, or to follow the trail downhill to early morning Mass or vespers in the dusky chapel fitted up in the ruins of the old mission. Here, too, were colors rich and warm. The flickering sanctuary lamp and the lighted candles glowed on a great oil painting of the crucifixion on the wall behind the altar. The Stations of the Cross also were done in oils in intense colors. I was not capable of judging whether these pictures were art, but they satisfied me. Padre Joseph Mut, himself a native of Barcelona, told me that the Franciscans had brought them long ago from old Spain.

We were the only members of the congregation that were not Mexican or Spanish. Men and women came to church in their picturesque native costumes: shirts or tunics of silk or damask, velvet breeches, lace *mantillas*, *serapes* striped with bright colors, and *mangas* with richly embroidered collars. Servants of the well-to-do spread rugs for their households to sit upon. The others squatted upon the bare floor. There were no pews or chairs. My father made a bench for us and we were the only ones in the congregation who did not sit upon the floor. Everyone sang. A Mexican orchestra—guitar, violin, triangle, tambourine, *castanets*—furnished the bizarre accompaniment for the hymns at Mass and vespers. After the religious services on Sundays, various groups would sometimes gather for *bailes* or dances. When at first I refused invitations to attend, thinking it was not the way to spend the Sabbath, they, knowing of American prejudices, would insist, "But why not? You are not American; you are *Islandes* (Irish)."

All went well while we lived like gypsies in our tent, until the results of my father's work began to show and it became known that we had come to stay. My father was a "squattie," or in the Mexicans' more poetic language, *injusto occupente*. They bore bitter hatred toward all squatters. From time to time different ones came threatening and claiming that we had settled on their property. To each and all my father declared that he would pay rent or buy the land from anyone who could show him a title to it.

One morning as he was driving away from the house, a group of sixteen or twenty *vaqueros* came galloping up the road and surrounded his wagon. With threats, curses, shouting, and gesticulation they ordered him to get off the place. I watched at the window of our house. My father sat there on the high seat of the wagon, cool, calm, determined, repeating again and again, "Show me a title to the land and I will pay." Finally they rode off sullen and still threatening. The people claiming the land instituted a lawsuit against my father. He hired a lawyer in Los Angeles. The case was tried in the local courts and then was carried on to Washington, D.C., and tried before the Supreme Court of the United

States. There Major Maginnis, at that time United States Congressman from Montana, presented my father's claims.[11] He won the case and a clear title to the land for us. Afterwards my father added by purchase a tract of forty acres to the first 160.

Money for first payments on all this expense came from selling vegetables and hay. My father had land that he could irrigate. During several dry seasons he had good crops.[12] The hay he sold for $20 a ton. He often drove to the market in Anaheim, about thirty miles north. One night we had watched for him until late. My stepmother, Kate, and Jimmy at last went to bed. I sat a little longer reading by the light of the kerosene lamp, hoping he would come soon. When I heard the rumbling of the big wagon on the hill, I ran down the road as fast as I could and opened the bars so that Pa would not have to get down from the high seat. I stood by the gate waiting for him to drive through. He did and then instead of going on to the barn he stopped, climbed down, came to me, and to my surprise—for he was seldom demonstrative—put his arms around me and said with a little sob, "Mollie, you look just like your dear mother standing there in the moonlight."

This made me happy and it made me sad. I loved having my own mother remembered and spoken of with such depth of feeling after all the years since her death; I longed to make up to my father somewhat for his loss of her. I was sorry, deeply sorry, for the kind, sweet, sensitive little stepmother. I knew, and had long known, that my father never loved Anne as he had loved my mother; he sometimes talked to me about her when we were alone. I knew that my father loved me above all else and wished and worked for my ultimate happiness. Our comradeship grew ever closer and we understood each other very well. I kept all his accounts. I shared to some extent his work in the field. When he sat down to rest and to smoke, it was my pleasure to make haste to bring him the old abalone shell in which he kept his tobacco, and to light his pipe. This little gesture of affection never failed to reward me with that look on his face of beaming tenderness.

In the midst of this struggle with the soil, with poverty, with the Mexicans over the title to the land, a letter came to me one day from Father Van Gorp at Helena. He said that he was writing at Mr. Ronan's request to say that Peter still wore my little gold ring and was still mindful of my farewell, "Keep it until I ask for it." Until I did so, he would consider that we were engaged. When I showed the letter to my father, he sighed wearily, heartbroken.

"I thought," he said coldly, "there was an end to that."

It was enough. I wrote to Father Van Gorp and told him to tell Mr. Ronan to send me my ring. I could not hurt my father. I could not add one more worry to his burden. Another consideration had weight, also. Through John Sweeney or some other Helena correspondent I had heard that Mr. Ronan was paying attention to an acquaintance of mine, Annie Brown.[13] Father Van Gorp wrote me a beautiful letter telling me of the respect and affectionate regard he had for Peter Ronan and how sorry he was that I was not going to marry him. He enclosed my ring. On its journey the ring broke through its wrapping and through the envelope. Some kindly postmaster rescued it, rewrapped it, and it reached me. (I wore it until my eldest daughter coaxed it from me. It slipped from her finger one day when she was playing in the creek at the old Flathead Agency. It washed away and was never found.)

Next came a letter from Mrs. Maginnis, written at Mr. Ronan's request, most beautifully, most effectively. Someone had told her that remarks of hers had influenced me to break my engagement. She declared that she would continue to do all in her power to bring Mr. Ronan and me together again. And so there was not, as my father hoped, "an end to that," nor could there be.

Though the feeling against my father as a "squattie" persisted, the Mexicans liked me. I was a Catholic. I sang in the mission-chapel choir. When Padre Mut bought an organ and tried to have that music substituted for the music of the Mexican orchestra, I played the organ. I met the villagers and the *rancheros* and their wives and children at church. They interested me and I enjoyed them. I learned to speak their language and so entered into their lives. I learned their games and their dances, the *contra* dance and *la jota*. They called me *la Mary*. Spanish girls of the same name were *Señorita Maria*.

The old Mexican men and women had such a tender way of greeting young girls. Usually when I went through the village plaza, Señor Don Juan Avila, a handsome, wealthy, old Mexican landowner, would address me from his spacious veranda, sweetly, lazily, "*Buenos Dias, corzoncita* (Good morning, little sweetheart), *Para donde va, mi vida?* (Where are you going, my life?) *Buenas tardes, mi alma* (Good evening, my soul)."

Any trace of ill feeling toward me as a squatter's daughter was entirely dispelled when I began to be a companion of Don Dick, their *alcalde*, or mayor. He was beloved by all the Mexicans as their trusted mediator in all their troubles among themselves, with *injustas ocupantes*, whether American or English, and with the United States land commissioners.

Judge Egan, as I always called him, lived at the hotel in the village or with his friend Pablo Pryor at Boca de la Playa, "the mouth of the beach." It was an adobe house two miles south of the mission and facing the sea. There was a cross on the hill above, as was the custom on the *ranchos* of devout families. Judge Egan gave me the key to his own ranch house, about a mile from the village, so that I might have access to and borrow at will from his library, a remarkable one in that faraway place and long-ago time. He had many of the classics and, most unusual for the time, always bought new books as soon as they could be had in Los Angeles or San Francisco.

We often walked or rode horseback in the evenings back to Capistrano's then remote, rugged, wild, cliff-escarped coast. He introduced me into the social life of the *pueblo* and the *ranchos*— the *bailes*, the barbecues, the *fiestas*. One grand *fiesta* commenced at Boca de la Playa in the morning with the lassoing of an ox that was then broiled whole. At noon in a grove of wide-spreading alder trees a meal was served on such a scale as to correspond with the meat course. "Then there gathered in clusters beneath the trees the beauty, wit, and manly valor of that whole region— Santa Margarita, San Luis Rey, Las Flores, Anaheim. While some indulged in the ancient Spanish games, others tripped the light and festive toe upon the green; and others still of the male portion contested for the championship in athletic sports only to leave it with the vigorous sons of Capistrano."[14] Late in the afternoon when the tide was out, we drove along the ocean beach.

A few daring ones ventured a boat ride, something not often done on that wild coast. We drove back to the *casa* for a bountiful supper of highly seasoned, rich food. Then we drove to the home of Don Juan Avila in the village of Capistrano and danced most of the night. The next day the festivities were transferred thirty miles away to Santa Margarita, ranch home of Señor Don Juan Forster, an Englishman, and his Mexican wife, Margarita, a sister of Pio Pico, the last Mexican governor of California. We went in carriages or on horseback. In the spacious, hospitable Spanish house on this vast ranch, twenty leagues square, we visited for several days.[15] This estate was run on an immense scale. Many, many Mexican peons and house servants did the work. I had my first experience of having my breakfast served to me in bed. It was called "the little breakfast," and consisted of a cup of chocolate and a piece of toast. How luxurious, how dreamy, how romantic I felt when the picturesque maid brought me my "little breakfast." About noon we all gathered on the *zaguan*, as they called the veranda, opening on the patio for another breakfast. Afterwards games were played, then some yielded to drowsiness and the *siesta*; others drove or rode horseback. There was another barbecue and a *baile*. So the gaiety continued through several days and, I might add quite truly, nights, before I returned to help my father in the field and my stepmother in the little adobe house on the hill, Casa Blanca.

Doña Margarita was a most gracious hostess. In appearance she was the typical Mexican woman, of medium height and very fat. She dressed in the very latest fashion and made lavish use of rouge, eyebrow pencil, and hair dye; nevertheless, she was imposing looking because of her grand bearing and manner.

Las Flores was the name of the rancho of Don Marcos Forster. I was taken there to visit by Judge Egan and Don Pablo Pryor and his wife, Rosita, the daughter of Don Juan Avila. Also with them I visited at a ranch called Cuajome not far from the mission of San Luis Rey and owned by Colonel Cave Johnson Couts. Mrs. Couts was one of three beautiful sisters of an aristocratic Castilian family named Bandini. Tonia, the daughter, was about my age.[16]

During the weekend that I spent at Cuajome, Tonia and I practiced together Leonard's "Mass in B Flat." We two sang it all alone that Sunday in the chapel at San Luis Rey, to please Father McGill who lived at Cuajome. Father McGill said Mass every morning in the chapel there but went on Sundays to the mission of San Luis Rey to hold services. Besides a chapel, Cuajome included a ballroom among its many rooms. Colonel Couts was a Southerner, devoted to his memories and to the traditions of his old home, and so in this California home one enjoyed the double magnificent hospitality of old Spain and of the old South. I can never forget the effect of exoticism produced by the two little Negro maids among the Mexican servants.

The Spanish and Mexican girls and young matrons from these great *ranchos* lavished a great deal of attention and money upon their elaborate dress. I could not afford to adopt their fashions, nor to vie with them, nor did I try. When I was not working in the house or in the field, I dressed in simple gowns of sheer white material, made, of course, by my stepmother and me. I was often in our little wash house by the arroyo washing those dresses and the chemises and many white petticoats that went with them, and often ironing them on the porch in the shadow cast by the kitchen cabin, for all the claim to charm that those dresses had was in crisp freshness.

At church, at the *bailes*, at the *fiestas*, on every occasion I appeared dressed in white with a little necklace of coral for ornament, or a gold chain and earrings, the latter a gift one Christmas from John M. Sweeney. I was accepted as being different because I was *la Mary*, and they approved of me because I had won the friendship of Don Dick.

Judge Richard Egan, Don Dick the *alcalde*, was my friend for fifty-four years. His life story is material for high romance. Born in Ireland, he stood more than six feet tall, splendidly erect and vigorous. His steady eyes were clear blue; his heavy hair and beard were wavy brown; he was more chivalrous than any caballero.

Judge Egan often told me that he could never live out of sight of the sea; once upon a time he knew every little inlet on the shore of South Carolina. I came to know that he had been left an orphan, brought to America by relatives. He went to school in Long Island, New York, and afterwards to South Carolina as a bookkeeper and assistant to the overseer on a plantation. The Civil War broke out. He joined the Confederate Army. When the Carolina ports were first bottled up by the Federal fleet, he became a blockade runner. After nearly two years of this hazardous service, one night Federal capture was so near that he plunged in open sea over the side and swam to a French vessel. The Federal fleet prevented any return to southern shores, and so he disembarked in France and wandered about Europe with a companion in expatriation, a Confederate army man, Colonel McCoun.

The two men settled on the Island of Capri until peace had been declared, but they found the South so intolerable under the rule of the carpetbagger that they sailed on a ship around Cape Horn, hoping to find a little, unknown island that could be all their own. When their ship weighed anchor off the Capistrano coast, Richard Egan and Colonel McCoun discovered the Spanish-speaking Mexican village of San Juan. At night the coyotes could be heard howling in the hollows of the hills; wild horses thundered past in herds, startling the villagers. In those places Federal law was yet far off. There were bullfights and dances; cavalrymen from Arizona bartered for horses; Mexican *rancheros* and *vaqueros* roistered together. There was reckless gaming, knifings in dark recesses off the plaza, and there were shootings.

The two Confederate soldiers, Richard Egan and Colonel McCoun, are said to have brought gold coin from the mint in San Francisco, enough to pay the United States government for a tract of land, buy what they needed, and live for a year or two. They saved enough to take them out of their self-imposed exile if they wished it, burying it secretly. They made a bargain with one another that if either wearied of the exile, he had to buy the other out. After two years, Colonel McCoun tired of this kind of pioneering and withdrew from the partnership to live in San Francisco, in Berkeley, and finally again on the Island of Capri. I met him once at the grand fiesta in his honor at Boca de la Playa and at Santa Margarita, of which I have told.

Judge Egan became more a citizen of San Juan Capistrano, a citizen in a larger sense, than any of its other citizens old or new. Rosita Pryor told me that he learned to speak Spanish well in a month. His life in continental Europe had made him understanding and delicately appreciative of certain Old World customs. He was bred a Catholic. He knew how to explain away the terror of what to the simple natives honestly seemed the sinister influence of the American invasion. He knew surveying. He knew law. He could give the Mexican and Spanish *rancheros* practical help in their trouble over their land titles; he became legal adviser for many of them and he was appointed *alcalde*. By his integrity, clear thinking, good judgment, unfailing tact, and broad sympathy, he brought to the community respect for American law; he was the law. It is a notable fact that with common sense as his guide, and "red tape" thrown in the discard, no decision of his was ever reversed by the superior court.[17] Already when we came to Capistrano Valley he was, as I have said, everything to everyone, the chief citizen.

In later years Judge Egan built himself the brick house which still stands in the heart of the village, directly on El Camino Real. Travelers, scholars, writers, and artists discovered the history, romance, and beauty of San Juan Capistrano through Judge Egan's hospitality. The poet Marah Ellis Ryan wrote of him and Helen Hunt Jackson came to him in search of background material when she was writing *Ramona*. Modjeska, the famous Polish actress of the 1880s and 1890s, was often his guest. She painted a watercolor of a corridor in the ruins of the old mission. It was her gift to Judge Egan and his, in turn, to me.

Through all my father's struggles in San Juan Capistrano, in every crisis, Judge Egan was there: the lingering illness and death of my stepmother, the cruel accident which made necessary the amputation of my father's right arm; and in other crises of which I cannot bear to speak. He was with my father during his last hours, drew up his will and settled all his earthly affairs. During thirty-five years he tended the plot in the old Mexican cemetery on the hill where they lie at rest, those dear ones, my father and stepmother.

School Days in Los Angeles

One day my little sister Kate came home from school sobbing as if her heart would break. Some children had told her that their *madres* said that I was not her own sister. It took the combined efforts of mother, father, and sister to soothe her first big sorrow, to explain to the satisfaction of the nine-year-old girl our true relationship and that love knits closer bonds than complete kinship of blood.

The first American public school in San Juan Capistrano had been opened after we had been living for some time at Casa Blanca. The square, one-room schoolhouse stood just off El Camino Real, between our house and the mission. Of our family only Kate attended. Teachers came and went without making, so far as I recall, any impression on the village—certainly none whatever on me. It was someone's idea, perhaps Padre Mut's, that I should take the teachers' examination and qualify to teach the school. I knew I was not capable. Well do I remember how Padre Mut went up to Los Angeles to make arrangements with Sister Scholastica, Superior of the Convent of St. Vincent de Paul, for me to attend during the school year of 1871–72. Since this was a time when my father was in desperate straits with not a dollar ahead, the arrangement was that I was to pay for my tuition and other expenses when I would be earning money teaching.

This photograph of Main Street in Los Angeles, California, was taken in 1874 from the Pico House, past which Mary and her classmates promenaded on their daily walks.
REGIONAL HISTORY COLLECTIONS, PHOTOGRAPHS OF HISTORIC LOS ANGELES,
UNIVERSITY OF SOUTHERN CALIFORNIA

Padre Mut made plans also to have me take music lessons so that I would be able to play the organ, to direct the choir, and to help him in his endeavor to have music for church services more sacred in tone, more suited to the dim religious atmosphere of the antique mission chapel than the tinkling instruments the Mexican orchestra afforded; the *señors* with their guitars could transpose even the "Sanctus" into the sentimental lilt of a moon-light serenade.

Friends of ours from Montana had, as we did, followed pio-neer trails into California. Mrs. Bridget McGrath (through whose back fence in Alder Gulch I had peeped at a prize fight), Martin Golden and James Kennedy (a brother of William and John

Kennedy) from Helena had visited us in Capistrano and we had visited them on our occasional trips to Los Angeles. Mrs. McGrath had taken me about the town and we had called upon the Sisters of St. Vincent de Paul; therefore I have no vivid first impression of arriving in Los Angeles and the beginning of that school term.

I could never be tired of strolling about the *calles de arboles*, the paths of the spacious, old-fashioned convent garden, watching the orange, lemon, and lime trees in their pageant of budding, blossoming, and bearing ripe fruit; basking in the fragrance of the flowers or, on hot days, in the moist breath of air from the gently playing fountains.

When we girls went on our almost daily walks, marching two and two in a long file, we used to pass the new three-story Pico House near the Plaza on the east side of Calle Mayor. Often we would see an old Mexican, a very old man with white hair and beard, sitting on the porch. I was interested when the girls told me that he was Pio Pico, the last Mexican governor of California, kin to some of the girls I knew and intimate acquaintance of Judge Egan and Pablo and Rosita Pryor. Upon the injunction of the Sisters we avoided the business center where many tough-looking characters lounged about the long, narrow porches and at saloon entrances. They slouched over their saddle horses at the hitching posts, half on and half off, with one booted leg hanging low and one toe touching the stirrup. Favorite walks were past the extensive two-story house of the Lanfrancos and what was called "the palace of Don Abel Stearns," a magnificent one-story Spanish dwelling with verandas and courtyards and fountains. One landmark that yet remains to remind me of those walks of long ago is the old Avila adobe on Calle Olivera, a little street running out from the plaza north of Marchessault. It was pointed out to me many times and the story told of how it was the headquarters of Commodore Stockton in 1847.[18]

One night we were awakened and terrified by the tumult of a Chinese Tong war raging up and down the street and around the convent walls. As long as we girls could hear the savage, sibilant shouting, screaming, and muttering, we clung around the Sisters. No one dared to peep out the window for fear of attracting attention and of directing the torrent of fury toward the convent.[19] On another night of terror the weird rumble preliminary to an earthquake startled us from sleep. Three distinct shocks rocked and swayed the building.

"Pray, girls, pray," said the Sister as she assembled us around her and prepared to get us out of the building.

"I can't pray. All you girls pray for me," gasped Pedra Mascarel, a beautiful Mexican girl, sitting up in her bed and trembling so that she could not get to her feet. No further shocks occurred. After all we did not leave the building. No serious damage resulted in Los Angeles, though much destruction was reported in the surrounding country.

I loved the Sisters and the sweetly ordered, studious, peaceful routine of the convent, with one day slipping past so like another that the year rolled quickly around. I was so intent upon my immediate objective, of preparing to pass the teachers' examinations, and so absorbed in a correspondence that developed toward the middle of the year, that my association with the other girls left scarcely an impression and certainly no lasting friendship. Some of them were beautiful *señoritas* of pure Castilian blood, some were vivacious Irish and French girls, some were nondescript Americans, and most of them were bronzed Mexicans. The name of the girl who graduated with first honors in the class of 1872, Guadalupe Dryden, suggested an intermixture of blood, as did the names of some of the other girls.

With Guadalupe's flashing mind went a disposition bubbling with fun and love of pranks. Boys from St. Vincent's College many blocks away used to come and serenade outside the walls, as close as they could get to the windows of the dormitory.[20] Guadalupe would take a sheet from her bed and wave it back and forth out the window in acknowledgement of the serenade. One night the Sister who slept in our dormitory, with white curtains drawn around her bed, suddenly pulled those curtains aside and caught the gay coquette in her girlish crime. Guadalupe's bed was moved from its nook by the window and placed close to that of the Sister.

Mary Burns, daughter of Los Angeles pioneer James F. Burns, liked fun, too. She managed an expedition one rainy Sunday morning when, after Mass at the cathedral, three young gallants who had carriages at the hitching posts politely asked the Sisters if they might not be permitted to drive some of the young ladies to the convent and save them a drenching. The Sisters consented. Mary and her boy friends were particular to choose a special group of girls to be rescued from the rain and I was one of the favored ones. Before we reached the convent we had enjoyed a thorough and gay tour of Los Angeles. Although, in 1871, it was emerging from a pueblo into an American town, most of the streets bore the names given by a simple people—the street of the grasshoppers, the street of the hornets, the street of the bull, because it led to the field where the bull fights used to take place, the street of Eternity because it led to the cemetery.

My special friend, more interesting to me than any of my class or schoolmates in the convent, was my music teacher Miss Rose Kelly. The reason was not far to seek. She had come to Los Angeles from Helena and she knew many of my Helena friends. She had been brought to teach in the academy in Helena by Mother Vincent who introduced her to Peter Ronan. In some way she was connected with the family of John G. Downey, afterwards governor of California. I was invited to his home and met his wife, a lovely Spanish woman, as I recall. Through this acquaintanceship with Rose and also through girls in the convent whose families were prominent in the social life of the town, I was asked to other homes, among them the home of the beautiful Doña Arcadia Bandini, the wife of Don Abel Stearns.[21]

My father came up from Capistrano to visit me. One evening I went with him to call upon our friend Martin Golden at his home on a little farm, covering several acres of ground in what is now the heart of the great city of Los Angeles. Lying upon the table was a letter in a handwriting too dear to me to be mistaken. My heart beat fast. I could not keep back the eager remark that I recognized the letter as being from someone I knew in Helena— Peter Ronan. Mr. Golden said that I was correct and read the letter to us; it told of the illness of a brother of Mr. Golden's in Helena and required an immediate answer. When Mr. Golden wrote he concluded, as I afterwards learned, by saying, "A friend of yours is here going to the Sisters' school." Then he related the incident of my recognizing the handwriting. At once came Mr. Ronan's reply, which was passed on to me. "I am glad to hear of Miss Sheehan," he wrote. "I had understood that she had not only forgotten my hand writing but my very name."

I was deeply stirred. And as this all happened in the dear, romantic long ago when Valentine's Day was regarded seriously, I yielded to an impulse and sent a missive. Back came this answer:

Helena, Montana
February 23, 1872

Miss Mollie C. Sheehan:
    On the evening of February 14th, I received an envelope, postmarked Los Angeles, and upon breaking the seal, found a book mark, on which were worked the words "Love Mary," and in the folds of a piece of paper were two leaves, one of which I took for a rose geranium; the other leaf was so bruised and broken I could not tell its species. At first I did not dare to

hope that your dear hand had traced the direction on the envelope, or folded the precious tokens in the piece of paper, fearing that some one who knew my heart's secret, had taken those unworthy means to open the wounds anew; but yesterday evening, I received from the mail a white envelope, on which was the monogram of "S" and which contains a description of a picnic at which your name was mentioned in a complimentary manner.[22] I immediately recognized your handwriting, and resolved to speak again, let what will occur or whatever pain your answer may inflict.

The language of the rose geranium, I believe, expresses "preference." Dearest Mollie, after all these years of sorrow, can, can I believe my senses? Was it indeed yourself who forwarded those precious tokens of remembrance, or am I made the victim of a wretched hoax, planned by some wretch to tear open the wounds which time cannot heal? If you did send those tokens, and if I am still "preferred" as the language would imply, avow it frankly, and I will hasten to your side and claim the hand you promised me in the happy past. Since I saw you last, time has dealt kindly with me, and I have tried to prove myself worthy of your love. In this I will not recount the pure and tender love I bear you, which neither coldness nor silence, the unhappy circumstances of our parting could efface— I still hoped on, loved on and will continue to do so until I am formally told that it is useless.

> I remain as ever
> Affectionately yours
> Peter Ronan

I never felt that I could deceive my father. I made my plans and, when next he came to visit me, I told him what I had done. I shall never forget that scene. It was late afternoon. We had walked on Primavera Street to where it began to skirt the foothills. We turned off, climbed a little hill, and sat down. I gave my father Mr. Ronan's letter to read. When he finished reading I told him that I must see Mr. Ronan again. If I found that he had changed or that I had changed in my feeling for him during the four years of our separation and that I no longer wished to marry him, I wanted to join the Sisters of St. Vincent de Paul. My plan was to teach for a year and then to go independently on money that I had earned myself to Montana to visit Cousin Ellen Tiernan at Sheridan, and while with her to arrange to see Mr. Ronan.

I concluded by saying, "I think, Pa, that I am old enough now and have sense enough to choose what I shall do."

My father was deeply affected. He answered, weeping as he spoke, "Sure, Mollie, if you wanted now to marry a tinker I wouldn't be the one to tell you no."

The correspondence with Peter Ronan went forward but not so my plans. I had not taken into consideration the generosity and fervor of my lover or circumstances in which fate or destiny or, to speak more truly, my own limitations, involved me. I failed to get my teacher's certificate. I did not pass the examination in mental arithmetic. I shall never forget how sad I was—sad rather than humiliated, for none knew better than I my incapability, how few and scattered and interrupted had been my terms of attending school, except for the one year with the Sisters of St. Vincent de Paul; how unplanned, unsystematic, discontinuous, totally inadequate my course of study, if course it may be called, had been.

My sorrow was threefold; I wanted to help my father; I was under obligations to pay the Sisters; I wanted to earn money to pay the expenses of the trip I planned to make to Montana. A neighbor of ours in Capistrano, a man named John Bacon who had large interests in land and sheep, came to tell me that he would loan me money to go to the normal school in San Francisco until I should be graduated and that I could have the loan for as long as I wished and could pay him back by degrees when I was teaching. Although I did not avail myself of his generous offer, I appreciated it deeply and have never forgotten John Bacon.

After his death, I burned the letters I wrote to Mr. Ronan during this time. His letters to me I kept so that the children might some day read them and through them come to have some slight firsthand knowledge of their father, of his manly sincerity, of his frank acknowledgement of belief in love, religion, and God.

When I realized that any plans of mine to go to Montana would have to be deferred for more than a year, I hinted to Mr. Ronan in a letter that perhaps business interests might bring him to California and that, incidentally, we might arrange to meet and see if after all we still felt the same toward each other. In reply this letter came:

> Helena, Montana
> April 7, 1872

My dear Mollie:

Your most welcome letter came to hand Easter Sunday, and as that is a day of general rejoicing throughout the Christian world, how much more a day of happiness for me it was in being doubly blessed by receiving a letter from you. On the evening of the same day I was shown by Father Van Gorp, your letter to him; he informed me that he would answer it the following morning, and I suppose you will receive this about the same time. I know not what he will say to you in regard to our matters; but I am satisfied that he will deal fairly with me in his language, for I firmly believe that his sacred calling is sufficient guarantee that he will act in accordance with his conscience and his God. You asked me to make a confidant of "no one" in regard to our correspondence, and, therefore, I did not inform him that I received a letter from you; but left it with yourself to explain when you write to him.

You speak, dear Mollie, of the changes that time may have wrought in both of us since we met, and almost hint that it would be agreeable to you to have me come down to Los Angeles. There is nothing on this earth that would afford me more pleasure than to see and converse once more with you. I will avail myself of that most delightful pleasure; but here I must pause and ask you to name the time when it would be most agreeable to you for me to visit. And in this connection I would say that, if you can make it so, I would like to have my visit agreeable to your parents also; you say your mother mentioned my name in a letter to you. Oh! Tell me, did she speak kindly or harshly of me? God knows I never gave her cause to be my enemy.

You asked me not to try to change your mind in regard to the course you have chosen to pursue in our mutual affairs, and I will try to curb my patience. In regard to what you say about keeping our correspondence to ourselves I entirely agree with you. Father Van Gorp, of course, excepted. He knows all about our affairs, except that you have written to me.

And now in conclusion, my dearest Mollie, let me thank you for that beautiful Valentine which I received from you and which came safe to me without a blemish. I had it put into a handsome frame, and will ever regard and prize it as a token from you.[23]

Please answer on receipt and give me your expression about the time you will expect me.

Adieu, dearest—and kindest regards to Mr. Golden and believe me as ever yours,

Peter Ronan

The requested invitation I did not extend. I feared to do so, to have him come that long, difficult, expensive journey only to have me refuse to marry him. I felt that I had changed so much. I feared that he had. I was not sure that my love existed as a reality rather than as a romantic fancy. I was torn between that remembered love and my desire to take the veil in the Community of the Sisters of St. Vincent de Paul. What had been the trend of my letters is revealed in this reply to me:

Helena, Montana
May 19, 1872

Dear Mollie:

Your welcome letter of May 4th has been received and I hasten to answer. I was sorely disappointed in not having received an invitation to visit you as I have been weaving bright dreams of happiness at the thought of meeting you this summer; but I will try to bear my bitter disappointment with patience and look straight ahead to the bright future which I can not but believe is in store for us.

You have given me your promise that in one year from the month of next June, you will either invite me to your home or you will come to Montana. I accept the pledge with joyful heart and soul to my business affairs, and in the fierce and ambitious struggles of life which I have marked out for myself this year, time will fly and the happy time draw near when we are again to meet. You speak of the changes that time may have wrought in both of us. I fear nothing for those changes, for I firmly believe that if any changes have been wrought in either of us they are for the best. I will avoid speaking further on this subject, in regard to myself—all I ask is your confidence, and the happy time will come when we will both kneel together and thank God that we had love and confidence in each other.

You spoke of having written to Father Van Gorp. I regret to say that he is away and is not expected to return for two weeks. Father Van Gorp, through his piety and energy, has made the very name of Catholic respected in this country. A convent, young ladies' seminary, and hospital now grace the hill where our old printing office used to stand, and preparations are being made to erect a brick church. Besides the large number of Sisters who came to establish the institution, six more arrived last week among whom was good Mother Mary Vincent, of whom you often heard me speak, and who used to correspond with me in the long ago when you were a little girl. Do you not remember the evening I took the letter she had written to me and read it to your father and mother and asked their counsel in regard to establishing a convent here? Well, I do remember it and can even now describe the pretty white "tunic" you wore. On the arrival of Mother Vincent, she sent for me and you may be sure I was glad to meet her. She inquired minutely into my business affairs, prospects in life, whether I attended to my duties or not, and finally dismissed me after imparting the information that she had appointed herself my guardian, and gave me an imperative command that I should visit her at least once a week and give an account of myself. God help her!

I will not bore you by writing much more, but in conclusion want to ask two favors—bearing in memory all the time your injunction in a former letter not to ask too much. One favor is that you answer this letter, and the other is (am I asking too much?) *your photograph.* Oh, Mollie, do not refuse this boon to me—I have no likeness of you, nothing to call up your dear face save the lonely lamp of memory.

> With kindest regards to old friends,
> I remain as ever
> Truly yours
> Peter Ronan

On June 14, 1872, I was graduated from the Academy of the Sisters of St. Vincent de Paul. The old scrapbook contains a clipping from the *Los Angeles Star* giving the citizens of the small town an account of that glorious occasion. The account reads most quaintly now, but so will accounts detailing events of today read sixty years hence. I delivered an address titled, "The Sphere and Influence of Women."[24]

It was a grandiloquent and effusive address in the manner of youth. Amusing as it is to read now, I must say I still subscribe to some of the sentiments expressed in that one and only address that I ever delivered, for they were heartfelt words and the thoughts back of them rooted deep. I took myself, what I had to say, and my graduation quite, quite seriously. I tried to look my best, and I played my best, and sang my best for that one dear, careworn man, my father, sitting far back among that great crowd of strangers.

Letters, Clippings, and a Journal of 1873

oward the close of the summer of 1872 my mind was made up and I sent a letter to Peter Ronan giving my promise to marry him. His reply, written amid circumstances so spectacular, so devastating that they might easily have changed instead of only delaying our plans, reveals the drama more authentically than can words of mine.

Helena, August 23, 1872

My Dear Mollie,

I just received your welcome letter of August 9th, which gives me the joyful assurance that you will accompany me back to Montana, as my own darling bride, and now I can talk to you as my own. You will never regret your choice, for from this day forth all my care and industry will be employed for your welfare; all my strength and power will be exerted for your happiness and protection. . . .

About the last week in September I will leave here for California, and when we meet we can talk over our future and set the day. Before leaving here, I will quietly and without letting anyone know except two or three intimate friends, furnish and prepare our home, and after the marriage is celebrated we will make a trip wherever our fancy may lead us, and then return to Helena. How do you like the programme? But I forgot you have something to say in the arrangement of it, and I guess we had better defer the matter until cozily and quietly seated together in some quiet retreat among the vines of California we make our arrangements for the future. . . .

There is a fearful cry! Oh God the office is in flames Adieu.

Saturday, August 24—Dearest Love, the enclosed tells the fearful tale—But, thank God, although yesterday I made a narrow escape from death I still have my health, my courage, my energy, and in a few days will again be established in business. This misfortune will not deter me from making my trip to claim you. I may be a poorer man than when I wrote the forgoing pages, but I know that will have no effect on you but to cling to me closer. Farewell, dear love, I will write you more particulars in a day or two.

> I remain as ever
> Your fond lover
> Peter Ronan

Visible in this photograph above the J. H. Curtis Building, Peter Ronan's Rocky Mountain Gazette *Office was one of sixty downtown Helena buildings destroyed by fire in August 1872. This photograph of the ceremonial laying of the cornerstone of the Masonic Temple was taken on June 14, 1872, only a few months before the fire.*

Still folded within the pages of that letter is a clipping from the *Helena Daily Herald* of August 24, 1872, a three-column story relating the details of the fire which swept over seven blocks, consumed sixty buildings and destroyed $140,000 worth of property. A map is given of the burned district. Incidentally, this issue of the *Herald* marked a milestone in the development of journalism in Montana, for this map was the first attempt of a newspaper in the territory to illustrate a story.

Although Mr. Ronan, in the postscript to his letter of that fateful twenty-third of August and also in letters following, minimized his narrow escape from death and his financial loss, as a matter of fact the partners in the *Rocky Mountain Gazette* suffered the greatest destruction of property. Because it was not Mr. Ronan's way to bewail the past or the inevitable, none of his letters makes reference to the fact that this was the second time within four years and four months that the newspaper plant had been totally destroyed by fire. On April 28, 1869, a few days after my father had set out with us from Helena, practically the whole of the business district had been wiped out by the first of the many disastrous fires that swept Last Chance Gulch.[25]

The same letter that brought me the story of the fire of August 23, 1872, enclosed also an advertisement clipped from the *Herald* promising that the *Gazette* would continue in a reduced format until new equipment could be ordered from the States. True to this promise, the *Weekly Gazette* was printed on September 2, 1872, on the presses of its honorable Republican rival, the *Helena Daily Herald*. The *Gazette* continued to be issued through this plant until equipment arrived on December 20, 1872. On September 9, 1872, I received this hopeful message:

> You have learned of the destruction of our office, for I was writing you when the alarm was given, and made a hurried postscript of the occurrence next day and enclosed the *Herald*'s

account of it. It was a heavy loss to me, dear Mollie, but I do not regret it half so much as the fact that the occurrence will cause a few more weeks delay in my visit to you. Major Maginnis will have to leave for New York this week to purchase the material for our office and will probably be absent four weeks. Immediately upon his return I will start for Los Angeles. Yesterday, while making out the bill of articles to be purchased, I told him that he should not make one unnecessary hour's delay in returning—and informed him why I was in such a hurry—in fact I blunderingly told him *I was going to be married this fall*, and when I told him *who* I was going after he fairly jumped with joy. This was the first time, dear love, that I betrayed our secret or my intentions.

Tomorrow evening I will write to your father and tell him of my intention. I will also inform him of our correspondence and pledges, and formally ask permission to bear his darling from him.

I feel most happy that if such a misfortune as the destruction of so much of my property was to happen, that it came before our wedding day, for it might have a tendency to cast a gloom over the first bright hours of our wedded life.

The formal letter to my father asking his consent to our marriage followed three days later. Though my father, with equal formality, gave his consent, the "four weeks" extended to four months before the presses and other new equipment had arrived and been installed under the skilled hands of Mr. Ronan. Among the local items of December 24, 1872, appeared the following paragraph: "Peter Ronan has gone off to California facing the blinding snows and fierce inclement weather in search of a more genial clime. Some of the boys say that his destination is Southern California, where verdurous spring reigns all the year, love wanders through bowers of perpetual verdure, and the *orange blossoms* are always in bloom."[26]

Judge Egan had established a telegraph office in Capistrano and was himself the operator. On the wire from Los Angeles one Sunday afternoon in January he took the message from Mr. Ronan to me saying that if it were agreeable to me he would come down on the next coach. I was in the mission chapel practicing with the choir when Judge Egan came and beckoned me to come into the arched cloister. I found him sitting waiting for me on the old stone bench; the same one is still there near the chapel door. I dropped down beside him and read the telegram. I felt faint. Suddenly, I was possessed with terror of the difference that the years might have wrought in us.

"It calls for an answer, Mary," said Judge Egan gently after we had sat for some moments in silence. I could not speak.

"What do you wish me to say in reply?" he asked.

"I don't know. I can't answer. You answer it," I whispered.

"But I can't," he insisted, "unless you give me some idea whether I am to tell him to come or not."

"Come. Tell him to come," I managed to decide, well knowing that I had made the first move to start the cycle of events that had led me to this crisis, well knowing, in anguish of spirit, that if the consequence of our meeting was for me to realize that I no longer loved Peter Ronan, I must have the courage to send him back on his long way alone.

He arrived in the stagecoach the next evening at early candlelight. My father went to the hotel to meet him. I waited in our field by the bars and watched them walking toward me over the hill trail in the gathering dusk. Mr. Ronan took me in his arms and kissed me, saying in the same dear, dear voice, "At last, Mollie, at last." Then for the dusk and my tears I could not see his face. When we went into the house I found that he had not changed at all in any way, not even in looks, during the four and a half years that we had been separated. I knew that for better or worse, I was ready to go with him to the end of life's journey.

Later that very evening while we were walking in the Capistrano moonlight, he took a plain gold band from his pocket and asked me to try it on. He had bought it, he said, in Los Angeles just before the coach was due to start. I slipped it on. It was perfect. An intense feeling swept over me of having been through this scene before, every detail of it, with us two standing alone together by the fence in the ambient moonlight. Mr. Ronan took a heavy gold ring set with a square-cut diamond solitaire from his little finger and slipped it on my finger, all the while laughing and saying, "Here, Mollie, is another engagement ring. This you will keep; this you are not going return to me, ever."

When I exclaimed that it was indeed handsome, much more so than the one I had returned to him, but for all that I would dearly love to have our first ring again. He said that could not be because he had given it to his sister Margaret along with the little gold cuff buttons monogrammed "M," which he had had made for me from the gold he had himself panned. The new ring, he said, betokened greater love than any ring he could purchase because his friends in Helena had given it to him, so with it he wished to plight again our troth. I accepted at once and have always held Mr. Ronan's idea that for us no other ring could symbolize a greater wealth of love.

During the week in which we made ready for the wedding and for my departure, we found time to visit all the places of interest about Capistrano: the mission, the beach, and the homes of my friends. When I was busy at home, Judge Egan entertained Mr. Ronan for me. Theirs were kindred spirits and a warm friendship commenced almost from the moment of their introduction.

My joy would have been as near perfect as human joy can be had it not been for my father's sorrow at the prospect of parting from me. He could not hide his feelings and sometimes he did not try. More than once he said in tones so tragic that they frightened me and stabbed me to the heart, "Anne and I can never get along without you." One afternoon he called me into the field where he was plowing. When we had followed the furrow to the end of the field, he bowed his head upon his strong brown hands and cried aloud, "You will never, never see me plow again, Mollie." Later, as we walked arm in arm to the mission chapel for my marriage, my heart was wrung with his weeping.

I had dreams of a white dress with a train, a bridal veil, and a wreath of orange blossoms, but when the time actually came I considered conventional things inharmonious with the simplicity and unconventionality of our way of living. We planned to approach the marriage sacrament at an early hour. I wore a pearl gray dress, one of the two new ones my stepmother and I had made. I wore with it a silver filigree chain with pendant cross, breast pin, and earrings to match—Mr. Ronan's gift to me; a plain hat purchased in Capistrano; and a sheer pink silk shawl, the gift of Mrs. McGrath.

The story of my marriage day and of a few days following is told in some pages of a journal I kept at that time. The pages were torn from an old notebook, and now for long, long years they have been tucked away.

Monday morning, January 13, 1873

I arose at daybreak. We were all quiet—our hearts were full. After I knelt and received the blessing of my parents, we all embraced each other and then went our way quietly to the chapel in the ruins of the Mission of San Juan Capistrano where we were joined in the holy bonds of marriage by the Reverend Joseph Mut. The holy sacrifice of the Mass was offered to us and we also received special benediction. I will never forget the words addressed to us from the altar.

"I know," said the Padre, "my dear young people, that you have complied with every rule of the Church, that you have received the holy Sacrament of Marriage in a state of grace, and I believe also that it is not any worldly motive that prompts you to marry, but pure and true love. . . ."

How impressive and solemn everything seemed. None was in the church save the priest, my father, sister, brother, and Mrs. McGrath. Every sound echoed through the quaint old rooms, and the statues with their great black eyes seemed as if they were alive, standing there to bear witness to the vows we had made.

On entering the church I leant on the arm of my father, when leaving on the arm of my husband.[27] We walked some way in silence. At last my husband said, "Mollie darling, God has blessed us, and a meeting like this has more than repaid our separation and suffering during the last four years." Those were, I believe, the first words my husband said to me after leaving the church.

When we reached home, Mother met us with a bright smile and kiss. Breakfast was on the table. Little brother and sister cried. They seemed to realize that I was about to leave them. Pete ran after Brother and I after Sister. We kissed them and laughed away their fears.

A poor and ragged stranger from Ireland had come to our house the previous evening. He told my father that among the peasants in the old country it was a sign of good luck to have a stranger come to the house where a couple was newly married.

Most of the forenoon Pete and I spent alone. At two o'clock the guests began to arrive. We had a nice dinner and many were the toasts drunk to us both in Spanish and English. At midnight our Spanish friends gave us a beautiful serenade. How beautiful and sad the *Adios* sounded that calm night.

Our Spanish and Mexican friends were disappointed with the simplicity of our marriage. They had expected to have their customs observed, with everyone in the village and from the surrounding ranchos invited to the wedding ceremony and to a day and night of feasting, toasting, dancing, and serenading. Mr. Ronan entered into the situation with much understanding, enjoyment, and merriment. Between him and most of the guests I had to act as interpreter of their exchange of compliments, pleasantries, and attempts at conversation.

January 14

We left home at 4 o'clock in the morning. We were in such a hurry that we found little time for tears. My dear father—how tenderly he kissed me. As the coach (my husband and myself were the only occupants) slowly wended its way from the fond scenes of home, I could not suppress my tears. I felt the fond embrace and the low, half-whispered words of love and encouragement from my devoted husband. As day began to dawn, the coach wended over the familiar and beautiful rancho known as *Boca de la playa*, owned by my friend Don Pablo Pryor. Further on we traveled over the lovely rancho of Marcos Forster, known as Las Flores where I spent many pleasant hours, and at noon we arrived at the Mission of San Luis Rey, where the coach halted for dinner, but my husband and myself preferred to walk amid the quaint old ruins.

How gloomy and grand those ruins stand, a monument to the zeal and courage of the Franciscan monks who founded it in the palmy days of glorious old Catholic Spain, but our reflections were cut short by the driver who announced that the horses were changed and all was ready.

After a ride over the country of some sixty-five miles from San Juan, we arrived at San Diego where we domiciled at the Horton House, the most elegant hotel of Southern California. There we spent the first week of our honeymoon in blissful happiness. During our stay in San Diego we were visited by a number of old acquaintances who came to wish us joy in our new path through life. Among our callers were Don Pablo Pryor, Don Juan Stewart and family, Don Miguel Padesno, and several others. Our stay at San Diego was very pleasant.

On the 20th of January we took passage on board the steamer *Senator* for San Francisco. We occupied the bridal chamber, a neat cozy room, and received the attention of officers and servants in a marked manner. At 5 o'clock we steamed out of the harbor of San Diego and proceeded on our voyage to San Francisco. That evening, Colonel C. P. Head of Prescott, Arizona, called my husband aside and begged him to take charge of a package for him that contained fifty thousand dollars in greenbacks. The money was deposited in my little satchel.[28]

On the morning of the 21st we arrived in San Pedro and the captain announced that we would lie in the harbor for several hours. We concluded to make an excursion to Los Angeles and visit the Sisters' Academy, the scene of my school girl days, and from where I had graduated the previous summer. A nice party consisting of Mr. and Mrs. Fisk of Illinois, Colonel C. P. Head of Arizona, and Mr. Harte of Western Missouri took the cars from San Pedro to Los Angeles and upon arriving, Mr. and Mrs. Fisk, my husband and myself took a barouche and drove to the Sisters' Academy where I was welcomed with tearful joy by the Sisters and some of my old schoolmates. After a few moments of happy converse, we looked over schoolrooms, dormitories and grounds. The orange trees were bent to the earth with ripe and delicious fruit. They were a subject of delight to my husband and the other visitors who had never witnessed such gorgeous splendor as the orange, lemon, lime and other tropical fruits and flowers presented.

After a wonderful parting from the scenes of so many happy hours of innocent schoolgirl days, and a tearful farewell to the Sisters and schoolmates, we took our departure and drove around and visited many places of interest in the city. We stopped at an orange orchard where myself and Mrs. Fisk plucked beautiful bouquets of flowers while our husbands filled a market basket with oranges from the trees for the voyage. The Sisters met us at the depot. They placed one of their pupils under our charge, Miss Emma Fleming, who was returning to San Francisco.

From Los Angeles we proceeded to Wilmington in the cars. There we found a big boat waiting to carry us to the *Senator* which lay in the harbor of San Pedro. On boarding the steamer, we found we had several hours to amuse ourselves before steaming out of the harbor. My husband availed himself of the opportunity to catch a fine lot of fish while I and some other ladies and gentlemen amused ourselves in our room at a game of cards. At six o'clock in the evening we steamed out of the harbor of San Pedro and on the morning of the 22nd at four o'clock cast anchor in the harbor of Santa Barbara.

January 22nd—On board the steamer *Senator*

We left Santa Barbara soon after daylight. In a few miles
to the west we came in contact with the asphaltum, flowing
from extensive springs near the coast. It runs down into the
ocean and spreads over the surface for miles. These springs
are worked to a considerable extent and this product is shipped
to San Francisco and other ports. After breakfast we passed
some hours.[29]

We spent a week or more in San Francisco. At the hotel where
we were staying we met our old friend James W. Whitlatch and
his wife.[30] With them and other old Montana friends we enjoyed
sightseeing, theatres, and supper parties. Mr. Whitlatch was then
at the height of his prosperity. Mrs. Whitlatch was a society woman
with much *savior faire*. Mr. Ronan wished me to have some new
dresses, and so under the guidance of Mrs. Whitlatch, I went to a
modiste and had three beautiful gowns made. One was of silk
poplin, light brown threaded through with a little gold stripe. It
was made with a tight basque and many tiny ruffles running around
the full length of the wide sweeping skirt. Another was of soft
green cloth, with a polonaise. The third was of the same kind of
material but black, made with a tight basque and a long training
skirt.[31] The flowing sleeves were scalloped at the wrist. With this
dress I wore white ruching at the throat and my filigree-silver set
for ornament. We must have thought the black dress the most
becoming for in it I had my picture taken in Helena. For a wrap I
liked to wear a shawl in the Spanish fashion over the left shoulder,
especially a fringed shawl with rainbow colored striping which
my parents had given me. Upon the insistence of my generous
husband, the San Francisco shopping expeditions included the
purchase of a black broadcloth cloak with a scalloped cape, a long
navy-blue ulster for coach travel which completely covered my

dress, a mink stole and muff, and hats to correspond with my various ensembles.

We traveled by train on the Union Pacific Railroad to Corinne, Utah, and from there by the Gilmer, Salisbury and Company stage line to Helena. That was a terrible trip. Although Mr. Salisbury had given orders that we be hurried through and that every courtesy be shown us, we were nine days on the way between Corinne and Helena. Besides cold and storms, and the condition of the roads in February, the horses were sick with a dreadful epidemic called epizootic.[32] We had warm clothes and greatcoats and were bundled in buffalo robes so that we were fairly comfortable in the coaches when we could not see or could forget the pitiful condition of the horses. Some days, chiefly on account of the sickness of the horses, but also because of the roads and the weather, we could travel for only a few hours at a time and then would put up at the first possible place for the night. Stations for changing horses were established every twelve or fifteen miles along the main route and lodging and eating places for the passengers were from forty to fifty miles apart. Some days we did not even make the distance between stations. I am not sure that we stopped a single night at one of the regular lodging places. One stop I remember as the most distressing of all. The horses were so weary and weak that they could scarcely stagger through the deep snow. It must have been at a wayside saloon that we spent the night. The proprietor made a bed of buffalo robes for me on the floor of a bare little room in the ramshackle house. I lay there and wept, weary and, though Mr. Ronan was with me, frightened at the sounds of carousal and drunkenness distinctly to be heard coming from the room beyond the log wall. By way of contrast I recall one neat, comfortable house where a pleasant woman served us a delicious breakfast with the unusual item of waffles on the menu.[33]

We arrived in Helena late in the evening of February 16 and went to the St. Louis Hotel. I was getting ready for bed when I heard music in the corridor. A number of Mr. Ronan's friends, who had heard of our arrival, had come with a band to welcome us.

"Are you too tired to meet them, Mollie?" my husband asked.

I was all eagerness to do so. Finally all left except John Caplice and Joseph K. Toole.[34] Mr. Caplice, Mr. Ronan's best friend ever since they had staked their claim in partnership in Alder Gulch, insisted we two would never be married again and that he for one intended to make a night of welcoming us home. He would not let Mr. Toole go. So we talked over old times, our marriage and wedding journey, and our plans for the future until Mr. Caplice decided to bid us good morning and to depart at about two o'clock.

The next evening our friends gave a reception in our honor. I clipped and kept in the old scrapbook the account of that occasion, which appeared in the Helena *Daily Herald* of February 18, 1873:

> Mr. Peter Ronan and bride arrived in Helena Sunday evening, and were received by a host of friends with a hearty welcome. At a late hour in the day on Monday it was determined to have a reception on that evening, and invitations were sent out through the city and suburbs to that effect. Although an impromptu affair, the friends of both responded in numbers which filled the halls of the St. Louis Hotel to overflowing. Not only was there a general exchange of congratulations, good wishes etc., but a social dance and splendid repast ensued, all of which carried the participants into the small hours of the morn. We shall neither attempt a description of the bride, or her toilette, or the many ladies and gentlemen assembled there and their habiliments.[35] Early residents of this section of Montana knew the bride as Miss Mollie Sheehan, a modest, handsome, entertaining young lady. As Mrs. Ronan she appears the perfect matured lady. . . .
>
> It was observed that Mr. Ronan was looking exceedingly well, and exhibited a countenance beaming with satisfaction

and contentment unknown to bachelors. Many fair ladies and noble looking gentlemen graced the occasion, but we doubt if from all the assemblage a better appearing couple could have been selected.

The evening was pronounced one of the most enjoyable had in the Metropolis during the season.

The next morning it was, I think, my husband came to me holding out the scrapbook that I had returned to him in the long ago. He opened it and, pointing to the blur of pencil marks, laughed and commanded, "Here now, Mollie, I have been wearing out my eyesight for the last four years and a half trying to make this out. Write it again." And he handed me a pencil.

I retraced the lines beginning "other skies may bend above thee," while he watched over my shoulder.

"Now we'll begin our scrapbook right," he said and pasted on the first page the notices of our marriage.

VICISSITUDES APLENTY

The quiet and peace of truly happy days afford little for the chronicler to record, and so I have little to relate concerning my first year of married life. A newspaper man's working hours do not allow many excursions into social life; added to this fact, during the year 1873 my husband was busier than usual trying to retrieve the fire losses of the *Gazette* and to reestablish the paper at its former point of prosperity. We did, however, go about a little socially, for I was interested in renewing old and making new friendships; our happiest hours, though, were spent alone together, often reading aloud. Mr. Ronan bought whatever books and magazines were to be had; I particularly remember *Harper's*. He brought home city newspapers from East and West on the *Gazette's* exchange—the *Boston Pilot*, *New York Times* and *Sun*, *Los Angeles Star*, and others that I have forgotten.

After having lived for three months at the St. Louis Hotel, we moved into a three-room house on the upper end of Wood Street. When I went into it, the house was completely furnished and everything in place. Our neighbors on the next corner, Mr. and Mrs. L. F. LaCroix, had assisted my husband in selecting the "parlor set" of black walnut upholstered in black horsehair, the carpets and other things.[36] I thought everything beautiful; to my eyes no house had ever looked so charming; to my ears the very

125

pans and kettles sang for joy; I was blissfully happy keeping house.

I do not recall that the social life of our community was particularly different from that typical of town life throughout the country, as I knew it through the vicarious experience of reading and conversation. As it was during the 1870s it continued to be during the 1880s and 1890s and even into the early years of the twentieth century, until the automobile and the World War changed our social order.

In an editorial titled "Homes," published in the *Rocky Mountain Gazette* of December 4, 1873, the following paragraph appeared:

> It is pleasing to note the increasing number of pretty homes which are dotting the suburbs of Helena and the lovely valley of the Prickly Pear. In the language of a contemporary, whether they contain two rooms or twenty, whether the "stately Mansard which covers all the modern conveniences" or the lowly cottage wrung from hard labor by hands—they are alike home where families can assemble about the fireside of mutual comfort and improvement.

What those "modern conveniences" included, whether inside plumbing, hot and cold running water, and furnaces, I cannot remember. Such things came among us gradually, but certainly to Helena, with the wealth that was then flowing from its mines, as soon as to any metropolis. I myself was long in having any of them, as circumstances kept me pushing into frontiers where "modern conveniences" had not yet been imported.

I do remember that our hosts and hostesses under some of those "stately Mansards" and in some of those low-roofed cottages, for instance the Maginnises, in their low-roofed, rambling cottage with unexpected steps up or down into equally unexpected rooms, were as refined and cultured and gracious as anybody one meets today, and as clever—though less consciously clever than is the present-day vogue. Dignity and reserve marked the manner of those who aspired to be known as ladies and gentleman. As long and intimately as I knew Major and Mrs. Maginnis, thus were they always called by me and by their other intimate friends— never Martin and Louise. At their table, at the tables of others living in Helena then, guests dined amid beautiful appointments though without the variety to the service that is now fashionable.

It was when I came to Helena as a bride that I first met those two great black robes, so prominent in the early history of Montana, Father Ravalli and Father Palladino.[37] Father Ravalli was theologian, philosopher, artist, artisan, sculptor, surgeon, physician, linguist of Indian tongues, and even student of *belle lettres*! One grows very humble thinking of the versatility of the man. He was stationed at St. Mary's Mission, Stevensville, in 1873, and journeyed now and then to Helena. I came to know him well later, between 1877 and 1884. When I first met him he was already past sixty and somewhat broken in health. This was because of the sacrifices he made and the deprivation and the exposure to all weathers he suffered in answering every call. Whether it was to minister as physician to the sick, maimed, or dying or to attend as priest to Indians, trappers, miners, and settlers, he was at the service of everyone with all his skill and knowledge and sympathy. His tremendous energy was still evident in his bearing and manner. Upon meeting him socially, one found his conversation full of merriment. While he was deferential and dignified, he also had a sweetly affectionate way; but most of all one was impressed with his great and fine simplicity. His large, soft, dark Italian eyes bespoke more the dreamer than the thinker.

Father Palladino was sent to Helena in 1873 as assistant to Father Van Gorp, whom he later succeeded as parish priest. Father Palladino's wisdom, tolerance, broad basis of common sense, and tender sympathy for humanity made him seem old at thirty-seven, his age when I first met him. He was only a little less versatile than

Father Ravalli, if not a sculptor or physician, he was a musician and a writer. He loved children; to give them surroundings which would aid them in developing healthily, happily, and normally was a special interest. In each parish where he labored, he carried out a sort of "playground movement" of his own, though to label what he did by any such phrase was unthought of by him or anyone else. In wintertime he used to make a rink for the children, which he would himself flood, scrape, and keep cleared of snow and smooth for skating. In summer the rink became a playfield and there again he organized, coached, and umpired various games and contests.

Father Van Gorp, whom I have already mentioned so many times, was also much beloved. He was a Belgian, a man of splendid physique and strikingly handsome; many remarked his resemblance to pictures of George Washington, especially to Stuart's famous portrait. Because he was familiar with the ways of men of the world and because of his genius for business, he was much sought after by prominent, successful, and worldly people. For all he was the grand gentleman, dignified and reserved, he was nonetheless a great and good priest.

A splendid clergyman of another following, famous in early Montana history, whom I never knew personally, was the Episcopalian bishop, the Reverend D. S. Tuttle.[38] Many of my acquaintances and friends talked about him with great admiration, and I went with Mr. Ronan to hear him lecture. He impressed me as a man of broad views and gentle speech.

One windy morning, January 9, 1874, Mr. Ronan got up early, went to the window, drew aside the curtain, struck a theatrical attitude in his fun-making way, and proclaimed, "on days like this ships go down at sea!" His jesting stopped short, for a moment he looked intent, then exclaimed with startling earnestness, "My God! There's fire at the *Gazette*." True enough in a few moments, fanned to fury by the wind, a terrible conflagration was devouring the business district and threatening much of the residence district, but not our home at the upper end of Wood Street. People were frantic with fear.

I was frightened for Mr. Ronan's personal safety but not about the plant, which was housed in a supposedly fireproof building. I had little time for thought; Mike Reinig, a German merchant whose home was threatened, brought his wife and two-day-old baby and placed them in my care. I put Mrs. Reinig and the baby in my bed. Several other people brought their children, bundled in winter wraps, and left them in my yard under my charge.

After hours of fighting the fire, Mr. Ronan came home weary, looking wan through the smudge and scorch on his face. He told me what had happened. The *Gazette* building had melted down in the flames, leaving nothing standing but the interior brick walls; all was lost, equipment, material, books, files, everything lost irretrievably. Then over the telegraph wires came the news that, in the aftermath of the panic of 1873, the company with which the *Gazette* was insured had been declared bankrupt on January 8, 1874! As I recall the plant had been insured for $30,000, though the estimated loss to the *Gazette* was given as $15,000.[39]

In all the fire consumed a million dollars' worth of property, burning about a hundred business houses and twenty residences. The greatest estimated loss was to the mercantile firm of Gans and Klein, $160,000. A loss not estimated in money value and never to be replaced was that of the manuscripts, notebooks, diaries, and pamphlets in connection with the history of the territory, which Colonel W. F. Sanders had collected in his library. These were totally destroyed. Likewise the files of the *Rocky Mountain Gazette*, those day-to-day chronicles of the times, were a double loss since the files of the *Helena Daily Herald* had been destroyed in the fire of October 1, 1871.

Stricken as he was, Mr. Ronan felt that many had suffered even more. At least our home had been spared and could afford shelter for those less fortunate, and he found it full to overflowing with refugee friends and neighbors. However, by evening the fire had sunk to ashes. All at our house, except Mrs. Reinig and her baby, returned to their own homes or to some other shelter from the bitter cold of winter. Although I, too, was in delicate health, for I expected my first child within four months, it was necessary for me to take care of Mrs. Reinig and her baby for several days. While they stayed in our little house with us, I made a bed on our "parlor" floor for my husband and me. In those early days we had to resort to all sorts of expedients to help one another.

Major Maginnis was in Washington serving the first of his twelve terms as United States Congressman from Montana and for some time Major Wilkinson had not been active on the staff of the *Gazette*. Mr. Ronan was not willing to undertake a third resurrection of the paper though friends came forward and offered to loan him the money to do so. Fred Cope offered him liberal inducements to transfer the *Montanian* from Virginia City and to establish it in Helena. Hugh McQuaid and J. C. Kerley endeavored to interest him along with L. F. LaCroix, former accountant for the *Gazette*, in joining their partnership as publishers of the *Helena Daily Independent*, which moved its offices from Deer Lodge to Helena and appeared as the successor to the *Rocky Mountain Gazette* on March 22, 1874.

Mr. Ronan refused to consider any of these proposals; what with the failure of the insurance company and the debts still accruing from the reorganization following the fire of August 1872, the further obligations that any of these plans involved looked staggering. Perhaps, too, a little superstition influenced his decision, for in an explanation of his refusal published years later, he concluded, "I had now had enough of journalism or it had had enough of me."

He determined to go back to prospecting and to mining, and he purchased, in partnership with J. R. Quigley, from E. Matlock, a hydraulic placer mine on Nelson Hill in the vicinity of Blackfoot City. This investment, he said laughing, was less likely than a newspaper "to light out in a cloud of smoke."

Blackfoot City

Early in the spring Mr. Ronan went to Blackfoot City to start operations on the mine and to prepare to take me there to live.[40] I remained in Helena for the coming of the child, a son, who was born on May 1, 1874. Some days before this event, my husband had returned to Helena to be with me in my ordeal. Dr. J. S. Glick and Dr. William Steele attended me; the latter had been the physician for my stepmother when my brother Jimmy was born and also long before that in Alder Gulch he had been with her when a little girl was born, only to die within a few days.[41] Trained nurses were unheard of; to care for me and for the baby Mr. Ronan had employed a woman named Sarah, who had had experience in obstetrics, a word never used in those days.

Father Palladino christened our first born son Vincent Rankin; the first name was, of course, for Mother Vincent, that grand woman so long a mother to Mr. Ronan and one, also, to me ever since he had brought me to Helena as his wife. Rankin was for a dear friend of Mr. Ronan's, David Rankin, who had mined at Diamond City in Meagher County in the boom days after the discovery of placer mines there in 1866. Mr. Rankin made his stake and returned to his old home, St. Louis.

Vincent was a beautiful, fair-skinned, blue-eyed, flaxen-haired baby, as healthy as he was beautiful. When he was five days old his father had to go back to the mine, leaving me in the care of our good neighbor and devoted friend, Mrs. L. F. LaCroix. By May 11, I was writing, "Thank God I am up today, sitting in the parlor with my good, good baby. There could not be a better child; he sleeps nearly all the time. The morning he was five days old he laughed and has every morning since." My husband's letter, written on May 12, was just as optimistic: "Everything looks prosperous for my mining interests and I will soon be taking out plenty of money."

At the end of the month he came and took the baby and me in a spring wagon the thirty off miles from Helena to our new home. It was a four-room log cabin situated on the side of a mountain, near a spring, and a mile or so from the mine. All our furniture had been freighted out from Helena. Soon we made the log cabin cozy, comfortable, and attractive.

We were thankful for the four miles that intervened between our home and Blackfoot City, a shabby mining camp that had seen its boom days. The "city" was built where Ophir Gulch widens into meadowland and rolling hills. It consisted of two rows of weather-beaten log cabins, about thirty or forty rods in length, with a street between them. More of the cabins were saloons, gambling dens, and houses of ill fame than the homes of families. Mr. Quigley, Mr. Ronan's partner, was proprietor of a general merchandise store. The one hotel consisted of a bar and a restaurant on the first floor and on the second floor a few dark, evil-looking little cubbyholes of rooms for lodgers. There may have been another store or two and a couple of butcher shops.

For us the days of summer and autumn passed like the incidents in a happy pastoral. While Mr. Ronan was busy at the mine, I was occupied with my baby and with my housework. It never occurred to me to be lonely or frightened. Once a week, when a meat wagon from Blackfoot City came down to the mine, I carried my baby out to the wagon to have him weighed while I was discussing with the vendor my purchases. Throughout the summer the baby gained regularly a half a pound a week.

My husband always loved a garden and had a way of coaxing things to grow, and so in our paradise in the wilderness he planted flowers and vegetables. He was also an enthusiastic fisherman and hunter. For our table we had a variety of fresh vegetables, fresh eggs, chickens, fresh mountain trout, and wild game. Because it was difficult to keep yeast I learned to make salt-rising bread. Friends discovered the delights of our mountain retreat and drove out from Helena to visit us. Except these visitors, I seldom saw a woman.

My husband and I spent the winter in complete seclusion. I was conscious of no hardship, of no monotony. Without was the endless variety of hills, glistening with drifted snow or somber with black forest patches and dark notches of canyons. Ragged lines of pines marched endlessly along the skyline. On clear days, far to the south, a jagged white peak could be seen stabbing the blue. Inside was warmth and congeniality, serious and silly talk, plans and hopes and laughter. Vincent thrived and grew; every day registering some absorbingly interesting baby change. I never had a worry at being so remote from a doctor.

Freezing weather put a stop to all work at the mine, so Mr. Ronan was at home with me most of the time. He read *Josephus* aloud to me and all of Shakespeare's plays; we had papers and magazines, for once a week Mr. Ronan would tramp out on snowshoes to Blackfoot City for the mail. We had horses and a sleigh, which he drove when he went for supplies. Sometimes if the roads were not too difficult, I bundled the baby in warm blankets and went along for a visit. Two or three times during the winter we drove to the "city" to attend a dance. One of the mothers in Blackfoot City stayed with the children, or we hired a nursemaid for the evening.

As early in the spring as the ice broke and the water ran, operations at the mine reopened. During the latter part of June my husband started with Vincent and me for Helena, for I was to have another child and we had made arrangements with Mrs. LaCroix for me to be taken care of in her home. At Blackfoot City, where we stayed over night before starting on the journey, we met Father Ravalli, who was also on his way to Helena. He was in ill health and was glad to accept our invitation to travel with us and to have advantage of the superior comfort and speed of our spring wagon over his own conveyance. It renewed our confidence to have him with us, for we did not know exactly how soon I might require the assistance of a physician. Father Ravalli rode on the front seat with Mr. Ronan, Vincent and I, in the back seat. At a ranch house about half way between Blackfoot City and Helena, we stopped for a meal and rested for two hours.

Mr. Ronan saw me comfortably settled with Mrs. LaCroix and then returned to the mine.

In less than two weeks, on July 8, 1875, a daughter was born. Dr. Glick attended me.

Everyone loved Dr. Glick. He put his profession before all other considerations. He was prompt at every call no matter what the weather or what the distance. How splendid he looked on the beautiful, spirited horses he kept for riding about on his calls. Once in his sad, broken, last years when his mind was beginning to fail, Mr. Ronan brought him to stay for a time at the Jocko Agency, hoping that happy surroundings might restore him some-what. Though sick in mind, he was not a difficult guest for he was gentle and tractable and childish play amused him. The pathos of his condition was intensely poignant to those of us who had known him in his vigorous days of supreme service.

Father Palladino baptized Mary Ellen, whose name had been chosen for months in advance of her coming. Mary was for the mother of Jesus, Ellen for my own mother. She was healthy, happy, good, and beautiful with red hair and dark, starry eyes; she bore and still bears a strong resemblance to her father. On the day that Mary was born a terrible storm raged at Blackfoot. The flume that brought the water to the mine was blown over, a bolt of lightning struck the tool shop where Mr. Ronan and a hired man were working. They were both knocked over and stunned; as a consequence the hired man was permanently crippled. Mr. Ronan used to tell with relish how a friend, hearing of the circumstance, said mournfully and in all seriousness, "Pete, you are the most unfortunate man. Think of it—flume blown down, struck by lightning, and a baby girl all on the same day!"

I was so anxious to go back to my home that when Mary was a week old I got up and dressed, determined to demonstrate that I was able to take care of myself and my babies. It happened that Mrs. Maginnis, just returned from Washington, D.C., came to call upon me that very day. She was beautifully dressed in the latest mode, and joyous. I shall never forget how pityingly she looked at me, weak and pale, holding my tiny baby in my arms and trying to soothe the toddling boy tugging at my skirt. I was too happy with my lot to resent her pity. It amused me then; but the memory of it came back to me with sadness in the lonely, childless, latter years of Mrs. Maginnis's life; yet I was glad for her, too, that once she had thought hers the happier lot.

When Mary was a month old, Mr. Ronan took the children and me back in the spring wagon to our home on the side of the mountain. He hired a young girl to help me with the babies and the housework. Throughout that summer and fall I remember nothing but days of health, happiness, and hope.

Every six weeks or so the sluice boxes would be scraped of their treasure. Always there was a fair "clean-up." Late in the autumn every indication pointed to a last big "clean up" of several thousand dollars worth of gold dust. Early in the morning of the day that was to conclude the season's work, the men went to the boxes and found that thieves had emptied them in the night and made away with all the precious dust. In that remote and inaccessible place stationing a guard at night had never been considered.

At breakfast that morning Mr. Ronan had said, "We will have lots of gold today." I was surprised when I saw him coming back before noon. To my questioning, he replied, trying not to look dejected, "Well Mollie, we're not going to have so much gold after all. The boxes have been robbed."

Much as I realized that the robbery meant that days and days of hard work and eager expectation were for nothing, and as sorry as I was for my husband and for his partners, I was not oppressed with the feeling that a calamity had befallen. I can remember the very attitude that I assumed gave emphasis to my words, "Well, we have left all that is sweetest and best. We have Manhood, Womanhood, and Childhood, united, loving hearts and willing hands!" Just as I was uttering this high sounding and entirely sincere speech, my friend Mrs. Hubbard stepped in and interrupted, "You are a very foolish girl and show that you don't know what life is." She was thirty then, enough older than I was to realize the struggle of trying to live and to bring up children on slender means or none at all.

The theft had been so carefully planned and carried out that scarcely a clue could be discovered; some Chinamen were suspected but not with enough evidence to prosccute. The robbers were never apprehended. Long years afterward Mr. Quigley happened accidentally upon a train of evidence that proved to his satisfaction, at least, that the prime mover had been a man with a wife and child who was prospecting a claim over the hill from ours. He was not suspected in any way at the time and even managed to get out of the country with his stolen gold dust without bringing the slightest suspicion upon himself. He had made neighborly calls on us now and again and stayed for an occasional meal. He was not the sort of person to interest us at all, but we never thought ill of him.

Before the winter closed down upon us we moved, household furniture and all, back to Helena. With that last big "clean-up," the vein of ore in the mine had pinched out. Friends, members of the Democratic Party, wanted Mr. Ronan to enter politics, to accept the nomination for sheriff of Deer Lodge County. He refused. However the sheriff of Lewis and Clark County, a man named Clark, appointed Mr. Ronan his undersheriff.

Major Maginnis conceived the idea of having Mr. Ronan appointed Surveyor General of the Territory of Montana, and set in motion the political machinery, which he thought, would turn out such a result. In the stormy presidential election of 1876, when Tilden was counted out seven to eight, his champions in the Democratic Party lost prestige, among them, in Montana, Mr. Ronan and Major Maginnis. So nothing came of the Major's idea with regard to a Presidential appointment. Meanwhile, we had spent an interesting and exciting year in Helena, a hotbed of political activity.

Our second son arrived on March 17, 1877. He was a little individual quite different from his brother or his sister, a brown baby with olive skin, dark hair, and eyes that even when he was tiny had the flash of his father's eyes. As when Vincent was born, again Mr. Ronan was determined that his son should not be called Peter, and so this boy was named in memory of Gerald, my little brother whose eyes were dark and deep, lost tragically in the long, long ago, and for the Saint Patrick on whose feast day he was born.

Out of a clear sky, without any solicitation on his part or on the part of any of his friends, came an appointment to Mr. Ronan from Carl Schurz, Secretary of the Department of the Interior, to

go to the Flathead Indian Reservation as agent to fill out the unexpired term of Major Charles S. Medary, who had been suspended
and summoned to Washington, D.C.[42] Mr. Ronan did not know
whether he wanted the appointment or not, but as it came at a
most opportune time when he was undecided whether to go on
prospecting some other mining claims he owned or to go back
into the newspaper game, he reported at once at the old agency in
Jocko Valley. From there on May 31, 1877, he wrote in part:

> My darling Wife,
>
> Tomorrow will be my birthday, and tomorrow I assume
> the reins and will commence the discharge of the duties of the
> Agent for the Flatheads and confederated tribes. I am very much
> taken with the place and I know you will be delighted. As one
> evidence of your liking the place I will state that one of the
> Sisters told me that thirty-two strawberries from the garden
> last year weighed one pound. The season is far in advance of
> Helena and we have vegetables of nearly every kind already.
> There are three bedrooms, a parlor and dining room, a large
> and convenient kitchen (furnished) with one of the finest cook
> stoves that I have seen in Montana. There are also two store-
> rooms off the kitchen; a good cellar, several closets, and a stream
> of clear, sparkling water running through the yard. We have
> four fine government milk cows. The doctor's office is well
> stored with all the drugs and medicines of a well-appointed
> country drug establishment. You will need your mirror, pic-
> tures, carpet, and parlor furniture, also your dishes and bed-
> ding, but you can dispose of everything else. I am almost certain
> that I will be able to leave here for you about the first of the
> week. I will take over a nice spring wagon belonging to the
> agency, which will convey you and Mrs. Lambert and the chil-
> dren in a very comfortable manner.[43] Kiss our darlings for me.

This letter was prelude to a trek and to setting up household
goods anew on another frontier.

BOOK THREE

Life among the Flathead

Tomorrow to fresh woods and pastures new.

—JOHN MILTON
"Lycidas"

The Flathead Indian Band poses in front of the Indian boarding and manual labor school at the St. Ignatius Mission. The Ronans maintained close ties to the mission and employed several of the school's graduates.

F. JAY HAYNES, PHOTOGRAPHER, MONTANA HISTORICAL SOCIETY PHOTOGRAPH ARCHIVES

The Jocko Valley

According to Duncan McDonald, the last factor at Fort Connah:

> The Flathead Agency is situated on a small tributary of the Jocko River. One mile to the rear a chain of lofty mountains rise abruptly from the valley—forming no foothills—and towering grandly above the scene. The mountains are covered with a dense forest of fir, pine and tamarack. Nearby are several clear mountain lakes, abounding in speckled trout, and from one of those lakes a waterfall or cataract over one thousand feet high plunges into the valley, forming one of the tributaries of the Jocko River. The valley is about five miles in breadth and twelve miles in length with excellent farming land, cultivated by Flathead Indians and half-breeds. Following down the Jocko to its confluence with the Pend d'Oreille River the valley closes, and the Jocko rushes through a narrow gorge. At the junction of the Jocko and Pend d'Oreille River, the valley again opens into a rich and fertile plain, where a large number of Indian farms are located.[1]
>
> St. Ignatius Mission, where the Indian boarding and manual labor school is established, is some seventeen miles from the Agency.[2] This Mission is one of the largest institutions of the kind in the U.S. and is presided over by a number of Jesuit priests, lay brothers and Sisters of Providence. A large convent, church, school house and dwelling are surrounded by a picturesque Indian village of some seventy snug log

houses, where principally Pend d'Oreille Indians dwell and cultivate the rich soil in the surrounding valley. The Mission Valley is a broad, extensive and well-watered plain with ranges of mountains on both sides. From the Mission to the Flathead Lake—a distance of thirty miles—and around its borders there are farming lands enough for thousands of settlers. The Indian name for the lake is Skalt-koom-see, which means Wide or Big Sheet of Water.[3]

Peter Ronan reported to the United States Commissioner of Indian Affairs in August 1877:

Flathead Lake is embossed in one of the loveliest and most fertile countries, surrounded by towering cliffs and mountain ranges. It is some twenty-eight miles in length, and has an average width of ten miles. In the center of the lake is a chain of beautiful islands, and upon its clear, broad bosom wild waterfowl of every description, even sea gulls, disport themselves. Around the foot of the lake is another Indian settlement where snug houses, well-fenced fields, grazing herds and waving grain, give evidence of the rapid advance of those Indians in the ways of civilization and thrift. Here the Pend d'Oreille River takes its rise, rushing and leaping through narrow gorges, and widening out into a broad stream, winding through lovely valleys for hundreds of miles, when it falls into the Pend d'Oreille Lake, a sheet of water larger than the Flathead Lake.

I have quoted at length because these descriptions reveal a situation for the Indians quite different from the present one. I bear witness to the fact that at that time many of them did have snug log houses, well-fenced farms, waving fields of grain, and grazing herds of horses and cattle; and there was evidence of husbandry and thrift and of the advance of the Indians in ways of civilization.

The confederated tribes of the Flathead, the Salish, Pend d'Oreilles, and Kootenais, at once bestowed upon my husband the title Scale-ee-hue-eel-i-me-kum, White Chief.[4] That he was indeed and more; he became their advisor, mediator, patriarch, and champion. So concerned was he in their affairs, in counseling them, in seeking to solve their problems, to get justice for them and redress for their many and grievous wrongs, and so successful was he in the administration of his office as an agent of the government that he spent the remaining sixteen years of his life among the Indians on reappointments through Republican and Democratic administrations.[5]

Once, in council with the confederated tribes, General John Gibbon, who looked upon the solution of the Indian question as dependent upon the transfer of the red man to the guardianship of the army, suddenly put the question to Flathead Chief Arlee: "Do you like your agent?" Arlee replied, "As agent of the government we respect him; as a friend and advisor and neighbor we love him; and I trust I may never live to see the appointment of his successor." With a few notable exceptions, that, for instance, of Major John Owen, always the understanding friend of the Indians, the history of the affairs of the Flathead Reservation under the various agents had been one of everlasting trouble, or misappropriation of Indian and government property and of constant court proceedings. Mr. Ronan, in writing to his people in Malden of his appointment as agent of the Flathead, concluded that this was the condition to a notorious extent.[6] He wrote, "No doubt your reading of 'Indian Rings' and thieving agents gives you the idea that it is hard for human nature to withstand the temptation of becoming a public robber, but make your mind easy on that score. I came into the office with clean hands, and with clean hands I shall go out."

True enough, just as my husband thought, I was delighted with the beauty of the place. There I spent twenty years, the most interesting and difficult of my life. Something stirring, exciting, dangerous, was always pending, threatening, happening. The old agency was isolated from civilization, but the situation was so lovely, and fishermen and huntsmen found the streams and country all about such a paradise for their sports, that after the first summer, as long as I lived on the reservation, I was never again alone in my home with my own family. As there was no hotel nearer than Missoula, a half day's journey by wagon or on horseback, and my husband was lavish in his hospitality, all comers were our house guests for as long as they chose to stay. Keeping my household organized, attending the needs of growing children, the insistent demands of a baby— during the most of those years there was a child under three years of age—counseling with my husband when, in our mutual concerns, we felt that two heads were better than one, all this combined to keep me in the midst of enthusiastic activity and burning with a sense of quickened and multiplied consciousness.

My difficulty came upon me in having to play the gracious hostess almost continually to members of Indian commissions, transcontinental surveys and railroad commissions, senatorial commissions on appropriation for the reservation, special agents of the government, generals of the army and other officers; a papal delegate, archbishop, bishops, and priests; an English and an Irish earl, a French count; sportsmen from abroad, the East and the West; scientists, millionaires, journalists in search of a story, celebrities, friends, relatives; and Indians—chiefs, tribesmen, and squaws with their papooses. There was no retinue of trained servants in the background to prepare and serve food and to dispense other necessities and comforts for this multitudinous and very human pageant of guests. My "help" usually consisted of a Chinese cook, an Indian laundress, and a young girl to act as nursemaid for the children and to help me with the sewing, for I made nearly all my clothes and the children's. I am glad to remember that in those busy years I never felt overworked or abused or longed for my little children to grow up. There was always something especially appealing about the worn little shoes, scattered about in the evening, which made me resolve that the next day I would try to be more patient and sweeter.

If I had the ability, the heart, and the endurance to capture and to relate the complete story of these years, to tell of the people and of the events that came and passed in perpetual flight into or beyond memory, my story would fill volumes. Since all that is actual is in a moment gone, reducing experiences to groups of impressions, I can only hope to trace faintly the main line of my story and to capture some of what is so fugitive by the aid of my old scrapbook with its accounts, in letters and newspaper clippings, of events as they were long ago recorded.

Mr. Ronan carried out the plan sketched in his letter of May 31, 1877, came to Helena in "the nice spring wagon," and conveyed Mrs. Lambert, the children, and me the hundred and fifty miles to the Flathead Reservation in a very comfortable manner, according to our ideas at that time. Mrs. Lambert with her little daughter Grace, who was just Mary's age, and I with my baby Gerald, not yet three months old, sat on the back seat. Mary, not yet two years old, and Vincent, just past three, sat beside their father on the journey. We spent the first night at Deer Lodge. At the hotel in the evening M. J. Connell, who was at that time a clerk in the store owned by E. L. Bonner, called upon us. During the second day we stopped a little while at New Chicago (hopefully named!)—then a settlement of some ten or a dozen houses— now I am told, no such metropolis! At the store of Archie A. McPhail, I met his wife, Annie McCabe, with whom as a little girl I played in Bannack, fourteen years before. We drove on and spent the night at a stage station—at Bearmouth, I think. At noon each day we would stop for a meal and a rest at a stage station.

Mrs. Lambert and I were young, happy, and forward-looking. We did not find the care of the children irksome at all. The weather was pleasant and sunny, so sunny that my wrist, exposed between my sleeve and glove as I held my baby, was all blistered. The country was beautiful beyond power of description. The spicy fragrance of June blossoms, especially of wild roses which hedged the road and of syringas, which almost overpowered it, delighted us into forgetfulness of burned wrists, arms aching from holding the baby, during hours and hours of jolting over rocky roads that followed river bottoms or clung along mountain slopes, of toiling up long, long grades or scraping down with brakes set, of pitching down steep banks into deep fords. Between Deer Lodge and Missoula, a distance of eighty miles, the Missoula River had to be forded about twenty times.[7]

On the evening of the third day of our journey we arrived in Missoula and went to the hotel on West Front Street kept by Mr. and Mrs. William Kennedy. The old friends were expecting us and greeted us warmly. Fifty-five years ago Missoula was a little village, and most of the log houses were clustered around the vicinity of Higgins Avenue bridge, where the Missoula Mills, the property of F. L. Worden, stood; the village extended a block or so east and west on Front Street, and north on Higgins Avenue.

Early in the morning we started on the last twenty-eight miles of our journey to the agency. At the mouth of the Coriacan Defile (now called O'Keefe Canyon), we stopped at the log ranch house of Baron O'Keefe, for through all the years, since the Alder Gulch days, I had kept up my friendship with Mrs. O'Keefe, née Hannah Lester, by letters, and since my marriage, Mrs. O'Keefe and her two little girls had visited in Helena. In spite of urgent invitations we did not stay long enough to get down from the wagon, for we were anxious to reach our new home.

Mollie O'Keefe, a girl of about twelve years of age, came down the roadway from the cabin and stood beside her mother at the gate of a zigzag rail fence, on which a bluebird perched and sang. Mollie was radiantly beautiful. Her wavy blond hair was caught back from her face and hung in ringlets about her shoulders. Her eyes were blue as the bird's plumage, her cheeks delicately pink, her skin clear as porcelain and smooth as satin. She was tall for her years, slender, willowy, and lithe. My words may sound extravagant; they are only futile in their attempt to picture Mollie O'Keefe as I saw her that morning, looking like the princess of the old fairy tales, who dwelt in the castle rather than the pioneer child who lived in the tiny log cabin in the shadow of the high hills that flanked the narrow canyon. She stood, a lovely picture; still I see her so.[8]

The weariest, most wildly beautiful stretch of our way lay through the narrow Coriacan Defile. Besides following the windings of the canyon, the road twisted and turned around great boulders; the roadbed was as rocky as a river bottom, in fact it lay along what must have been an ancient riverbed. We traveled next for four or five miles through the dense, majestic Evaro woods, slaughtered years ago; down Evaro Hill to the ford of Finley Creek, then a roaring torrent for none of the water had been diverted for irrigation. Just beyond the ford we emerged from a grand grove of yellow pines, and I saw for the first time the fruitful valley of the Jocko.[9] It was lovely and lush in June growth, the grass and flowers spread knee-deep across the prairie; here was a great blue patch of lupine; there, a rippling splotch of pink clarkia. A band of wild horses, grazing in this luxuriance, raised their heads, startled, whinnied, and broke into a gallop. Pitched against backgrounds of occasional clumps of trees, smoke-stained tepees could be glimpsed. Best of all, in the distance, at the end of a road that looped in long curves almost across the valley from west to east, was visible a little settlement, the agency, our home, a cluster of houses showing white in the late afternoon sunshine.

Directly to the east and to the south of the agency buildings, not two miles away, rose, so abruptly that they seemed to lean forward, great wooded pyramids of mountains, their dark blue intensified by deep shadows. To the northeast, in a gap in the mountains, was a magnificent view of one of the jagged snow-capped peaks of the Mission Range and a glimpse of a waterfall on its craggy side, barely distinguishable from the snow.[10] To the north were rolling brown hills; back of us, to the west, were higher wooded hills and mountains. So beautiful the valley was, it seemed to me that day I had entered a place like unto the garden of paradise.

At the agency stockade gate Harry Lambert waited to welcome us. We went into the house described in my husband's letter and found a delicious dinner prepared and ready to be served to us by the cook. Mr. Ronan had hired a clean efficient white woman to cook for us, the sister of Ovando Hoyt, the agency miller.[11] We were tired, but not too tired to be gay during our house-warming dinner. Then Harry took his wife and little daughter to their cottage just across the way.

When Mr. Ronan had had sufficient time to make improvements, the agency settlement, built in a hollow square, covered in all about an acre of ground. It consisted of our residence in the center of the south side of the square; on the west were the agent's office, a storehouse for government supplies for the Indians, a cottage for the government clerk, a granary, and a long narrow building with living quarters for the Indian interpreter and the agency employees (miller, sawyer, carpenter, stableman, etc.). On the north there was a barn, a carpenter shop, and a blacksmith shop; to the east a grist and sawmill. In the southeast corner was a house that included the residence, office, and drugstore of the agency doctor. In the yard back of the agent's residence were various small buildings: an icehouse, milk house, smokehouse, chicken house, washhouse, etc. All the residences were weather boarded and enclosed with low picket fences; the yards were planted with flower gardens and shade trees. All the buildings and fences in the settlement were painted white or whitewashed, except the sawmill, which was red; the roof, too, of the big barn was red. A picket fence six feet high enclosed the whole agency square; in the center of each side—north, east, south, and west—was a gate wide enough for a wagon to drive through. At night these gates were closed to keep out wandering stock. A fence-enclosed vegetable garden, a pasture with a zigzag fence, cattle sheds, while the houses for the sawyer and blacksmith were outside the stockade to the north and west.

In time Mr. Ronan set out an orchard on the ground between our house and the doctor's. In it were several varieties of apple trees (among them the McIntosh Red), wild plum trees, currant, gooseberry, raspberry and blackberry bushes, and strawberry plants. In the midst of the orchard he had built a little cottage for the gardener. Back of the cottage was a big root cellar, and still farther back was a pond for water storage in the summer time and from which to cut ice in the winter. He devised a system of water works: a cold stream was run through the milk house; cold water was piped into the kitchen sink. A bathroom, with a big tin tub, was improvised in a small room off the kitchen. Hot water had to be carried in pails from the large tank attached to the kitchen stove and emptied into the tub; cold water was carried in pails from the sink. But the water drained out through a rubber tube into a narrow irrigating ditch—a truly great convenience!

After a number of years the government allowed a sufficient appropriation so that additions were built on to several of the residences. On account of the numerous official guests that it was necessary to entertain, the two-story addition to the agent's house was somewhat pretentious for the times, consisting of a large "parlor" and several bedrooms. The house came to have, during most of the years that we lived in it, eleven rooms, besides a fair-sized storeroom, pantry, bathroom, and three hallways. The largest of these the children named "the hall of death" because in it were many mounted trophies of the chase: a black bear, a mountain goat, elk, moose, deer, and caribou heads. Practically all the lumber used in these buildings was turned out in the agency mill and most of the building was done by the agency employees, with the carpenter as head contractor.[12]

Straight across the prairie to the north, scarcely two miles away, out of Big Knife Canyon, came tumbling and roaring the cold, sparkling waters of the Jocko. Often in the late afternoon Mr. Ronan would walk, ride horseback, or drive to the Jocko and return in perhaps an hour with twenty or thirty trout hanging from the crotch of a willow branch, in plenty of time to have them cooked for supper. All about just outside the agency stockade were quantities of prairie chickens and pheasants. We would drive out a little way with the children in the spring wagon and Mr. Ronan would shoot the birds from the wagon. The children loved to be lifted down to run to get the birds. Even that first summer sturdy little Vincent did this sort of retrieving. In season for each we went on gay expeditions to gather huckleberries, chokecherries, wild plums, Oregon grapes, and elderberries. These I preserved or made into jelly or jam in great quantities and put them away in gallon earthen jars.

We needed to use every resource. We were provided with shelter, heat, light, some staple supplies such as flour and sugar, and we were privileged to utilize for our own household products from the government demonstration farm, garden, and orchard. My husband's salary was $125 a month, payable in quarterly installments. Oftener than not, however, until the railroad came through, the payments were delayed a month or two or three. The currency to pay the salaries of all the government employees on the Flathead Indian Reservation and allotments to the Indians was expressed to Missoula, where my husband had to go to receive it and then drive back with a pouch containing thousands of dollars over that lonely, twenty-five-mile stretch of hill country, mountain, forest, and canyon to the agency. The trips to Missoula for the money were always made secretly. Sometimes Mr. Ronan took with him a trusted guard, but oftenest he made the trip alone, always armed. He was never accosted by robbers, but I was never a moment at ease until his perilous errand was done.

We kept hearing stories of the trouble which had been rife since May among the non-treaty Nez Perces, led by Chief Joseph, and the white settlers in the Wallowa Valley in Idaho, backed by the United States soldiers under the command of General O. O. Howard.[13] Except for an uneasy feeling when I listened to these rumors, the first weeks at the agency passed like a happy dream. When I sat by the "parlor" window or on the long, narrow porch across the west side of the house, rocking my baby or sewing, I could see my husband going about the agency square with hired men or colorfully blanketed Indians. When he was not off on trips of inspection, he could be home for every meal.

In those happy-go-lucky, idyllic days before a household budget was heard of, we would have regarded it as a breach of hospitality to have submitted to the Department of the Interior an expense account for the ubiquitous inspectors, special agents, and other officials on government business who stayed at our house and sat with us at table for days, weeks, and sometimes months at a time. As a matter of fact, it never occurred to either of us to do so. I suppose we were simple, unsophisticated, and unbusinesslike. We were products of our times, and every stranger was welcomed like an invited guest. Our latchstring always hung out.

Thunder Traveling Over the Mountain and the Nez Perce War

Soon storm clouds gathered, the terrible red clouds of war. Every day brought us new rumors that the trouble between the Indians and Whites in Idaho was spreading.[14] The Nez Perces and Flatheads were friends and allies. Many Nez Perces lived on the reservation. Arlee himself, the war chief of the Salish, who lived not a mile west of the agency in the old log house that was built for the first agent of the Flatheads, was the son of a Nez Perce mother.

One morning, a few weeks after our arrival at the agency, I was sitting on the porch drying my hair, which was heavy and wavy and hung below my knees. Arlee stalked up the steps followed by one or two of his men and the interpreter, Baptiste Marengo. They inquired for Mr. Ronan. I arose, shook my hair back from my face, and started into the house to find him. I heard a moccasined tread behind me and felt my hair gathered together by a hand at the nape of my neck. I was terror stricken. There flashed to mind my childish fears when I was trekking across the plains and the awful tales of scalpings related by emigrants around campfires at night. Fortunately, I did not have time to cry out or to show my fear in any way, for quickly I felt a second hand below the first, and so hand below hand the length of my hair, my first experience with the Indian way of measuring. While the measuring was in progress, Baptiste spoke, saying to me that the Indians liked long hair, that Arlee had never seen any so long as mine, and that he wanted to tell the tribe how many "hands" long it was.

Though abrupt on this occasion, Arlee sometimes displayed the deferential manner of a courtier. One day when he was holding a council with my husband, my little auburn-haired Mary, who talked quite plainly from the time she was toddling, broke in upon the conference. Arlee patted her benevolently on the head—no people ever loved children more than did the old Indians. The war chief said in his own language, "We call her Ich-i-queel-kan (Red Hair)." Baptiste repeated to Mr. Ronan what Arlee had said, and he told Mary what the chief was calling her. She stamped her baby foot and cried pettishly, "He is Red Hair himself. Me not Red Hair!" Arlee asked what displeased the little girl. When he was told that she did not like to be called Red Hair, he said in Indian, with a gallantry that Lord Chesterfield himself might have envied, "Tell the little girl, then, that after this we will call her Khest kom-kan (Pretty Hair)." And so they did always. At once, indeed, the Indians had given us all names, and by them they called us and spoke of us always. I was No-ke-no Scale-ee-hue Eel-i-me-kum (Wife of the White Chief). Because of his blond hair Vincent was called Ich-i-pee-a-kan (White Hair). Gerald's flashing dark eyes gained for him the name of Eel-i-kan-oop Cha-kloos-tas (Eagle Eye).

One day Eagle of the Light, a Nez Perce chief, arrived unannounced at the agency with eleven lodges of his people. He had kin upon the reservation. He said that he had broken with Thunder Traveling Over the Mountain (the Indian name for Chief Joseph) and with White Bird and Looking Glass, and that at the last council, which the Nez Perces held to decide whether they would commence a war of revenge by massacring the usurpers of their home land, the settlers in Wallowa Valley, he had pleaded against this action. The braves gathered in the council lodge received his advice with scorn and derision. Eagle of the Light then tore off his insignia of rank as a Nez Perce chief, trampled it under his feet and strode forth. He called together his family and the few Indians who held to his views and they left the Valley of the Winding Waters. They had traveled over the mountain trails of the Idaho Clearwater, through Lolo Pass, Missoula Valley, and O'Keefe Canyon to the Flathead Agency. He requested that he and his band be allowed to remain on the reservation. Mr. Ronan granted his request, not without grave misgivings, but during all the bloody scenes that were to follow for his tribe, Eagle of the Light remained encamped with his followers near Arlee's house true to his promise of friendship.

One day a runner came with definite information that Chief Joseph and his band, flushed with victory over the United States soldiers in Idaho, were on the warpath and were headed to Montana on their way to Canada. Mr. Ronan was away from home on business. Ovando Hoyt, the miller, really a better carpenter and painter, was doing some renovating about our house. He was a Spiritualist.[15] Whenever I passed him, going about my household affairs, he would stop his work and, embellishing his revelations with much waving of arms and gesticulating with a paint brush, relate to me the visions that had been vouchsafed him of the Nez Perces sweeping in carnage across the reservation and over the entire state of Montana. Without my husband to reassure me, this was very distressing.

Excitement possessed us all. The very air was charged with fear when a runner brought us the news from Missoula that on July 20 the Nez Perces had appeared in the Bitterroot Valley, forty miles from the reservation, and that on July 23 they had actually appeared in war array outside Captain Rawn's encampment in

Lolo Pass.[16] The *Missoulian* issued an extra on July 25, which carried the headline, "HELP! HELP! WHITE BIRD DEFIANT. COME RUNNING!"

The *New North-West* of Deer Lodge, dated July 28, 1877, came to us several days late, carrying a story of the presence of Chief Joseph, White Bird, and Looking Glass in Lolo Canyon, with three hundred and thirty warriors; of Captain Rawn, the Seventh Infantry, and a volunteer force being entrenched in the canyon; of the call for more troops; of the coming of the Deer Lodge volunteers; and of Governor Potts' arrival at Missoula, twelve miles from Lolo Canyon, to ascertain the true situation. Mr. Ronan was in the midst of the stir, riding back and forth between the agency and Missoula to keep informed, and here and there about the reservation, to check on the whereabouts and activities of the Indians under his charge, especially of Eagle of the Light and his following.

My baby Gerald suddenly became very ill. No doctor was at that time assigned to the agency; there was no one to send to Missoula for a doctor, so Mr. Ronan went himself with a team of fast horses. While he was gone a runner brought the news that the Nez Perces were headed through Missoula and across the reservation into Canada over the Kootenai Trail.[17] He said that all the women and children in Missoula had been gathered in the courthouse with guards picketed, and already the Indians had launched their attack on Missoula.

I have no words to express the intensity of my feelings. I scanned keenly every Indian that chanced into the agency square, trying to pierce their stolidity and to detect a look or an action that betokened friendliness or enmity. When, in the morning, I found that the baby was much better and could be left with Mrs. Lambert, I went about among the agency employees to see what news or hope they could give me that my husband was safe and that the march of the Nez Perces was not in our direction. My terror was increased, for I found that the men had all stopped their work and were putting their firearms in readiness for use.

By noon Mr. Ronan returned with reassuring news. He said that there were no Nez Perces in Missoula and that there was no fighting. The women and children had been gathered in the courthouse under guard merely as a precaution. He was assured, he said, of the friendly attitude of Arlee, "the renegade Nez Perce," as Charlot, Chief of the Bitterroot Flatheads, called him. Furthermore, Mr. Ronan declared that among the two hundred volunteers entrenched with Captain Rawn were many Flathead Indians.[18]

For all he said, that night I saw him, when he thought I was asleep, slipping guns, ammunition, and even a hatchet into the wardrobe in the bedroom. We only pretended to sleep that night; our ears were alert for sounds of hoofbeats and war whoops. At last morning came and runners from Missoula to say that still there was no sign of the Nez Perces.

That morning old Michelle, Chief of the Pend d'Oreille, and a band of his warriors pitched their tepees just outside the agency square. He and a group of his headmen came ceremoniously into Mr. Ronan's office. Through an interpreter Michelle announced to the White Chief that he and his people would stand with Arlee and with the whites against the Nez Perces. He had sent a message, he said, to Joseph, that should he try to cross the reservation, it would mean the annihilation of his band. If the wife of the White Chief were frightened, he would picket a guard of his warriors around the house until all danger had passed.

I was summoned to the council. The Indians sat about the office, some in chairs, some squatted upon the floor, solemnly passing around the circle a tomahawk with a bowl and pipe stem, each one drawing and puffing in that slow, enigmatic way that I came to know as typical of the Indians. I stood beside my husband. I could scarcely conceal my trembling. The interpreter repeated to me Michelle's message. In the Pend d'Oreille chief's rugged old countenance and kindly attitude was that which commanded belief and respect. My courage was restored. My self-possession returned. After a brief consultation with my husband, I asked the interpreter to thank Michelle and his men and to say that I would not require a guard. The encampment of Pend d'Oreille so near the agency and their chief's pledge of friendship was assurance to me of safety for my little children and myself.

After his next trip to Missoula, Mr. Ronan brought back the news of the ultimatum that Charlot, though the Flatheads and Nez Perces were friends and kinsmen, had issued to Chief Joseph. Charlot rode with a guard of warriors into Joseph's camp.[19] He refused to shake the outstretched hand of Chief Joseph; the hand of Looking Glass he spurned, saying, "No. Your hand is reeking with the white man's blood. I will never shake hands with you again." To Joseph he turned and spoke, "Joseph, I have something to say to you. It will be in few words. You know I am not afraid of you. You know I can whip you. If you are going through the valley you must not hurt any of the whites. If you do you will have me and my people to fight. You may camp at my place tonight, but tomorrow you pass on."

After several days we heard that Looking Glass had made an offer to Captain Rawn to surrender all Nez Perce ammunition if his band was allowed to pass in peace.[20] Next we heard that early in the morning of July 28 Joseph had broken camp. With his entire following of warriors, squaws, and papooses, along with the equipment and stock belonging to his band of non-treaty Nez Perces, Joseph had skirted Captain Rawn's entrenchments and had pushed northward along the wooded slopes of the Bitterroot Mountains. For more than a week couriers kept bringing us news of the leisurely march of the Nez Perces through the Bitterroot

Valley. "In view of all the circumstances, it was the boldest, most fearless, audacious, and confident tactical movement we have known."[21] Then came the news of the terrible carnage of the Big Hole, beginning at daybreak on August 9, 1877. By little and little the news reached us of the retreat through the Yellowstone Park, across the Missouri, and north across the state toward Canada, of the encounters with General Miles and with General Howard in the Bears Paw Mountains, of the escape of Chief White Bird and forty bold warriors across the British Miles on October 8, 1877, to save the sad remnant of his tribe of eighty-seven warriors (forty of them wounded), one hundred and eighty-four squaws, and one hundred and forty-seven children.[22] Chief White Bird was reported to have said, "I have said that in my heart, rather than have war, I would give up my country. I would give up my father's grave. I would give up everything rather than have the blood of the white men upon the hands of my people."

My husband, as a result of his conferences with the Jesuits, who knew the Indians so well, and also because of the acquaintanceship and investigation that he had been able to make among the Indians even during his first two months of office, believed in the sincerity of Chief Joseph and regretted the course that was being pursued with him. Hostility had been forced upon Joseph. Many whites began to realize that he was indeed a man with a grievance, a man to be greatly respected and admired.

We followed with interest all that befell Joseph, his removal with his people to Fort Leavenworth, later to Baxter Springs, Kansas, where many of the Indians sickened and died. Through all the years of Mr. Ronan's service among the Indians, echoes of this tragedy kept coming to him; and more than that, he listened frequently to poignant appeals from Nez Perce friends of Joseph's on the reservation to do all in his power to bring an end to that tragic exile.

"Take me back to my old home," the broken warrior chief kept pleading, "where I can see the tall mountains and can count the stones in the bottom of the mountain streams." Because my husband believed that the plea of Chief Joseph and the pleas of his friends were based on just claims, he did exert his utmost in behalf of the dispossessed Nez Perces. Among those who came to him was Tukalikshimei (No Hunter), the brother of Looking Glass, with the proposal that the Nez Perces be released from their exile and assigned to the Flathead Reservation.

Tukalikshimei was a splendid, big, upstanding Indian of the finest, most clean-cut type of Nez Perce. He wore a handsome fur headdress, fitted tight about his forehead, with a lynx tail hanging down his back. At the close of their conference Mr. Ronan asked Tukalikshimei if in exchange for money he would give the headdress to him as a reminder of their mutual esteem. The Nez Perces agreed to do so.

Among Mr. Ronan's papers are two sheets headed "Tukalik-shimei—No Hunter" in Mr. Ronan's handwriting. The speech is written, in part, as follows:

> Tukalikshimei, though that is my name I am old Looking Glass's son and brother of the one who was killed. My friend, I hear very well what you say; you are truly an Agent Chief. Though I do not know you personally, you have a good name among your people. You speak well of my children, that they might grow in this world, and therefore together we sent a letter to Washington and now both of us are giving news about our people. Peace and friendship are good and we should love them. I think that your proposal of having a place to live is very good. You think so and I also think so, and we should have a place where our children might grow. . . .
>
> When General Howard said now we are done fighting, I was very glad, so much so my body had life again; my ears could hear and my eyes could see. I was then glad, because now we only hear of peace and friendship. . . . My heart aches

every moment of every day for the death in battle of so many whites and Indians, and I beg you and all white friends to make my heart live again, and I should like that the chiefs in Washington would see my heart and I would be glad. I do not hide anything. I show my heart as it is.

Another one, when peace was restored, who came to plead this same cause was Eagle of the Light, the Nez Perce chief of whom I have already spoken. He had first presented the case to Brigadier General O. O. Howard and to other commanding officers in the United States Army. They responded with noncommittal letters, in general reading, "I am not prepared to judge of the advisability of granting the petition. . . . Possibly the remnant might be gathered to the Flatheads." Each one passed the decision on to the next, and Eagle of the Light sought the agent of the confederated tribes of the Flathead in council assembled. My husband preserved the speech as the interpreter repeated it to him:

> My heart is sad now because I lost all my children, all my brothers, all my women, in the war. It was not my fault that my children and my tribe were killed in war and made prisoners. I was opposed to war, and because I opposed it in the councils of my nation I was compelled to leave my tribe and to come here and ask permission of you to live among the Flatheads until peace would come. Now I will speak as clear as the light of the morning, as in the morning the sun is clear after the darkness of night—so will my words be clear. I know that all the Nez Perces that are now prisoners in the south, among whom are some of my children and relations, are very sad because a great many are already dead and the rest are fast dying in a climate they are not used to; as I beg of you Great Father of the white people in Washington, to give them back to me. I am a chief, as well as you, and when war is over we could agree that brave men and women and children should not die if it can be helped. That is the reason I say again—give me back my children! I speak for Chief Joseph and his fellow

prisoners. I was chief of those Indians before Joseph was, and left my people because I believed in peace.

Mr. Ronan recommended to the Commissioner of Indian Affairs that Joseph and his band be sent to the Flathead Reservation. His recommendation was not acted upon in every detail, but at last, in 1885, the broken Chief Joseph and the sick and impoverished survivors of his audacious tribe were sent to spend their last days on the Colville Reservation in northern Washington, near, at least, to their old home and where they could "see the tall mountains and count the stones in the bottom of the mountain streams."[23]

In the very midst of the furor and excitement of the Nez Perce trouble, the first of our long series of distinguished visitors arrived, Bishop O'Connor of Omaha, whose dioceses then extended into Montana. Accompanied by Father Palladino from Helena and Father Van Gorp, superior at St. Ignatius Mission, the bishop drove from Missoula and reached the agency at noon on July 22, 1877. The members of the party spent a few hours looking over the mills, workshops, office, storehouse, garden, and farm. They were our guests at dinner before they proceeded to St. Ignatius Mission. Mr. Ronan had dispatched Indian runners the length and breadth of the reservation with the message that the "Chief of the Black Robes" had arrived and would say Mass and speak to the Indians at St. Ignatius Mission on Sunday morning, July 23. Mr. Ronan went to the mission with the bishop and his party. This is some of his account of the occasion, preserved in the old scrapbook:

> The chiefs and headmen of the three confederated tribes—Flatheads, Pend d'Oreilles and Kootenais—accompanied by their warriors, squaws, and papooses, came flocking in. At nine o'clock Sunday morning his Grace celebrated Mass

in the commodious Mission Church and addressed the Indians in English which was interpreted to them by Father Bandini.

"I am very happy, my dear friends, to be with you today. One of the principal objects of my long journey from the East was my hope of visiting this place, and I assure you, my dear friends, I am not disappointed. I am truly edified by your devotion to your religion and the duties it imposes.

To love our enemies requires courage. A coward can hate. It requires a brave man to forgive. The Indians are brave in the chase; they are brave in battle; they are brave against all danger. Show your courage and your bravery by forgiving your enemies. For love of you the black-gowns left their homes and far-off country and came to dwell in your midst and to teach and advise you. I will not ask you to love them, for I see you do love and revere them.

Your Catholic brethren in the East love you, and the great heart of the American people and the Great Father in Washington love you and regret the wrongs you have had to suffer. The American people condemn the action of bad men. You have a good Agent, Major Ronan, one of your own faith, loved and revered by his friends, and respected by all who know him, without regard to creed or country. Goodbye; God bless you all, my children."

It interests me to note how the bishop studiously avoided a direct reference to the Nez Perce War and even more any reference whatever to the news that three days before the Nez Perces had been seen in the Bitterroot Valley. It was whispered that the Salish would not remain true to the promises of their chiefs to protect the white settlers and not side with Chief Joseph. Indeed, on the very day Bishop O'Connor was pleading for peace and brotherly love, the Nez Perces, in war array, were warily skirting the entrenchments of Captain Rawn.

After the excitement following the surrender of Chief Joseph had subsided, except for minor troubles with police discipline and the necessity of expelling some whites from the reservation, peace reigned in our little domain and the year rolled happily around to July 1878.

One sultry day a trooper from Fort Missoula galloped into the agency with his horse in a lather. He bore a message for the agent that the band of warriors under White Bird, who had escaped into British Columbia, were on the march over a trail of blood on their return to Wallowa Valley. Mr. Ronan sent out trusted Indian runners to ascertain the facts. Meanwhile good riders and fleet horses were kept in constant use between the agency and Missoula.[24] Each day added to the excitement. Messages came that the Indians had killed some men on the Dearborn River and others on Deep Creek, which was a day's travel from the Dearborn in the direction of Missoula. They were reported to have come through Cadotte Pass and to be headed through the Swan River and Blackfoot country for the Jocko Trail on to the reservation.[25] Next a messenger brought word that they had taken a trail to the Bitterroot Valley by the way of Rock Creek, where they had murdered three more men.

The rumor spread that the murderers were from the Flathead Indian Reservation, probably from among the band of Eagle of the Light, and that a general uprising of the Indians was about to take place with the confederated tribes of the Flatheads joining in the revolt; even the Columbia River Indians, under Chief Moses and Spokane Carez, were said to be on the warpath and marching toward Montana.[26] People on isolated farms and in small settlements like Philipsburg were deserting their homes and thronging to Missoula for protection.

While these wild stories were spreading and growing, the runners sent out by Mr. Ronan had brought back the information, which proved to be true, that the hostile Nez Perces were from White Bird's band and that they numbered not more than nineteen, seventeen men and two women. They had crossed the

North Fork of the Sun River and were following an Indian trail leading through the Bitterroot Valley to Lolo Pass and thence to Idaho. Mr. Ronan dispatched this information to the commanding officer at Fort Missoula together with a description, which he got from trustworthy Indians, of the route which the Nez Perces would likely follow. Soldiers under the command of Lieutenant Tom Wallace were sent to intercept the Nez Perces.[27] This they did on July 25, on the North Fork of the Clearwater. Six of the Indians were killed and three wounded. Later, official messages announced that "authorities of Idaho had hunted to death" the ten Indians who made their escape.

Immediately, when Mr. Ronan had heard of the rumored disaffection of the Indians on the reservations, he called a general council. He gave the particulars of the murders that up to that time had been committed by the Nez Perces, presented the Indians' situation as he saw it, and predicted the disastrous outcome. Michelle, chief of the Pend d'Oreille, was the spokesman for the Indians. He renewed the words of friendship that he had spoken the previous summer when he had offered to be personally responsible for the safety of my little ones and me. He rose among his confederates, supporting himself on his crutches, shook his grizzled locks back from his face, and spoke with convincing earnestness:

> A few days ago a messenger came from the camp of Sitting Bull with word that if I valued the lives and welfare of my Indians, to gather them together and leave the Reservation, if I did not feel like joining him and making war upon the whites; that after he had done his work among the settlers, myself and my people could come back again and occupy our lands without fear of obtrusion from whites, as they would be wiped away. . . . I told the runner to say to Sitting Bull and his council that the Pend d'Oreilles, Flatheads, and the Kootenais of this Reservation were friends of the whites—that years ago when I was young the Indians of this nation had met the Sioux

in war and were enemies. We are now quietly upon the land assigned to us by treaty with the whites, supporting our children as well as we can; our homes we love, our lands are beautiful, the crops are ripening and we will soon be gathering them in. We are not well armed and have nearly forgotten the modes of war, but a mouse though small if trodden upon will turn and bite. Tell your chief if he comes this way we will give them battle, and make common cause with the white people.

When asked what he thought about the murders just committed by the Nez Perce band, Chief Michelle replied:

> I think that White Bird, whose voice was always for war, has arranged with Sitting Bull and has sent out this small marauding party to pass through Montana and onto Lapwai Reservation in Idaho, committing in their route murder and outrage, with an endeavor to incite another uprising among the Nez Perces and all other Indians west of the mountains, with a view to joining forces with Sitting Bull, who has promised to help them in their war against the whites. This is only my opinion. Perhaps this band of murderers broke away from White Bird without his consent. I am now ready to pick out Indian scouts to accompany white settlers or white soldiers and assist in the capture of this band of Nez Perce murderers.[28]

Eagle of the Light spoke on behalf of himself and of his followers and promised that the attitude of peace and friendship, which had persisted throughout the year, would continue. Thus we always found our Indians loyal and true. Seventeen Nez Perce warriors, in desperation to get back to their homes in the Valley of the Winding Waters, had terrorized the people of three states: Montana, Idaho, and Washington. I am not condoning the murders that they committed, but it was my experience always to find the Indian more sinned against than sinning.

One day in mid-July when this excitement about the Nez Perces was at its height, two strange Indians, heavily armed, dismounted at our gate, tied their horses to the white picket fence, and stalked into the sitting room. I was alone in the house with my three little children and the nurse maid, Minnie Sullivan. Minnie at once recognized that the warriors were Nez Perces. One of them, who walked with a limp, a grim, bruised, battered-looking man with a soiled and bloody bandana bound around his forehead, asked in English for Major Ronan. While Minnie hastened away to find him, the Nez Perces told me that they had come from a camp on the Jocko lakes. I was terrified. In my mind this confirmed the rumor that White Bird's hostiles (we did not know how few in number they were) had indeed come over the Jocko trail and would soon surround the agency. In a few moments Mr. Ronan entered the room. The Indians greeted him and then sat in silence for some time before the spokesman took three letters from his beaded pouch and gave them to Mr. Ronan. When my husband finished reading, Captain George, for that was the spokesman's name, told his story.

He had not joined the retreat of the Nez Perces from Idaho the previous summer. A young warrior of Joseph's band had carried off his sixteen-year-old daughter from his home at the crossing of the Camas in Idaho. She was with the Indians in all their battles, including the Battle of the Big Hole, where fifty Indian women and children were among those killed; she was among the fugitives in the retreat across Montana. Her abductor was one of the band that escaped with White Bird; and he took her with him to the camp of Sitting Bull. Captain George had traveled in search of his daughter on horseback more than two thousand miles before he arrived at the agency that morning of July 14, 1878. One of the letters, written by General Nelson Miles, read in part:

> The bearer 'Captain George' (so-called) is a Nez Perce who came through with General Howard to get his daughter who was in the hostile camp. He was very useful as an interpreter at the surrender of Chief Joseph and his band of warriors and after

the Nez Perce camp was secured. I sent him to Sitting Bull's camp for his daughter, and with a message to White Bird and the band who escaped. He secured his daughter, got as far as Carroll, or near there, where he was foully dealt with by miserable white men—he was shot in several places, as his unhealed wounds will show, and his young girl used worse. I presume he was left for dead, but succeeded in reaching the Crow camp. His daughter was taken, I understand, to Benton, where she remained at last accounts.

If the white men who committed the crime are caught, I would suggest that you report to department headquarters, as the department commander ordered the affair investigated.

A second letter, dated July 5, was from Major James T. Brisbain, the commanding officer at Fort Ellis, Montana.[29] The third letter was from an officer at Fort Benton and commanded safe passage for Captain George from there to Flathead Agency; it enlisted the assistance of the agent in searching for the Nez Perce girl and restoring her to her father.

Mr. Ronan found quarters for Captain George and his companion. He directed them to remain on the agency grounds while he made investigations among the Indians. He knew that it was dangerous for them to travel through Missoula County, as they might be taken for members of the hostile Nez Perce band that only the week before had passed through the country leaving death along their trail. In a few days some Salish Indians reported to the agency office that early in the spring a young squaw, answering to the description of the daughter of Captain George, had been rescued by members of their band from her white captors near Fort Benton. They had brought her with them over the Indian trail through Cadotte Pass to the reservation and had sent her, under Indian escort, over the Lolo Pass to her home at Camas.

Mr. Ronan sent out a runner to gather more information about the girl and he himself started to Lolo to meet a camp of

Indians who were reported coming over the trail from Idaho. On the way he met one of the Bitterroot Flatheads, John Hill, or Tah-hetcht, which in Indian means Hands Shot Off. He said that eight days previous he had camped at the lodge of Captain George at the crossing of the Camas, beyond the Bitterroot range of mountains. The girl was at home with her mother, brought by a band of Salish braves who took her from the white men at Benton. When Mr. Ronan returned with this news, Captain George's impassivity gave way to emotion. He was wild with delight. He said that Tah-hetcht was his friend; he would not lie to him; he knew that it was true that his daughter had been restored to him. Mr. Ronan sent Captain George to Fort Missoula and from there Major Chipman sent the brave, devoted Indian father safely home under military escort. I wish I had kept the letter of thanks that he sent back to Major Ronan, to conclude fittingly this true story.

This incident and the continued and growing friendliness of the Indians, including Eagle of the Light and his band, during all these turbulent times, sealed our trust in my husband's charges. That trust was never betrayed in all our years among the Indians, not even was it betrayed in small matters. Indeed, as the years passed, we came never to shut a window or door in our house except against the weather, and no door or window was ever locked. The Indians might stalk into the house at any time of the day; they never came with sinister intent, nor took anything, nor did any harm. They either stated their business to some member of the family or told what their "hearts" wanted. Their hearts wanted many things, but they accepted denials with stoicism, or they squatted down idly in silence until the spirit moved them to depart. If I requested them to go they did so quietly and without offence. Of course, I always endeavored to put such requests tactfully and to accompany them with little gifts such as a bit of sugar, a piece of bread, or an apple.

ONE SMALL DOMAIN

Hugh McQuaid of the *Helena Independent* wrote after a visit to our small domain:

> To those who are not familiar with the duties of an Indian agent, it might seem that those duties are light; but he who spends a few days on the Reservation will find that the man who listens to the never-ending complaints brought to him by rude minds; who adjudicates local disputes; who supplies the petty wants of thousands of Indians, has his hands and head about as full as they can carry of straight-forward business. And the agent who listens to their troubles, and uses his best judgment in all business transactions with them receives the reward of their respect and filial love, which they show in various ways.

In order to keep up with his numerous duties and ahead of the demands upon his time, my husband used to rise very early to plan his day's work and to audit accounts. He especially liked the early morning hours for writing his monthly and lengthy annual reports to the Commissioner of Indian Affairs and such publicity as he had time to prepare for the papers. When we were alone in the evenings, now and then, he would read his reports or articles for me to critique, and sometimes, as in the old days in Helena and at the mine, we had leisure to read poetry and other things.

When winter came we were isolated, but not nearly so much as we had been at the mine at Blackfoot, for living right within the agency square were two agreeable women neighbors, Mrs. Lambert

Before a church was built at the agency in 1889, the Ronans took their children some seventeen miles to the St. Ignatius Mission chapel, shown here in 1884, to celebrate feast days such as Christmas and Easter.

F. JAY HAYNES, PHOTOGRAPHER, MONTANA HISTORICAL SOCIETY PHOTOGRAPH ARCHIVES

and Mrs. Choquette, the latter of whom was the wife of the doctor who had been appointed for the Indian Service.[30] With my three little ones, it was a comfort to me to know that the doctor's home and office could be reached within two minutes.

Picnics and fishing expeditions to Jocko River, Finley Creek, or the "big woods" north of the agency were favorite family diversions when the season permitted. Sometimes in the years that followed we packed our camping equipment in covered wagons, ourselves and the little ones in spring wagons, mounted the older children on horseback, and cavalcaded gaily across the reservation on a two-days' jaunt to Flathead Lake. There we would camp for several weeks, usually on Polson's point. Once or twice Mr. Ronan had our outfit ferried across the Pend d'Oreille River. We established our camp on Dayton Creek so that he might take the opportunity to get better acquainted with the Kootenai tribe, most of whom lived in that vicinity. He built and equipped a storehouse in this place, still standing on the knoll in 1929, which he used as a place to distribute government rations to the Kootenais. Once Mr. Ronan chartered an old-fashioned steamboat and took the family on a tour of Flathead Lake. I recall that we made an overnight stop at Demersville, a thriving settlement at the head of the lake that quickly died when the Great Northern Railroad bypassed it.

In the winter we entertained and were entertained by the agency families at dinner, supper, or an evening gathering. The bachelor employees were frequent guests at our firesides. Sometimes we danced among ourselves with Dave Polson furnishing the music with his fiddle.[31] These dances were always held in the dining room of the agent's house, an attractive old-fashioned room, as was the sitting room, both having wide open fireplaces, low mantelpieces, and wainscoting around the walls.

Before the little church was built at the agency, on such Feast Days as Christmas and Easter, if the weather and other considerations permitted, my husband and I took the children and drove to St. Ignatius Mission. He and the boys would stay at the house of the Jesuits and I, with my little daughters and baby, for there was always a baby, would stay with the Sisters of Providence. Thus I came to know so well those noble, sweet women who founded the school for girls at St. Ignatius, Mother Mary Infant Jesus,

Sister Mary Edward, Sister Paul Miki, Sister Remi, Sister Jane de Chantal, and Sister Mary Trinity were among my best friends in the community. Mother Infant Jesus—what an efficient, grand woman she was and what a loving mother to me! Those visits shine in my memory as bright incidents and precious, comparable to the experience of the young matron who takes her children and goes into the peace and order and freedom from household responsibilities that her own devoted mother's home affords. Always I was transported back to the dear days of my girlhood in the convent in Los Angeles, to such a sense of quiet well being.

Occasionally we spent a day or two in Missoula. We visited oftenest with the Kennedys; sometimes in later years, when I came to know them well, with Mr. and Mrs. F. L. Worden or with Mr. and Mrs. Hammond.[32] On one eventful visit during our first year at the agency, we were tendered a reception by the citizens of Missoula. I kept the newspaper notice of so notable an occasion:

> The past week has been a gay one in Missoula social circles. On Friday night a complimentary part was given at the courthouse to Major and Mrs. Ronan, and the attendance must have been particularly gratifying to the Major and his accomplished lady, evidencing as it did, the esteem in which they are held by our citizens.[33]

Among our most frequent visitors were the army officers from Fort Missoula. Colonel John Gibson, Major Jordan, Captain Frémont in the early days were all charming, cultured men. Later, there was a host of others. In those days members of the Army circles were regarded as "America's aristocracy." Indeed, in the hurly-burly of frontier life, Army officers were the only group of men who had any leisure in which to cultivate themselves. Once, when we visited at Fort Missoula, my husband and I were guests of honor at a supper given by Lieutenant and Mrs. Cook in the log house that still stands at the fort.[34]

As Mr. Ronan had to drive about the reservation much on business, at least two teams of spirited driving horses and several excellent saddle horses were always in the barn or in the pasture just outside the stockade. Mr. Ronan was a good judge of a horse. Endurance and speed were essential qualities. Speed, as estimated over fifty years ago, was essential to his efficiently directing the affairs of the reservation. Sometimes he would come in from one trip to find that he had to take a fresh team or saddle horse and start out at once upon another. As I look back on it now, it seems to me that in mounting saddle horse, wagon, or sleigh, one almost had to make it in a flying leap, so restless and prancing were the horses Mr. Ronan chose. Sometimes, depending upon the distance and other circumstances, the children and I made these trips with my husband, in a light spring wagon, or in winter, cozily bundled in buffalo robes in a sleigh with jingling bells.

I drove and rode these spirited horses, but a safe old reliable one was always on hand. All of the children learned to ride as soon as they could sit on a horse and hold the reins, usually by the time they were five years old. Most of the children learned on Nig, a blooded horse that was gaited, swift, high-spirited, and so intelligent that he understood that he was to be gentle with the little ones. Old Brown was slow, safe, and sure; Cherry was a treacherous little bucker; Buckskin was wild, beautiful, and noble. These were a few of a long line of equine favorites.

Ovando Hoyt, agency miller and Spiritualist, was frightened away by the Nez Perce trouble. With him went his sister, our cook. Jack Griffith, who had worked for us in Helena and whom I had taught to cook, took her place. Between Jack's erratic comings and goings we had various Chinese cooks. Gee Duck stayed with us for four years; Wah, a splendid character, came next and stayed for five years. Women never stayed. They were nervous about the Indians and also found the place too isolated. Only two others besides "Miss" Hoyt stayed longer than a day or so. Bridget, a true descendent of the Irish king Brian Boru, was a haughty creature. When we had company, she swept about the dining room in long, rustling trains to show her equality with any among "thim prezunt." Matilda Swanson was an ideal Swedish housemaid and a sweet, lovely character.

The old mill whistle blew, and punctually thereafter the bountiful meals were served. Breakfast was at eight o'clock. The usual menu was oatmeal, fried potatoes, home cured ham or bacon, and pancakes or waffles served with hot cane-sugar syrup or cold chokecherry syrup. Maple syrup we had occasionally as a very special treat. Twelve o'clock was the dinner hour and six o'clock the supper hour. These two meals were to be distinguished each from the other only by name, not at all by menu, which consisted usually of soup, meat from our own storage, chicken, or wild game of all sorts, vegetables fresh from the garden or from the winter store in the root-house, and dessert. Just as surely as the breadbox was kept supplied, so was the cake box. I taught each cook in turn a quick, easy recipe for a gold and a white cake. The two cakes required two dozen eggs from the constant supply in our own hen house. With fresh cows in the pasture and our own store of ice, ice cream was frequently on the bill of fare. Raspberries, blackberries, and strawberries grew in the orchard. The most aromatic, delicious wild strawberries grew in profusion along the irrigating ditches in the fields. The orchard supplied apples, but peaches, pears, bananas, and oranges were rare delicacies. I made quantities of mincemeat that was so much praised by my husband, children, and guests that I became very proud indeed of my ability in this particular cuisine, and delegated the making of the mincemeat to the cook only as an extraordinary evidence of trust.

Our table was usually spread with a white cloth, although when red-and-white cloths were in vogue I used them for a time on the breakfast table. The children did not like these cloths. To me, heavy satiny damask gave an exquisite satisfaction. We used a dozen numbered ivory napkin rings. Silver ones came as gifts to various members of the family from various people on various occasions. Our silver table service was plated; I never had solid silver until the children grew up and began giving it to me as gifts. I had one beautiful set of dishes, used only on gala occasions. They were white trimmed with wide bands of cerulean blue and a narrow line of gold. My husband and I sat across the table from each other, not at the ends, that separated us too far since the usual number at the table was sixteen. My husband served the plates from the big tureens, platters, and vegetable dishes placed beside him. He always found pleasure heaping the plates and heaping them again for our hungry horde.

Indian women proved to be satisfactory laundresses and even learned to do the ironing well. First came Milly, a Kootenai woman. When she was asked each week what her wage should be, she always turned to her two little girls to seek their advice and to learn their wishes. They invariably demanded sugar. Sometimes I was able to persuade Milly, against the demands of the little girls, that money or something other than sugar would be good for a change. Usually the little girls triumphed. Milly finally went back to her tribe. She had many successors through the years, each one serving faithfully or less faithfully until some personal or tribal vicissitude took her away. A few stand out distinctly in my memory.

Tok-a-pee, a Spokane Indian, had wandered onto the reservation. She had two little girls to support, Qui-a-maw and Chew-chew-cha-some. She could never tell me what these names meant in English. Tok-a-pee was a truly lovable creature, beautiful in her dusky Indian way, light and graceful as a fawn. Poor Tok-a-pee! Tuberculosis took her swiftly, but not before Qui-a-maw had reached her teens, married, and could care for Chew-chew-cha-some.

Agatha Granjo was a mixed blood, a shade fairer than most mixed bloods. She was a large, benevolent, clean-looking woman with beautiful wavy hair. She loved my children and was most affectionate with them. Even when the little girls were well grown, she used to take them on her lap and caress them. In later years we were "washed and ironed" by Old Sophie who used to flit about as if her moccasins were winged, her shawl never drawn tight as is usual with squaws, but always slightly a-flutter in the breeze. Katherine Barnaby was last of a long line. Many times married, openhearted and honest, her daughter Felicitas served us as second girl for a short time during my last year on the reservation. Felicitas later traveled around the country with groups of Indians appearing in various places. Her beaded costumes were beautiful.

From the beginning at the agency we employed Indian girls, beautifully trained by the Sisters at St. Ignatius, who helped me with plain sewing and who could be trusted as nursemaids with my children. A few weeks after we were established at the agency, we engaged as nursemaid Minnie Sullivan, a white girl about sixteen years of age, who had been brought up by the Sisters of Providence. Hers was a pathetic story. As a tiny child she had lived in Missoula with her parents and a brother. Her young mother fell ill with tuberculosis; Minnie's father placed his wife and the children in the care of the Sisters. He disappeared. When months and months had passed and nothing had been heard from him, the Sisters took Mrs. Sullivan to St. Ignatius Mission to see if the change would benefit her. She died there and was buried in the old mission cemetery. The Sisters brought up the children. They let Minnie come to us on condition that we would assume entire responsibility for her until she should reach maturity. This obligation we assumed.

Minnie was a great help to us in those first days. As she had grown up among the Indian girls at the school at St. Ignatius, she understood and spoke the language well.[35] When Indians opened the door and stalked into the house and sat down for long periods of silence, she would find out if there were anything I could do to terminate the ordeal. One instance stands out distinctly because it was among my early experiences before I began to take the ways of the Indians quite for granted, and also because it is typical of their poetical way of begging.

One cold rainy day a grizzled, blanketed and be-feathered old warrior stalked in. After a guttural greeting, he planted himself beside the fireplace. He sat so long in silence and got so thoroughly dry and warm that he became intolerable in more sense than one. Minnie had been reiterating at intervals, "Stem-a-spoo-oose?" (What does your heart want?) This was the only way, according to Indian custom, to put the abrupt question courteously. At length he replied in his language, "My throat is thirsty for sugar and my heart is hungry for fifty cents."

A prepossessing stranger appeared at the agency one day and announced that he was Minnie Sullivan's father. So, indeed, he was. Minnie was delighted. Her father seemed happy to be restored to a daughter so pretty, so blooming, so sweet mannered. After the visit he went to Butte to work in the mines. From there he wrote to Minnie often. He sent her occasional presents, among them a compendium of English poetry, which I still have. At last he wrote her to come live with him. He sent some pretty blue material for a dress that I had made up by a dressmaker in Missoula. Minnie was delighted and anxious to go.

On one of the first warm days in the spring of 1879, we went for a picnic on Finley Creek. Minnie waded in the water. Next morning she had a severe cold and from that day, she was never well. She developed tuberculosis. We wrote her father of her illness, but he never answered the letter. She was ill for a year and a half before she died. I gave her a room just off mine so that I could tend her at night. I knew so little of tuberculosis, a very common ailment in those days. I had no realization that I might be endangering the health of my family or my own. I took every precaution for cleanliness and for sanitation, as we then understood it. As a matter of fact, not one of my children ever had the slightest tendency toward tuberculosis.

One day early in 1881, Minnie seemed much better. She got up for dinner and dressed in her pretty blue dress, but how pathetic she looked, how different from the rosy, healthy girl for whom the dress had been made. Two nights later she called me. When I went to her I realized that she was sicker than usual. During the few minutes that Mr. Ronan was gone for Dr. Choquette, she died, murmuring softly, "Oh, if I ever get well, I will stay with you and work for you always." She was buried beside her mother in the cemetery at St. Ignatius Mission. We sent a notification of her death to her father's address, but we never heard from him.

Indians, like children, expected to be given gifts, but seldom if ever gave gifts. When they did, it was with the expectation of immediate return of the courtesy. Old Andre was second chief of the Pend d'Oreille, chief of the Indian police and when his health failed, he became a sort of tribal supreme court judge. One day an Indian messenger arrived from St. Ignatius where Andre lived, leading a fine looking dog. He delivered the message that Andre had long desired to show respect for the agent in some fitting manner. He was now poor and old and going blind. He had probably not long to live upon the earth. He therefore sent a token of the regard in which he held the White Chief, his favorite dog, Chew-shoo-nooks. He desired the messenger to say that Chew-shoo-nooks was a white man's dog. Mr. Ronan accepted the gift and asked the meaning of the dog's name. The messenger did not know. Chew-shoo-nooks was the dog's name and that was all. Perhaps he had the same difficulty that we would have had if we had been asked to explain the meaning of Fido or Toby. Mr. Ronan soon called upon Andre at the Mission to extend in person his thanks for the gift. He inquired into the old man's health, supplied his needs and made certain that Andre was as happy and comfortable as possible during his last days.

Chew-shoo-nooks was duly installed as keeper of the dooryard and as comrade and protector of the children. He was an intelligent dog and seemed to understand the transfer. We always called him by his Indian name, unabbreviated. He lived to an old age, ripe with fruits of service and loyalty. The children were more devoted to him, I think, than to any other canine in a long succession of favorites, some of them pedigreed stock, gifts to the children from their father's white friends and illustrious visitors.

Indians, Customs, and Religion

An interesting character of whom I saw much was Arlee, a Nez Perce, whose Indian name, translated into English, was Red Night.[36] He had married a woman of the Salish tribe, settled in the Bitterroot Valley, and agreed to government terms. To the bitter and never-ending indignation of Charlot, the hereditary chief of the Flatheads, Arlee moved to the reservation with a following of Flatheads whose war chief he had long been. Arlee came from a long line of fighting men. His father had been killed by the Blackfeet in 1817 when Arlee was only two years old. While he was still a young man, Arlee had achieved a great reputation as a "brave." In carrying out the family tradition, no less than three of his sons were killed fighting against Crows and Blackfeet.

Arlee was sixty-three years of age when we came to the agency. He was a fat and pompous monarch and fashionable with his fringed buckskin shirt and leggings, fantastically beaded vest, belt, pouch, and moccasins, and bright-colored blanket folded around his protruding stomach. Topping all this magnificence, he always wore a brass dog collar around the crown of his hat. I never saw him without an eagle's wing in his hand. This he carried with a grandeur that endowed it with all the symbolism of the scepter.

My observation led me to the conclusion that when an Indian was chief he was so by virtue of being a chief among men. This was true of every chief I knew well personally. It was especially true of

Eneas (the Indian pronunciation of St. Ignatius), the Kootenai chief.[37] Though his tribe was the poorest, the most miserable, inferior, and dirtiest of the confederated tribes on the Flathead Reservation, Chief Eneas was otherwise. His Indian name was Big Knife. He was tall, handsome, clean, and commanding in his brilliant striped blanket and weasel skin pendant.

I shall say a word about one other of our interesting neighbors. In 1877–78 Duncan McDonald, then a handsome young man of twenty-eight, was conducting a trader's store just outside of the agency square. We saw a good deal of him and also of his father, Angus McDonald. The elder McDonald was a splendid, intelligent old Scotchman who came to Montana in 1838 and established a trading post for the Hudson's Bay Company on Post Creek, about halfway between St. Ignatius Mission and Flathead Lake.[38] He remained on the reservation after the company had abandoned the post by right because his wife belonged to the confederated tribes through her father, an Iroquois, and her mother, a Nez Perce. So devoted a friend was he that once, when I made a trip to California, he rode horseback the thirty-five miles from his home on Post Creek to the agency just to bid me good-bye and wish me a happy journey. Another time he presented me with a gold nugget shaped like a harp, and so, he thought, particularly appropriate.

Duncan, much sought after by those who studied the tribal customs, history, legends, and language of the Salish, was not aware of the advantage of capitalizing on his Indian ancestry and inheritance. He was anxious to appear to be a pure-blooded Scotchman like his father. As his father had done, so he took an Indian wife and was, so long as she did live, a devoted husband to her. In Louise's veins ran the blood of the Salish, Nez Perce, Kootenai, Iroquois, and French forbears. Her Indian name was Queel-soo-ee, meaning Red Sleep. According to Duncan, one of the peaks in the Bison Range near Dixon has been given her Indian name.

Our third son was the first white child born on the Flathead Indian Reservation on November 1, 1878. We christened him Matthew James for his two grandfathers. When the baby was a few days old, Michelle, chief of the Pend d'Oreilles, stalked into the sitting room just off my bedroom where Mr. Ronan was seated. The chief was accompanied by five or six important tribesmen, dressed in their brightest blankets, and by the agency interpreter. The Indians squatted in a semicircle and brought forth the pipe of peace. Michelle took a long-drawn puff and passed it on, and it went around until it reached the White Chief. He, too, took his long-drawn puff, thus completing the circle of peace.

Michelle broke the long silence, speaking solemnly in Indian. When he ceased the interpreter translated. The Indians had heard of the birth of the white papoose. They rejoiced for now they knew that their friend the White Chief had, indeed, established his home among them. It had been agreed in council that if the papoose were to be adopted into the tribe and to take the Indian name of Chief Michelle there would be perpetual peace and friendliness between the family of the White Chief and the Salish and their allies. Mr. Ronan ceremoniously requested that he be excused to inform me of the honor which they wished to bestow upon our son.

The Pend d'Oreille chief had been named Michelle when he was baptized by a Jesuit missionary. His Indian name was Whee-eat-sum-khay (Plenty Grizzly Bear), a name to be proud of because the grizzly bear is the most respected, feared, and emulated of all the animal kingdom. To say "he has the heart of a grizzly bear" was the greatest compliment that could be paid a brave. Michelle's Indian name had not been earned in combat with grizzlies but had been bestowed upon him as a tribute to his acknowledged courage by the Lower Kalispels, the name of whose hereditary chief had been Plenty Grizzly Bear.

How we laughed! Such a beautiful baby—blue eyes and soft brown curls—and to be called Plenty Grizzly Bear! Major Ronan returned solemn faced to the council. In my name as well as his own he accepted the honor proffered. Each member of the delegation expressed individually his gratification; the interpreter repeated each speech. The long ceremony closed with a request to see the papoose. The savages filed respectfully through my bedroom and passed the dainty blue and white crib of little Whee-eat-sum-khay. As each looked into the crib, he voiced his approval saying, "Shay!"

"And now," said Michelle sadly as he took his departure, "I have no name."

Mr. Ronan was puzzled but found the explanation the next day when he went with the interpreter to Michelle's camp. The Pend d'Oreille chief was sitting in his tepee in dejection, his head bowed and covered by his blanket. He wore squaw leggings. In answer to Mr. Ronan's question he told that his fringed leggings, arms, and pony had been taken from him because he had made himself nameless in giving his name to the white papoose the day before. As long as he remained unnamed he must be in this dejected and reduced state. When Mr. Ronan protested that they could remain friends without this sacrifice on his part, Michelle replied proudly that he made the sacrifice of his name with a big heart, that relief would come presently, for the Indians had that morning dispatched two runners to the camp of the Lower Kalispels whose principal chief had lately died, and whose name, interpreted into English, was the Man Who Regrets His Country, requesting that Michelle be permitted to assume the dead chief's name.

Within a few weeks the answer came from the Lower Kalispels that if the Pend d'Oreilles and Flatheads would send them six ponies in payment for six which had been stolen from them by members of one or the other of these tribes, some eight years before, they would look favorably upon the request for the loan of their dead chief's name. The ponies were sent and the transaction was terminated in a satisfactory manner.

On Christmas Day in 1878 Mr. Ronan was summoned to St. Ignatius Mission, and amid much form and ceremony the proclamation was made before the confederated tribes of Flathead, Pend d'Oreille, and Kootenai that henceforth the son of the White Chief should be a member of the confederated tribes and bear the name Plenty Grizzly Bear, and that Michelle, the chief of the Pend d'Oreilles, should henceforth be called in Indian the Man Who Regrets His Country.

In the springtime at the season for digging camas and bitterroot, the Indians moved all their belongings and went to localities where these plants were found. Camas grew on the reservation in abundance but for the bitterroot it was necessary to go to Missoula or to the Bitterroot Valley. The bitterroot was dried, pounded up, and used as a condiment. The camas root was put in some sort of container or even in a hole lined with rocks and baked for a number of days, buried underground beneath the campfire. The dry outer skin, like that of an onion, was peeled off and the camas root eaten whole. It was sweetly insipid, with a sort of pungent smoky taste. Huckleberries, serviceberries, and chokecherries were dried and stowed away in bags for winter use. Chew-a, a favorite spring delicacy among the Salish, was the peeled stem of the tender young silken-sunflower, of the variety known as *balsam orrhiza*. They gathered and dried kinnikinnick and red willow for smoking although they preferred tobacco.

In the summer months many of the tribe would cross the Rockies and spend several months hunting buffalo. Each year they would report greater and greater scarcity as a result of the slaughter of the buffalo by the whites. My husband suggested to them the idea of trying to herd some of the buffalo from the plains onto the reservation and to raise them, for he felt that the industry for which the Indians were most suited was stock raising, and he tried to encourage them to follow this occupation. After one of the hunts, a half breed drove in a buffalo bull and two heifers through a pass in the mountains. They were purchased by Charles Allard and Michelle Pablo; that was the beginning of the famous Allard-Pablo buffalo herd.[39]

When the tribes on the Flathead Reservation followed their own nomadic way of living, moving their tepees from place to place on root-digging, berry-picking, and hunting expeditions, they were a clean, healthy, picturesque people. Most of them could not learn clean and hygienic ways living year in and year out in the same house.

The Salish by nature were a superior tribe of Indians.[40] The Christianizing and civilizing of them had begun thirty-seven years before we came to live among them. I found them most uncommunicative with regard to their tribal and family histories and customs. It was not so much that they would not tell as they did not know. Theirs was a fast-fading culture, a culture handed down by word of mouth. I found that the older men and women of the tribe could tell me scarcely anything of the lives of their fathers and mothers. I think that this condition would have existed anyway, but that with regard to their customs and legends, among the generation of Indians that I knew, the condition was particularly acute.

I learned to speak the Salish language, although not fluently, from day-to-day meetings with them. I learned to understand their wants as well as to make my own known. Even during the time that I was living among them, I observed the changes in the language caused by association with whites. Older Indians spoke with deep gutturals and gave emphasis by a prolonging and intense accentuation of syllables or sounds whereas the younger generation spoke in softer tones and with less color and contrast.[41] The memories and traditions of the generation just before were being more quickly lost because of the eager interest in the new ideas and ways of living that the missionaries brought among them. At this time and for a number of years previous, the policy of the Department of the Interior was rather to do away with, than to foster, the language, traditions, customs, and handicraft of the Indians. The influx of white settlers tended to overwhelm the Indian himself as well as his culture.

The most beloved of our Indian neighbors was Michel Rivais, the blind interpreter who was officially appointed to that position and came to live within the square during our second year at the agency. He was a born linguist, with a remarkable command of Canadian French and many of the Indian tongues. Michel's English translations were quaintly phrased. His natural intelligence and gift for language had been cultivated by the Jesuit missionaries.

Michel Rivais was born in 1837. He was the son of Antoine Rivais, a French Canadian trapper and Emilia, a Pend d'Oreille squaw. Michel's wife was a clean, kindly Nez Perce squaw. They had lost two children, and were devoted to the son and daughter that remained. Before he was forty-five years of age, he became totally blind as a result of rheumatism. Everything that medical science could do was done at government expense, through the efforts of Mr. Ronan and Senator G. G. Vest of Missouri, to restore Michel's eyesight. He could see dimly enough to grope his way to the office when he first became interpreter but within two years was in total darkness. He was quite helpless in his blindness and always had to be led. He walked stumblingly, timidly. Ironically enough, his Indian name was Chim-coo-swee, The Man Who Walks Alone. His devoted wife usually guided him about, for his fine-looking son and daughter died within a short time of one another when they had scarcely reached young man- and womanhood.

Michel's wife and children were always the most picturesque and beautifully dressed of the Indians around the agency. Mother and daughter did beautiful bead and handwork. Most of Michel's salary as government interpreter went for the purchase of gay blankets and shawls, silk handkerchiefs, and a most vivid and varied assortment of velvets and silks for Indian tunics and leggings.

I enjoyed listening to Michel talk in his quaint way. He related to me many legends of Coyote, a sort of tutelary spirit, and other tribal stories, which always I was intending to set down verbatim and never did so. Best of all he liked to tell how the Flathead were the first Indians in Montana to embrace Christianity and civilization. He would grow so eloquent and his fervor would send such a light into his eyes that they seemed to regain their lost sight. He told the well-known story of the expeditions that were sent to St. Louis, Missouri, in search of the black robes, of the arrival of Father De Smet, their accomplishments at St. Mary's Mission, and how the black robes had befriended him and taught him from the time he was little more than a baby.

Michel was about medium height, slender, with the fine features of his French father and the bronze color of his Indian mother. His straight black hair he wore in the long bob we associate with a page or herald of medieval times. His costume was quaint and all his own. It was neither the dress of the white man nor that of the Indian, but a nondescript assortment of the two modes.

The Jesuits had taught Michel to sing and to play the violin. He had a fine old instrument; where he got it I do not know. On summer evenings he used to sit on the sill of his open doorway and play softly and plaintively, sometimes improvising. Michel's voice was melodious and true. At church he led the Indians in the congregational praying and singing. They sang simple Masses in Latin; the praying was in Indian.

The missionaries had translated some of the psalms and other portions of the Old and New Testament into Indian and set them to tunes of old tribal chants. The missionaries adapted the Indians' own customs into the celebration of the religious rites that the Jesuits had introduced to the Indians in Christianizing them.

This congregational singing and praying had a wild and savage sound, especially when the men joined in. The missionaries adapted the Indians' mourning song and they would chant and howl it all night in the tepee where a death had occurred. The missionaries incorporated this song into the services at the church on Memorial Day and on All Soul's Day (November 2). It was one of the most haunting of the tribal songs with the wanton rhythms of the winds and the weird sounds one hears at night in the lonely places in the forest.

The festivals of Christmas and Easter were celebrated with great tribal gatherings. Mr. Ronan gave this account of one such celebration:

> The square in front of the Mission church was crowded with people, old and young, from the well-clad thrifty-looking cultivators of the soil to the wild followers of the chase. Some were dressed in scarlet blankets with broad beaded belts, others were in gaily trimmed buckskins with beaded leggings and headdresses of eagle feathers. Some had their dwellings around the Mission and the Agency while others had come long distances to perform their Christian duties.
>
> At twelve o'clock, as the Mission bell rang out on the clear crisp air, there was a volley of rifles and pistols from forty Indian police and the doors swung open. The church was soon filled to capacity and a large number knelt in the biting air outside. Four Jesuit missionaries officiated at the altar which was richly festooned. The responses to the chanting of the High Mass were sung by Indian girls from the Mission school.
>
> On New Year's Day many Indians of the reservation filed through the Agent's house and shook hands with him, his wife,

and the little ones wishing them a Happy New Year. In the dining room a table groaned under the weight of boiled ham, roast pig, bread, and vegetables and an attendant served each one as he filed out into the yard, where guns were fired and other demonstrations of joy were indulged in.[42]

Our contribution to the New Year's festivities was not always so bountiful, but we always had something for each one who came even if it were only an apple. Usually our well-wishers began to arrive before we were up in the morning. They thought nothing of walking into our bedrooms and shaking hands with us while we were still lying in bed.

A great event of the year 1879 was the coming of Archbishop Charles John Seghers of Oregon. He and his party were guests at our home for a day and a night. As there then was no church at the agency, the Archbishop said Mass in the mill, which was the custom whenever a large number of Indians were expected to be in attendance. On most occasions, when a priest came to the agency to say Mass, I arranged an altar in our living room.

At St. Ignatius Mission on the following day, the Archbishop was received with much pomp and pageantry. Peter Ronan wrote:

> Two miles from the Mission the party was met by a cavalcade of some two hundred mounted Indians of the Flathead Reservation. They arranged themselves in a line and, as the carriages of the Archbishop, missionaries, Agent, and others passed, they fired a salute and ranging themselves on either side of the Archbishop's carriage, whipped their horses. The whole cavalcade came over the hills to the Mission at racing speed. Father Giorda halted them at the Indian burying ground, some five hundred yards from the beautiful Mission Church. The Archbishop walked beneath a silk and richly embroidered canopy, borne by four men and followed by eight Jesuit missionaries in rich vestments. A procession formed of at least eleven hundred Indian men, women and children. Just

ahead of the Archbishop two little maidens walked backwards strewing flowers in his path. At the church, benediction was given and a choir of Indian girls sang the responses. Eleven hundred Indians knelt to kiss the Archibishop's ring and receive his blessing.[43]

Celebrations of this sort were arranged for the Indians as a substitute for their war and scalp dances, which my husband was under government orders to prohibit. It was the opinion of officials in the Department of the Interior that observation of such tribal rites tended to undo the work of civilizing the Indian. As a matter of fact, sometimes they danced themselves into a frenzy, then they would chant their wild war songs and howl out their grievances against the whites and against each other until they were in a bad and dangerous mood. More often, though, the dancers endangered their own lives rather than the lives of others. They would dance until they were in a state of uttermost exhaustion and susceptibility to cold, pneumonia, and other diseases. Whenever the weird beating of the tom-tom resounded, my husband went, alone sometimes, into the midst of the dancers and by sheer weight of courage dispersed them.

When Archbishop Seghers returned to the agency, July 25, 1882, to lay the cornerstone of the little church which still stands, another grand gathering of the tribes was arranged.[44] The Archbishop's party coming from Missoula was met at Finley Creek by a procession. At the head was Mr. Ronan in a carriage. Next came Arlee on horseback, in habiliments of state, brass dog collar and all, majestically bearing his eagle's wing. Beside the Chief, eight-year-old Vincent skillfully reined a pony that pranced and pawed and tossed his head as if proud to display his own and his rider's festive caparison, beaded, fringed, glittering with tiny round mirrors and a-jingle with bells. Indians and half-breeds followed on horseback, for the most part, though some drove wagons.

The procession presented a fantastic appearance; the thrifty looking half-breeds in their best clothes, dark trousers, shirts, and broad-brimmed black hats lent contrast to the wild followers of the chase in bright-colored blankets with beaded belts, or elaborate buckskin costumes, and headdresses of eagle feathers. The Indians halted, dismounted, and knelt for the Archbishop's blessing. When they had remounted they fired a salute with their guns, then they ranged themselves on each side of the carriages and the whole party proceeded to the agency where the American flag waved. Anvils, substituted for artillery, rang as the Archbishop alighted from the carriage. From the porch of our residence, he addressed the Indians. He remained as our guest overnight.[45]

MÉLANGE

To my great happiness in the fall of 1879 my dear father came from San Juan Capistrano and spent a year with us. My joy had its poignant mixture of pain; my father had suffered much since I had last seen him on my marriage day. A few months after I left San Juan my stepmother had developed tuberculosis. After a lingering illness she died in June 1878. Soon after her death my father had a dreadful accident. He was coming home from Anaheim, driving as usual in his high-seated wagon, the six mules with one line. On a steep grade he put his foot on the brake. It gave way and he pitched forward onto the road. The wagon passed over his right arm and crushed it. A passerby picked him up unconscious. He was taken to the hospital at Anaheim and there his arm was amputated. Though he was ill during most of the year and a half until he came to me, he carried on with the same indomitable spirit that had been characteristic of him through all the vicissitudes of frontier life; he even learned to write with his left hand, which was a little crippled as a result of the accident. With his poor left hand my father drove, his only companion my young sister Kate, all the way from San Juan Capistrano to Sheridan, Montana. My brother Jimmie did not accompany them. At Sheridan, he and Kate visited Cousin Ellen Tiernan. They came on to the agency by stagecoach. When my father went back

The Ronan family poses in 1884 in front of the agent's house on the Flathead Indian Reservation where they made their home, Peter from 1877 until his death in 1893, and Mary until 1898. Children pictured include Vincent (b. 1874), Mary (b. 1875), Gerald (b. 1877), Matthew (b. 1878), and Katherine (b. 1881). The young man sitting on the right of the photograph is likely Mary's brother James Sheehan, who came to live with the Ronans in 1883. Not pictured are Margaret (b. 1883), Isabel (b. 1887), and Peter (b. 1890).

to California, he traveled by stagecoach to Corinne and on to Los Angeles by railroad, for Kate did not return with him. She had become engaged to Philip Hogan, a rancher living near Missoula, whom she married in January 1881.

A month after Minnie Sullivan died in my arms, on March 18, 1881, twin daughters were born to us, Louise and Katherine Josephine. Lovely Louise lived only fifteen days. The Indians named Katherine Es-nees-e-lil, The Twin. When she grew up, pretty, fair haired, brown eyed, low voiced, and sweet mannered, she was more often called Soo-i-noompt (Good Looking).

As in Helena in my first years of married life, so at the agency no trained nurse was to be had when the babies were born. The agency doctor attended me. His wife, Mrs. Lambert, spent a few days with me until I was able to be up. These services we exchanged, for Mrs. Choquette had a baby, and three babies were born to Mrs. Lambert while she lived on the reservation. After Dr. Choquette went into business in Missoula, Dr. Adamson came to the agency. He was an Englishman, a very fine doctor, with a splendid practice in Lake George, New York. He had sought the appointment as doctor for the Flathead Indians, thinking it would be an interesting experience and also because he needed a rest and change. With him came his wife and child and his wife's sister, Miss Jackson.

My nursemaid was now Anastasia Mourjou, a prize pupil of the Sisters. She was of mixed blood, and from the Sisters had learned to love the white people's way of living. She was refined, serious, dignified, and religious. Father Joseph Guidi, S.J., once told me that he had written the story of her life and sent it back to Italy to be published as an example of what it was possible for Christian education to accomplish for an Indian girl. Jack Griffith, the cook, used to tease Anastasia by drawing pictures of her as Psyche with a lighted taper in her hand, for one of her duties each morning was to carry the lamps and candles into the kitchen and clean and renew them for the coming evening.

At Christmas time, 1882, Anastasia went home to spend the holiday season with her parents. She never came back to me, as she became sick and died of "quick consumption" within three months. During her illness, Mr. Ronan and I would drive to her father's ranch house often to see her and to take her little delicacies from the table and other things to please and to amuse her. At that time we were all excited about the building of the Northern Pacific Railroad. The last time I saw Anastasia, "Nama," as the children called her, I could not keep back the tears. She looked so wasted and so pathetic. She noticed and said, "Don't cry, Mrs. Ronan. You know, I'm sure if I have a ride on the railroad train I'll get well right away." She did not live to have this quaint wish come true.

Anastasia's last wish reminds me of another anecdote of Mr. Ronan's about the coming of the railroad. While the Northern Pacific was negotiating with the Flathead for the right-of-way across the reservation, a shrewd old Indian came to Mr. Ronan and said he hoped the bargain would be closed and the money paid over before the track got to Bad Rock, an enormous rocky promontory jutting into the Pend d'Oreille River. This rock gave the Indians a great deal of trouble in their journeys and they were obliged to get over it by a precipitous trail. The old Flathead was sure the railroad would have to stop there. Mr. Ronan told him to go see how the railroad would get by Bad Rock. He went and saw an explosion of giant powder, which threw the whole rock into the river and opened the road around the promontory. The Indian returned to say that he was ready to believe anything the white man might tell him since he had seen the mountain jump into the river.

A third nursemaid, one whom the children especially loved, was gay, pretty, curly-haired Agnes Polson, the daughter of Dave Polson and his Nez Perce wife Mary. Nothing in the appearance of Agnes suggested the Indian. She looked like a French girl and a very pretty one. Her pert little ways amused Mr. Ronan and furnished him with many of the stories people used to ask him to repeat and repeat. Once when Agnes had returned from a trip to Missoula with her father, she told us that he had taken her to the theatre. In answer to Mr. Ronan's query as to how she enjoyed it, she replied, staccato, "Oh, very much, Major. My father got us reversed seats!" Some ladies were visiting at our house one day. We happened to be comparing the ages of our children. Agnes, who was omnipresent, for she loved company and gaiety, interrupted to mention the year in which she was born. Intending to convey a reminder of her manners by the hauteur of my tone, I said, "Did your mother tell you so, Agnes?" "Oh, no ma'am," Agnes answered smartly, looking very bright eyed. "She wasn't there."

Agnes would have the limelight. When the officers came out from Fort Missoula, she always hastened to put on her most becoming frock, to dress the baby in daintiest array, to send the other children to play out-of-doors; then, in the summer, she posed herself and the pretty baby on the clematis-embowered piazza or under the silver maple tree on the front lawn. If it was cool, she set herself off on the red bricks of the hearth of the wide fireplace in the sitting room through which the guests had to pass to reach the dining room. She never failed to be noticed and to have herself and the baby admired. Agnes' little ways never grew tiresome or annoying. She was amusing, not bold. After a time Agnes married a brother of Anastasia's, Joe Mourjou. They separated and she married again, L. C. Hitchcock, a businessman in Polson.[46]

My children Vincent and Mary were taught at home, at first, and next by Robert McGregor Baird, a Scotchman of refinement and of scholarly attainment, who had come to clerk in the trader's store. I engaged him to teach the children in the late afternoon and early evening hours. I can see that group now—handsome, black-haired, black-bearded Robert, sitting in the low rocking chair with one of the children standing on either side of him. "These," he would say gently, as he pointed out the vowels, "are little men. They can stand alone." Later Mr. Ronan had Mr. Baird appointed government clerk, and Miss Jackson taught the children.

Robert McGregor Baird shrouded his past and everything about himself in mysterious silence. Others besides my husband recognized his ability. In 1884 the Eddy, Hammond Company offered him inducements to leave the government service. He was robbed and brutally murdered in British Columbia in October 1884.[47] Something of his life story we came to know through a letter from his brokenhearted aunt, Charlotte Balfour, of Bruntsfield Place, Edinburgh, Scotland. She answered Mr. Ronan's letter to her, telling her of her nephew's tragic death. Mrs. Balfour's name and address my husband had chanced to notice in an advertisement that appeared in one of the Helena papers inquiring the whereabouts of Robert McGregor Baird.

Isabel Clarke followed Miss Jackson as the children's teacher. Her life story, too, is one of great interest. She was the sister of Helen P. Clarke, first school superintendent of Lewis and Clark County. It was she who sent Isabel to me as a teacher for my children. Helen and Isabel were the daughters of Malcolm Clarke and his Blackfoot wife.[48] The girls had been sent to the East and grown up among their father's kin, people of culture and means. They had been educated in a convent of the Ladies of the Sacred Heart. For years "Syvie," as the children called Isabel Clarke, was a beloved member of our family. After her followed P. M. McHale, an old newspaperman, and after him, Clem V. Carter and Anna F. Carter, brother and sister who were cousins of my husband's. When they were in their teens, Vincent and Gerald were sent to Gonzaga College, Spokane, Washington. Mary went to St. Vincent's Academy in Helena. Later, Mary and Vincent had a year in the public high school in Oak Park, Illinois.

As did the house servants, Indian neighbors, and teachers, the government employees, special agents, and others that circumstances brought into our lives furnished endless material for comedy, tragedy, and romance. This was especially true of government clerks, whom we knew most intimately, since, because of the situation at the agency, each in turn became a member of our family circle.

I wish to include a personal letter of Father Anthony Ravalli, S.J., for the sake of the glimpse it gives of the sweet, affectionate, humorous, genial man as well as the patient, long-suffering, saintly priest.[49] I include it also because of the hitherto unwritten bit of history it gives about the naming of Ravalli station on the Northern Pacific line through the Flathead Reservation.

Stevensville, 1st July, 1883

Dear Mrs. Ronan:

My dear Lady!

I would gladly in these few words I send you to indulge in some innocent mirth, as distant echo of the joyful moments of your hospitality, moments already passed away for me; but I feel obliged to set them aside, and in order not to abuse your time, . . . to go directly to the principal cause of my addressing myself to you.

I cannot see in what manner I could ask this than by intrusting it to your delicacy and feeling. Colonel Lamborn of the R. R. Co., out of kindness for me, though personally unknown to him, has called the R. R. station at the bifurcation of the main road with the trail to the Mission after my name. Such attention on his part deserves from me some grateful acknowledgement of the fact. But wishing to present him with my thanks by an indirect way, I would it be done in such a manner as to avoid either a show of private complacency from my part, or some kind of depreciation of his favor in his choice and preference. As I am informed that occasionally he accepts the offer of your hospitality at the Agency, you have at hand the opportunity of bestowing on him in the proper shape the favor that I ask of you.

Oh, my dear Lady, for how much I may be obliged to you for the above favor, I pray and entreat you from the deep bottom of my heart of your fervent prayers for me! How much I am in need of help for my poor soul in the long trial in which Providence keeps me! I shall not be ungrateful . . . of your prayers. . . .

My love to my dear friend Pete, and my most tender caress to your sweet children. Please remember me to Mr. Baird,
and to all my friends at the Agency. Believe

Dear Lady
Your truly friend
A. Ravalli, S.J.

Among my mementos of Father Ravalli I have a muzzle-
loading, double-barreled shotgun. The metal parts of the gun
were found by an Indian on a hunting expedition in the Mission
Mountains, back of the old Hudson's Bay Company's post on
Post Creek, and brought by him to Mr. Ronan. The Indian said
that the gun had lain so long that when he picked it up the
wooden part crumbled. The gun was of fine workmanship, with
scrolled silver work around the breech and stock; behind the
double hammers was a plate bearing the inscription "Lord S."
in gold letters, and also in gold letters, between the barrels immediately in front of the breech, the maker's name, "A. V. Lebed-
Ano-er-Privi-Aprague."

Mr. Ronan often speculated about the ownership, and the
mystery, or tragedy, of which the gun might be the mute evidence.
Because of my husband's romantic interest in it, Father Ravalli
took the gun to Stevensville, assembled it, adding to the parts a
wooden stock, beautifully carved by himself with a deer head on
the grip and fine scroll work along the sides of the stock. On the
right he set in a silver nameplate with ornamentation of filigree;
on it he inscribed "Peter Ronan—1879." All this he did when
confined by illness to his bed.

For the lapse of another fifteen months after he wrote me
the letter, dear Father Ravalli continued to suffer on his cross, the
bed of a paralytic. He died on October 2, 1884. At his request he
was laid to rest in the old burying ground at Stevensville among
those with whom he had lived and labored during forty years.

The coming of the Northern Pacific Railroad indeed brought us in closer touch with civilization, with kin and friends, with medical and military aid, but put an end to the old idyllic days. "An immense crew of railroad constructors is now at work west of the reservation, consisting of 7,400 with camp followers, gamblers, ex-convicts, and lewd women. They are rapidly advancing to the borders of the reservation, accompanied by portable saloons, gambling houses, etc." This was the information dispatched by Mr. Ronan to the United States Indian Office, Washington, D.C. "Merchants and traders of all descriptions also advance with the construction party, and when the border of the Reservation is reached, the question will arise whether this trade can continue in Indian country." The question did arise. Trouble and contention followed. The drama of the laying of the "iron rail" and of the sending of the "fire horse" thundering across the reservation is not for me to recount. In that drama I played a role almost entirely behind the scenes—that of the wife, mother of many children—watching, listening, waiting fearing, hoping, coming front stage sometimes in the mask of the smiling hostess.

Three months after the driving of the golden spike at Gold Creek, Montana, marking the completion of the Northern Pacific Railroad, with my husband and our baby girl, Margaret Theresa, born on that momentous day of September 7, 1883, I went to visit my father in San Juan Capistrano.[50] We traveled on the Northern Pacific to Portland and from there by steamboat down the Columbia River, across the bar into the Pacific Ocean, and down the coast to San Francisco; thence by train to Santa Ana and by carriage to San Juan. I pleaded with my father to return and make his home with us. With sturdy independence, he refused. "No, Mollie," he said, "I must stay and keep the old place. Some day you and the children will need it."

But my half-brother James Sheehan, Jimmie, came back with us. He brought an exotic air into our home, for he had grown up among the Spanish and Mexican people in San Juan and had so completely assimilated their customs and language that he scarcely seemed the American-born child of Irish parents. His speech never lost its suave Spanish accent.

A pretty little story is connected with the Indians' naming of Isabel, my fourth and last daughter. We named her for her god-mother, Isabel Clarke Dawson. The Indians called her Sku-ku-leil (Sunshine). It was on February 5, 1887, that Sku-ku-leil came to gladden our hearts. For weeks previous to her birth the weather had been cold and gloomy. The sun seemed to have vanished from his accustomed place. The Indians said, "The heart of the sun is sad or angry, and he has turned his face away from the earth." The morning after the little girl's arrival the sun shone out gloriously all over the land; then the Indians said, "Behold: the sun is pleased again since God sent upon the earth this little child; she has brought joy to the home of the White Chief; she has brought back to earth the sun; we shall call her Sunshine."

Well suited is Sku-ku-leil to the name the Indians gave her— a warm ray rests in her chestnut hair, soft is the light shining in her dark gray eyes, and never did a child have as a birthday gift a nature more tender and sunshiny.

In October 1887, I took my eldest, Vincent, and my youngest, Isabel, and went again to visit my father. He met me at the railway station in Santa Ana. The conquering spirit of the pioneer was manifest as of old. With his crippled left hand he was reining to control a team of horses that champed their bits, tossed their heads, and pranced in the harness. He was still living at Casa Blanca, the adobe house I had helped him build. There the children and I stayed with him although Judge Egan had insisted on turning over to my father, for our entertainment, his roomy, comfortable brick house.

Again I begged my father to return to Montana to make his home with us, but he repeated his sturdy refusal. When I bade him good-bye, we had seen each other for the last time. Within less than a year, October 1888, after a brief illness, he died.

My father was right about the ultimate value of his ranch, which, for various reasons, he left to me but which I chose to share with my sister and brother. We sold it to Judge Egan in 1899 for $7,000. This we considered a fair price at the time. In 1917, when my daughter Margaret visited Judge Egan in San Juan Capistrano, he told her that he had refused an offer of $100,000 for my father's property. "Only a lonely old fool could sit here year after year holding on to his property and letting prices soar and the world turn itself topsy-turvy," he said.

One more child and the tally of my family was complete. Peter, my youngest, was born September 22, 1890. I had my way and named the boy for his father. The "Little Major," agency employees called him. After all the years of protesting against the name of Peter, how proud the baby's father was to have a namesake. As with all the children, except Matthew and Isabel, so Peter got his Indian name for a characteristic of his personal appearance: his deep blue eyes. Cha-cha-maska-chick-a-kloostas meant, to his intense chagrin during all his funny little boyhood, Heavenly Eyes. The whole family was under dire threat if ever the secret were revealed to his gang!

I said that I had accounted for my whole family. This is not quite true, for since 1886, one dear boy, not yet named, had been making his home with us much of the time. This was William L. Murphy, or Willie as we called him. His mother had died when he was little more than a baby. When he was nine years old, his father died. My husband attended the funeral of his friend Con Murphy and there he saw the stricken, sensitive, delicate little boy. His heart went out to the lonely orphan and he brought him home for me to mother with my own vigorous brood.

A series of Indian murders previous to 1890 filled my days and nights with such fear that I cannot pass over them without a word. In 1882, I was terrified when my husband, the agent, walked alone into a council of forty sullen Indians and demanded that they surrender to him the Indian desperado, Koonsa.[51] He handcuffed the prisoner and accompanied only by a driver, delivered the murderer safely to the county jail in Missoula.

A loud startling knock at the door awakened us from sleep one dark December night in 1885. Joseph T. Carter, the agency clerk, delivered the message that there had been trouble with two drunken Indians at the trader's store at the Arlee railway station, that the trader V. B. Coombs and the postmaster, a man named Bader, had killed one Indian and wounded the other. The friends of the two Indians had assembled and were threatening vengeance, and that an armed posse had been summoned from Missoula.

Major Ronan had Chief Arlee and several head tribesmen notified to meet him at the scene of the tragedy. After several hours he returned home to say that all was quiet. The Indians had also agreed to return home to say that all was quiet. They agreed to let the wounded Indian be taken along with the white men to Missoula for trial. We had scarcely settled down to try to get a little sleep when again a more startling knock echoed through the house. The messenger had come to report that no sooner had Major Ronan left than a party of armed Indians, accompanied by the father and relatives of the dead Indian, had assembled at the station and informed the sheriff that he could take the white men to Missoula, but that they would hold the Indian and try him according to tribal laws. When the sheriff resisted, he and his deputies were disarmed. The wounded Indian was placed upon a horse behind another Indian, who galloped off with him. When an eastbound train thundered into sight, the Indians gave their arms back to the sheriff and his deputies and ordered them onto the train to return to Missoula. The white men did not dare disobey. With the sheriff and his posse, all the railway employees at Arlee, even the telegraph operator, took their hasty departure. The settlement was abandoned. We knew that as the news of this trouble reached Missoula, a detachment of soldiers from Fort Missoula would board a special train for Arlee. I feared the blood and carnage their coming would surely mean. The breaking down, perhaps forever, of the confidence and friendship we had been building up among our Indians during twelve years.

Why not trust them as we wished them to trust us? I told my husband that I was not afraid to take that risk. I knew it was on my account that he was not making the move to prevent the coming of the soldiers. That within his heart he was assured that he could command his words. Because he knew that I was sincere in my urging of him and because in his judgment, it was wise to settle for himself this insubordination among the Indians, he sent my brother Jimmie on a fleet horse to Evaro to send telegrams to Colonel Gibson at Fort Missoula, Sheriff Robert Land, and Railroad Superintendent F. W. Gibson, that the Indians were on the train and no trouble was expected. The telegrams reached Missoula just in time, for the soldiers were already on the train. Meanwhile, Joseph T. Carter had ridden back to Arlee and had taken charge of the trader's store. He was the only white man left that day at the railway station.

The Indians proved worthy of our trust. They brought the wounded tribesman to a house near the agency, where Dr. William Dade, the agency physician, dressed his wounds. A council was called. My husband explained the trouble that might have arisen from their defiance of the officers of the law. Unless they agreed to turn the prisoner over to civil authorities, trouble would surely ensue. After ten hours of heated discussion, they surrendered the wounded Indian. A few days later, when the prisoner had regained some strength, my husband delivered him to the authorities at Missoula, where he was discharged, as were Coombs and Bader, on grounds of self-defense. The two white men never again risked returning to the reservation. I have given so much space to this incident because of my part in it, a part of which I am proud, for I was really timid, and when the safety of my children was at stake, I found it difficult to let my head rule.

This was not the end, however. Revenge rankled in the hearts of the relatives of the dead Indian. The bodies of the two murdered white men were found near the mouth of the Jocko. Larra Finley, a half-breed desperado, killed an Indian at the head of Flathead Lake. He was captured, confessed to the murder, and reported that Pierre Paul, Lala See, and Antley were the murderers of the white men, whose bodies had been found at Jocko. They had committed the crime to even the score of the Indians on account of the tribesman whom Coombs had killed. These three Indians were hunted far and wide. They eluded capture even when three companies of the Twenty-fifth United States Infantry had been called to Ravalli. All were, at last, tracked down, tried and hanged along with a fourth Indian, Pascale, who had murdered a man for plunder on the lonely road between Dayton Creek and Demersville.

This fourfold hanging in Missoula on December 19, 1890, was observed with pomp and circumstance attendant upon a great civic ceremony. It was attended by invitation only, and invitations were issued to dignitaries all over the state of Montana. The *Missoula Weekly Gazette* of December 24, 1890, scarcely in a spirit of goodwill, devoted almost its entire eight-page issue to a rehearsal of every detail of the event, even to the distinguished list of "those present."

DEATH'S DECREE
THE MURDERED WHITES AVENGED
THE DEVIL HAS HIS DUE
Pierre Paul, Lala See, Pascale, and Antley are good Indians
now. They were hanged this morning.

The spirit which led the newspaper reporter to use these head-lines and this lead to his story grieved Mr. Ronan as did the grim details of the awful occasion. He felt the deep heart gash for the simple children of the forest who, under his charge, had fallen in evil ways as a result of drinking the white man's firewater.

Little Claw of a Grizzly Bear

In his little book titled *History of the Flathead Indians, Their Wars and Hunts*, my husband has told from firsthand knowledge the story of the grievances of Charlot, Slem-haj-kah (Little Claw of a Grizzly Bear), the hereditary chief of the Bitterroot Flatheads, and of the various treaties with the government which bereft him of his ancestral domain in the Bitterroot Valley. He wrote of the senatorial committee, headed by Senator G. G. Vest of Missouri and Congressman Martin Maginnis of Montana, that held council with him in the fall of 1883 and offered him inducements to move with the tribe to the Flathead Reservation. He also told of Charlot's refusal to go there alive.

"We are only a few. We are poor and weak," said Charlot, gazing steadily at Senator Vest. "You would not talk to us in this way on the plains when we were many and strong."

"We do not come here to threaten you," replied Senator Vest. "We come as friends to act fairly and honestly with the Indians. We know you are the white man's friend, and we came here to see how you and your people could be benefited. Your brothers want you and your people to come with them upon the reservation and to cultivate the lands and become prosperous."

"My hands and those of my people are free from the white man's blood," retorted Charlot. "When the Nez Perces came here we protected the whites. Why does the white man take his heart from us now?"

Again Senator Vest assured the Indians that he knew they were the friends of the whites and that the Great Father in Washington wished to deal fairly with them.

"We do not wish to leave these lands," said Charlot. "You place your foot upon our necks and press our faces into the dust. But I will never go to the Reservation. I will go to the Plains."

"Joseph, the Nez Perce chief, and his band attempted to go the plains," replied Vest. "Look where he is now. There are no more plains. The white men are as thick as leaves. Either get a patent to your land or go upon the Reservation, where you can raise plenty to eat."[52]

Charlot then made a speech, saying that the Indians would not take out patents, would not pay taxes. He referred to the terms of early treaties, which had not been fulfilled, to the forging of his mark to the Garfield Treaty of 1872.[53] He concluded by taking off his old battered hat, throwing it upon the floor, and shouting, as he glared into the eyes of Senator Vest, "You may take Charlot to the Reservation, but there will be no breath in his nostrils! Charlot will be dead! He will never go there alive!"

Before the council broke up Charlot did agree to go out to Washington, D.C., to talk the matter over with the Great Father. Arrangements were made. He, Michel Rivais, the interpreter, and four of Charlot's head men accompanied Mr. Ronan to Washington, D.C.; on the 18th of January, 1884, the delegation took its departure from Missoula. Every day during his stay in Washington, Mr. Ronan either wrote to me or sent me clippings from newspapers about the Flathead delegation, their appearance, reception, entertainment, and futile counseling. The newspaper clippings were read to tatters by the agency employees. The letters I have preserved tell an intimate personal story of my husband's experiences.[54]

After all that had been said and done in Washington, nothing was really accomplished toward the removal of the Flatheads from the Bitterroot to the Jocko Valley. No pecuniary reward, gifts, blandishments, or persuasions of the Honorable H. M. Teller, Secretary of the Interior, could shake Charlot's resolution to live out his days and to die in the homeland of his forefathers.

On the evening of March 7, 1884, my husband arrived in Missoula with the Flathead Indian delegation. He procured wagon transportation and sent them home, sent runners into the mountains to call the members of the tribe to meet in council, for most of them were hunting game, their only resource for food. After many consultations, backed by authority from the Department of the Interior, Major Ronan was able to make certain promises to each family that would consent to move to the Jocko reservation. Regardless of what Charlot did, each family had a choice of 160 acres of unoccupied land, assistance in the erection of a house, and assistance in fencing and breaking a field of at least ten acres. Each family would receive two cows, a wagon, harness, plow, and all other necessary agricultural implements. In addition, the government promised seed for the first year, provisions until the first year's crop was harvested, and the right to sell lands in the Bitterroot Valley, which any had patents, and the improvements included thereon. Twenty-one families agreed to move and did so. The Department of the Interior fulfilled these promises to the letter and, furthermore, authorized the construction of an irrigation ditch to cover the lands settled upon by the Bitterroot Valley Salish. The government issued supplies and assistance to get their farmlands in condition to yield them a living. Ten more families, seeing the prosperity of the twenty-one that had moved, appeared in the Jocko Valley with all their goods and chattels. For these ten families Major Ronan had no authority to do anything. That authority could have been granted to him only by an act of Congress. To my knowledge, no such act caring for these destitute families was ever passed. My husband did all in his power for them. From that time until his death, they became his special charges. Even when Charlot and his band finally consented to come to the Jocko Valley, by some unfortunate oversight in the offices in Washington, D.C., no provision was made for the poor, wandering ten families.

Arlee died on August 8, 1889. His funeral was a grand occasion and Indians gathered from far and wide to attend. He was buried in the Indian cemetery behind the little church of St. John Berchman's at the agency. His body was borne in state from his home, a mile west of the agency, to the church. Hundreds of Indians and half-breeds, on horseback, in wagons, and on foot, formed the motley cortege and chanted the Salish song of mourning all the way from Arlee's house to the church. At the head of this funeral procession, in front of the funeral cart, rode Mary on Nig. The horse pranced, danced, champed at his bit, and tossed his black mane. Mary's long, unbraided, auburn hair, so much admired by the dead chieftain, rippled in the wind.

After the high requiem Mass and the funeral orations, at the side of the open grave, the coffin of Arlee was opened. Hundreds of mourners passed in single file and each one shook the cold hand of the departed chief in farewell. When the coffin had at last been closed and lowered into the grave, the long file again passed and each one stopped for a handful of earth and dropped it in. The boards of the coffin gave back a hollow echo. Following the burial a great feast, lasting a day and a night, was held at Arlee's house at the expense of his heirs and relatives. Mighty was the eating, accompanied by great bawling, orating, chanting, and muffled beating of the tom-tom. All the debts and credits of the dead chief were settled and all his earthly effects distributed among his heirs. These were the customs among the Salish when a tribesman or woman of property died.

Immediately following Arlee's death, Major Ronan entered into negotiations with Charlot. If he would agree to come to the reservation, all the promises that the government had made to him in Washington, D.C., in 1884, would be fulfilled. Furthermore, he would again become chief over all the Flatheads, as he had been in the days before Arlee accepted the terms of the Garfield Treaty and was made chief of the reservation Flatheads.

Charlot never recognized the chieftainship of Arlee and never again spoke to him after he deserted the Bitterroot Flatheads and went to the reservation. The chance of having to face Arlee or of humbling himself to speak was gone forever. Arlee was dead. Charlot was impoverished and his great, once powerful tribe was reduced to scarcely three hundred poor individuals. He wavered in his decision never to leave the Bitterroot Valley alive.

In autumn, in reply to Peter Ronan's report to this effect, the Department of the Interior sent General H. B. Carrington as Indian Special Commissioner to make final arrangements with Charlot. The general's message to the stubborn old chief was, in a letter to Major Ronan dated October 22, 1889, "If Charlot would lead his people and say so, on paper now, he would have a light heart once more, and feel that the spirit of Victor, his father, had spoken to him, saying, 'Charlot, save our people!' The tribe would be happy. Only men who are jealous of Charlot and other Indians who are jealous of the Flatheads would talk foolishly. Brave men and wise men would say, 'Charlot is a wise chief, and has the courage to conquer his own opinion, when change comes, for his people's sake'."

These words fell persuasively on Charlot's ears, since they lent a semblance of magnanimity to a reversal of his decision, but really dire necessity drove him to abandon the Bitterroot Valley to the whites. The historic letter from General Carrington at Stevensville to my husband, dated November 3, 1889, records this historic decision. The general wrote, in part:

Charlot has given me his hand and his signature. He says that he will go to Jocko with "Big Heart" and take his people with him there. He cannot longer refuse. . . .

I wish I could express my thanks to Michel [Rivais] as I think he deserves.

To François, the noble, discreet, and Christian man who has been my interpreter since Michel left, the Government can never do too much honor. There are thirty-two families in the Bitter Root, says Charlot, who will need provisions. . . .

To have part in doing them justice, after so many whites have suffered, is a great privilege, indeed.[55]

Though Major Ronan and General Carrington made every effort to induce Charlot to come at once to the reservation, he did not do so until 1891. His coming was, under the existing circumstances, best for himself and best for his people. The persuading of him to do so was a triumph in diplomacy for my husband. Yet, I have scarcely witnessed so utterly sad a scene as that historic spectacle of October 17, 1891. Of my impressions that day I wrote:

It was a unique and, to some minds, a pathetic spectacle when Charlot and his band marched to their future home. Their coming had been heralded and many of the Reservation Indians had gathered at the Agency to give them welcome. When within a mile of the agency church, the advancing Indians spread out in a broad column. The young men kept constantly discharging their firearms, while a few of the number, mounted on fleet ponies, arrayed in fantastic Indian paraphernalia, with long blankets partially draping the forms of the warriors and steeds, rode back and forth in front of the advancing caravan, shouting and firing their guns until they neared the church, where a large banner of the Sacred Heart of Mary and Jesus was erected on a tall pole. The Reverend Philip Canestrelli, S.J., the good priest with outstretched hands blessed and welcomed the forlorn-looking pilgrims.

Chief Charlot retained his habitual expression of stubborn pride and gloom as he advanced on foot, shaking hands with all who had come to greet him. . . . All assembled in the agency chapel for the benediction of the most Holy Sacrament. After benediction, the good and learned Father Canestrelli, who spent many years laboring among the Indians, addressed them in their own language.[56]

A house was built for Charlot a few hundred yards north of the agency square. He came often to sit upon my hearth or to be served a meal at our dining room table. He was taciturn. Years of brooding upon his grievances had left a sullen stamp upon his dark, heavy-featured face. I came to know that he liked me and my family. Often a look of benevolence lighted his face when my children spoke to him with courtesy befitting a king in exile, for so they were taught to do. Sometimes he broke the long silences to request that one or the other or all of my three red-haired daughters, Mary, Margaret, and Isabel, be called into his presence and bade to unbraid their long hair for him to feast his faded eyes on its bright color and to feel with his bronzed old hands its soft texture. The little girls, for all the chief's admiration, did not enjoy this ceremony but they always played their parts in it graciously.

Charlot bore himself with reserve, dignity, and pride of race. As I have said, like a king in exile. But, alas, sometimes—perhaps not unlike many another monarch of an elder day—he was dirty! Once when he visited me in a most unusually dirty shirt, I erred so far in the delicacy and taste becoming a hostess so as to get one of my husband's clean shirts and to tell my guest of far and high lineage, to change his shirt. Said he proudly in his language, "The white man may like a clean shirt, but the Indian likes the dirty shirt." When I apologized, he relented so far as to put the clean shirt on top of the one he wore.[57]

I made the mistake of discouraging my children from speaking Indian. In the days when we were so isolated, when the children heard so little but Indian and broken English, I was fearful that they would never learn to speak their own tongue correctly. By constant association, however, the children could not but pick up some knowledge of the Salish language, the names of all sorts of common things, phrases of greeting and farewell, of approval and disapproval, queries and answers pertaining to all sorts of every day happenings.

On account of their years of friction with the white settlers in the Bitterroot Valley, the Indians of Charlot's band were less tractable than those whom we had been living among since coming to the reservation. Nevertheless, my children continued to be free as free could be to wander afoot on horseback, alone or in groups, as far as their fancies led them. Never once in all the years was one of them frightened or accosted in any but a friendly way. Mary even camped alone for days with her brothers at such remote and lonely places as Finley Creek Lake, Jocko Lake, and Lake Mary Ronan.

Peter Ronan on Mount Ronan, Mission Range, Montana
86-6, UNIVERSITY OF MONTANA

LAST YEARS AT THE AGENCY

The years from 1890 to 1893 marked a period of peace and the highest point of prosperity for the confederated tribes of the Flathead Reservation since the coming of the whites among them. Major Ronan's troubles were mainly with unscrupulous white men who sold whiskey to the Indians and who tried to infringe upon the rights of the Indians and the lands set aside for them, and with those who objected to Indians hunting off the reservation.

The railroad had made the agency more accessible. The older children had formed friendships at school and had begun to invite visitors, and so our procession of guests doubled and trebled. Among those of the latter years I shall name only two, both of them charming women and gifted writers, now deceased. Their memory is kept fresh by the warm, affectionate, beautiful letters I have from them expressing appreciation of such hospitality as my husband and I extended to them, and by an autographed book from each of them. *Boots and Saddles* was presented with the compliments of the author, Elizabeth B. Custer, whose husband played so tragic a part in the history of Montana's Indian wars, and *Rainbow's End*, by Alice Palmer Henderson, a correspondent for St. Paul, Minneapolis, and Chicago newspapers. In one of her articles, she published this impression of her visit with us:

A train man hoarsely yelled "Missoula." So we were some-where. The hour to Arlee was easily passed fussing with my belongings, and at something like one o'clock I stood in the cool night air and followed a tall figure, through a darkness that was palpable, to a carriage. Five miles of mystery and Montana's electric air, then the barking of dogs from an Indian's tepee, then the cheery lights from the agency, then the cor-dial voice of Major Ronan himself welcoming me to the Flat-head Indian Reservation; lastly, a homey room, strewn with the beautiful, long-haired white skins of the Rocky Mountain goat, with white curtains at the windows swaying invitingly, and an old-fashioned feather bed to whose embraces I yielded myself in that unknown which is ever so near us. This was the beginning of it all. . . .

The next morning was Sunday. Just as the sun ray had laid his fingers across my eyes with "Guess who—it is the Day," the sweet little brown-eyed daughter of Major Ronan brought me in some hot water, and the sunny one timidly handed me a bou-quet of the exquisite wild flowers which grow in such profusion thereabouts. Afterwards, I found those two little acts to be the keynote of the household harmony—"helpfulness and courtesy."

What New York clubman sat down to a better breakfast? Mountain brook trout just out of the icy water and venison, not to mention plenty of gay conversation and fun over Wah, the Chinaman, who was constantly rushing in and out noiselessly like a celestial Mercury. "Wah likes meals conducted on strictly business principles," laughed Mrs. Ronan. "Hold onto your plate until you have done, or he will whisk it off while you are talk-ing. I cannot break him of the habit. Often in the midst of a story he will swoop down on the Major's plate and before you realize it his cue [sic] is disappearing through the door."

. . . As we sat on the porch, the Indians began to gather for the [church] service. They came afoot, the squaws carry-ing their papooses on their backs, or on small Indian ponies which they tethered here and there. They all wore the bright-est yellows, purples, and reds obtainable, and the braves, es-pecially, strode along wrapped in their striped blankets, their long hair in tiny braids, with all the superiority of mind that consciousness of being well dressed confers.[58]

Newspapermen besieged Major Ronan for copy. He wrote a series of articles for the *Anaconda Standard* and another series for the Helena, Montana, *Journal*, which the editor, George E. Boos, compiled into a slender volume titled *Historical Sketch of the Flathead Indian Nation from the Year 1813 to 1890*. Among many requests for and acknowledgments of the book are letters from E. W. Halford, private secretary, on behalf of President Grover Cleveland; John W. Noble, Secretary of the Interior; Charles L. Lusk, Bureau of Catholic Indian Missions; Elizabeth B. Custer; Alice Palmer Henderson; Major Evan Miles, United States Army; and Father H. Allaeys requesting permission to translate the book into Flemish for publication in Belgium.

My husband's always robust health broke. He had lived so abundantly, had crowded so much thought, activity, sympathy into every day, that there is little wonder he had exhausted his energy. Some of his mining claims had begun to look promising. He had homesteaded a tract of land around Lake Mary Ronan. The Indians who guided him to this remote, beautiful lake northwest of Flathead Lake could tell him no name for it, and so he named it in honor of his wife and eldest daughter. He had formed a partnership with Henry Bratnober, who realized a large fortune from the sale of his interest in the Drum Lummon Mine at Marysville, Montana, to raise cattle. Mr. Ronan felt that he could provide for the growing demands of a large family better out of the Indian service, and had decided to retire at the expiration of his term of office in 1893.

In June of that year my husband attended the World's Fair at Chicago and accompanied Vincent and Mary home from school in Oak Park, Illinois. A physical examination revealed such an alarming condition of the heart that the doctors recommended an immediate change to a lower altitude. Since I was too ill to go with him, Major Ronan took Gerald and spent a short time in

Seattle and Victoria. He arrived at home unexpectedly on August 20, 1893. He seemed to be much better and in the best of spirits. That evening he died suddenly. He was laid to rest in St. Mary's cemetery in Missoula. Thus I found myself thrust upon a new, dim, and desolate frontier. My life partner was gone. I had four boys and four girls to rear and educate, slender means, and many legal entanglements. Such a frontier as this, indeed, many another lonely woman has had to find her own way through.

My husband's clerk, Joseph T. Carter, was appointed to finish Major Ronan's term as agent of the confederated tribes of the Flathead Indian Reservation. He was then reappointed for a term of four years with Vincent as his clerk.[59] And so with my children I continued to live at the agency. Scarcely a day passed but some of the Indians came to our house and asked to see Major Ronan. This meant that they wished to be admitted to the room where hung a large portrait of him. Sometimes they knelt before it and prayed. Sometimes they wept, but most often they sat impassively for a long period gazing at the picture of their beloved friend.

In the quaint church of St. John Berchmans just outside the stockade, Mary was married to Joseph T. Carter on August 21, 1895.[60] When Joe's term as agent ended, in 1898, I brought my family to Missoula and made my home here because the University of Montana had been established and thus a college education was a possibility for some of the children. I have lived ever since in the little house on Pine Street where I now reside.

Epilogue

One day in May 1932, I answered a knock at the door of my home. A white man said that some Indians were asking for Mrs. Ronan. I stepped down to the sidewalk. Screened by a large lilac bush lush with blossoms were two miserable, dirty, feeble, old Indian men. One was blind, shockingly so, with empty sockets and shrunken eyelids. His companion handed me a crumpled, soiled piece of paper. It read: "Sisters of the Sacred Heart Academy. Blind Michel wants to see Mrs. Ronan."[61] When I assured him that I was she, Blind Michel put two silver dollars in my hand and clasped it with both of his moist, withered hands. I had difficulty in understanding him or making him understand me because he and his companion were Kootenais and because he could not see my signs and his companion was dull about interpreting them. At last, however, what he was saying became clear. More than forty-five years ago he had stolen a blanket and a hammer from me. (I had never, that I can remember, missed these articles.) He was old now and was going soon to Kolinzooten, God. He let go of my hand, pointed upward, and turned his suffering, sightless face toward the sky. He wished to go with all his earthly accounts settled. He had come to make restitution for his theft. We passed the money back and forth between us a number of times before I made him understand that I thought him a good man, that I liked him, that my heart was good toward him, that his restitution was accepted, and that now I, because I liked him, gave the two dollars back to him as a present. He knelt on the cement walk and sobbed and prayed aloud, asking God to bless me. Finally he went down the street as happy as a child, with one hand on the arm of his companion and the other clasping his two silver dollars. This incident corresponds with my earlier impressions of the innate goodness and honesty of Indian nature.

Over the years I have spent some months with my married daughters at various times in Salt Lake City, in San Francisco, in Santa Cruz, and in Los Angeles. To the east I have never traveled farther than Helena, Montana. Vicariously I have lived wherever the fortunes of my children have led them and thus I have lived more deeply than ever I did as an individual. In the joys and successes of my children I have risen to rapture unknown before. In their suffering, failures, and sorrows I have felt anguish unutterable, not to have been endured but for the faith that through our many tribulations we enter into the kingdom of God.

Notes

Introduction

1. Carolyn Dufurrena, "The Fight to Save Virginia City," *Colonial Williamsburg*, 19 (Winter 1996–97), 29.

2. Paula Petrik, *No Step Backward* (Helena: Montana Historical Society Press, 1987), 96.

3. Michael Leeson, *History of Montana, 1739–1885* (Chicago: Warner, Beers and Company, 1885), 97.

4. See Glenda Riley, "Frontierswomen's Changing Views of Indians in the Trans-Mississippi West," *Montana The Magazine of Western History*, 34 (winter 1984), 20–35.

5. *Daily Missoulian*, May 27, 1935.

Foreword

1. "The Pioneers," in *Contributions to the Montana Historical Society*, 10 vols. (1876; reprint, Helena, Mont.: State Publishing Company, 1903), 4:134 (hereafter *Contributions*).

Book One: Into the Land of Gold

1. The Sheehans lost track of these relatives.

2. Gold was discovered in Gilpin County, Colorado, in 1859.

3. Freighters used a jerk-line in place of reins to guide the lead horse or mule. Ed.

4. Mary Ronan never saw this old Irish drinking song in print. She sang it as her father taught it to her.

5. Herbert Howe Bancroft, *History of Nevada, Colorado, and Wyoming, 1540–1888*, 39 vols. (San Francisco: The History Co., 1890), 25:592. According to Bancroft, gold was discovered in the vicinity of Empire City in 1860, and the

town was surveyed and laid out in town lots and blocks. Katherine E. Sheehan married Phillip Hogan, a farmer, whose property was four miles west of Missoula. The Hogans had two children: Mary, who married Fred Marshall and moved to Los Angeles, and John. Katherine died in 1903.

6. Central City was one of several gold camps clustered in the area in the 1860s. It was named for its central location between the gold camps of Nevada and Black Hawk. Ed.

7. Theatrical performances were well established in Denver by the late 1850s. Ed.

8. Mary's husband's name was Coleman. Paris Pfouts was prominent among the Virginia City vigilantes. See Thomas J. Dimsdale, *Vigilantes of Montana* (1866; reprint, Norman: University of Oklahoma, 1953); and Nathaniel P. Langford, *Vigilante Days and Ways* (1890; reprint, Helena, Mont.: American World Geographic, 1996). Denver in 1863 "wasn't much more than a frontier post, a crowded and disorderly collection of log and clapboard houses, mostly of pitch pine . . . built up solidly on both sides of Cherry Creek and across most of the sands of the creek too. . . . There was a waterway of perhaps ten or twelve feet, while the rest of the land was laid out in town lots. Many of the cabins there had been built up on piles, leaving little clearance for wet weather, and there was a bridge on Blake [Street] about six feet high for floods." R. C. Pitzer, "Fire and Flood in Early Denver," *Frontier*, 14 (January 1934), 148.

9. The line is from C. W. Sanders, *The School Reader*, 3rd ed. (New York, 1869).

10. This familiar excerpt is from "Try, Try Again," in W. H. McGuffey, *New Fourth Eclectic Reader* (Cincinnati, Ohio, 1866), 95.

11. Black Hawk was Chief of the Sacs and Foxes and led the Black Hawk Rebellion in Illinois, 1830–32. Mary lived on the Flathead Indian Reservation from 1877 to 1898; her husband, Peter Ronan, was the Indian agent. Ed.

12. The town of Bannack, later Montana Territory's first capital, sprang up after John White discovered gold there on Grasshopper Creek, July 28, 1862.

13. Bannock, a flat cake made of oatmeal or barley, originated in the British Isles. Travelers on long journeys across the plains made "shanter's bannock" of biscuit dough baked in one large loaf. Ed.

14. Seymour Dunbar and P. C. Phillips, eds., *The Journals and Letters of Major John Owen, Pioneer of the Northwest, 1850–1871*, 2 vols. (New York: E. Eberstadt, 1927), 1:311–15.

15. A few years later, Nelson Story drove the first Texas longhorns into Montana. See Michael P. Malone, Richard B. Roeder, and William L. Lang, *Montana: A History of Two Centuries*, rev. ed. (Seattle: University of Washington, 1991), 148. Story became a wealthy, influential citizen of Bozeman. Leeson, *History of Montana*, 1,163–64. Helen Sanders mentions these burros in Nelson Story's account of the hanging of George Ives. Helen F. Sanders,

History of Montana, 3 vols. (Chicago: Lewis Publishing Company, 1913), 2:868. Ed.

16. Alexander Toponce, *Reminiscences of Alexander Toponce, 1839–1923* (Salt Lake City: Century Printing Co., 1923), 53–56, gives the name of Jack Gallagher among those who made the trip with him, leaving Denver in February 1863 and arriving in Bannack on May 14, 1863. Following Gallagher's name on his list, Toponce notes: "After he got to Montana sided with the hard bunch and was hung." I distinctly remember Jack Gallagher in our party. Mary C. Ronan.

17. Thomas S. Preston, *The Life of Mary Magdalene or The Path to Penitence* (New York: P. O'Shea, 1861).

18. An arrastra is a simple stone mill wheel that sits on a stone-paved floor. Horses, oxen, mules, or men turn the wheel, crushing rock beneath it to release the gold trapped in the rubble. Ed.

19. Bill Fairweather and Henry Edgar panned the first pay dirt on May 26, 1863. In their party were Barney Hughes, Tom Cover, Henry Rodgers, Mike Sweeney, and Lew Simmons. They arrived in Bannack on May 30, 1863. The stampede for Alder Gulch left Bannack on June 2 and arrived in the gulch on June 6.

20. Alder Creek flowed into the Ruby River, formerly known as the Passamari, or Stinkingwater. Lewis and Clark named Stinkingwater the Philanthropy River; it was later called Ruby River for the garnets, or Montana rubies, found nearby. Early maps of Montana give it the name of Passamari, corrupted from the old Indian word Pah-mamar-roi, meaning "cottonwood grove by the water," according to Granville Stuart, *Forty Years on the Frontier*, ed. Paul C. Phillips, 2 vols. (Cleveland, Ohio: Arthur H. Clark Co., 1925), 1:154 n.

21. Langford, *Vigilante Days and Ways*, 127.

22. Dimsdale, *Vigilantes of Montana*, 18, notes that "In his wildest excitement, a mountaineer respects a woman, and anything like an insult offered to a lady would be instantly resented, probably with fatal effect, by any bystander."

23. Frances Gilbert Albright, daughter of Virginia City brewer Henry Gilbert, offers another picture of life. See "A Child in Virginia City, in 1863," in *Way Out West* (Norman: University of Oklahoma Press, 1969), 187–92. Carrie Crane married N. P. Christensen and made her home in Sheridan, Montana. Ed.

24. The Sheehans' cabin is the core of the building that soon became the Goldberg Store. Much later, it became the McGovern Store, and so it is known in Virginia City today. Ed.

25. The description of Jack Gallagher here seems to conflict with Mary Ronan's previous one in "The Long Trek." Langford, *Vigilante Days and Ways*, 164–71, relates much of what is known about Gallagher. Wilbur F. Sanders prosecuted George Ives in a trial held at Nevada City, Montana,

for the murder of Nicholas Thiebalt. Ives was convicted and hanged on December 23, 1863. His trial served as catalyst to the forming of the vigilantes. Henry Plummer was sheriff of the Bannack district and hanged there by the vigilantes on January 10, 1864. Ed.

26. St. Peter's Mission was moved four times within the Sun and Teton watersheds. It was eventually sited on Mission Creek west of Cascade in 1866. Ed.

27. Helen F. Sanders, *History of Montana*, 1:567.

28. Stores in the mining camps stocked rock candy for miners to make rock and rye, a popular drink made of whiskey, rock candy, and fruit. Ed.

29. During the winter of 1863–64, Thomas Dimsdale opened a private school for the children of Alder Gulch. He was also editor of the *Montana Post*, the first newspaper of consequence in the territory. The tiny cabin where Dimsdale held school was moved and preserved at nearby Nevada City. Mary Ronan's textbooks were Sander's *Fifth Reader* and Ray's *Arithmetic*. Dimsdale died on September 22, 1866, of consumption. His grave, surrounded by a wrought iron fence, is in Virginia City's Hillside Cemetery. *Vigilantes of Montana* was the first book published in Montana. See *Rocky Mountain Gazette*, September 28, 1866; and *Contributions*, 1:267, 5:281. Ed.

30. The five were buried side by side in unmarked graves on Boot Hill overlooking Virginia City. The graves were not marked until 1907. See "Road Agents Graves on Boot Hill Remained Unidentified for Years after 1864," *Madisonian*, May 24, 1963. Ed.

31. Margaret Ronan notes, "Though Mary C. Ronan declares that this experience is as clear in her mind as those connected with the historic executions of the five road agents and of Slade, I cannot account for it among the executions which are recorded."

32. The vigilantes hanged Joseph A. "Jack" Slade, former division manager for the Overland Stage, freighter, and local Virginia City character, on March 10, 1864. See Helen F. Sanders, *History of Montana*, 1:229. Also see Harriet Sanders's account of Slade's funeral in W. F. Sanders and Robert W. Taylor, *Biscuits and Badmen: The Sanders Story in Their Own Words* (Butte, Mont.: Editorial Review Press, 1983), 28. Margaret Ronan notes that Mrs. Margaret Gilbert, who came to Virginia City as a sixteen-year-old bride, made the same statement regarding Slade. In June 1930, she recalled that Slade came to Virginia City in the employ of her husband Henry Gilbert, and she expressed resentment at the execution, recalling the incident as if it had happened recently. Ed.

33. Dimsdale, *Vigilantes of Montana*, 136–46, 151–57; Langford, *Vigilante Days and Ways*, 217–23, 231–32. Both describe the capture, confession, and execution of Dutch John Wagner.

34. The Creighton family later endowed Creighton College in Omaha, Nebraska. The Creighton Stone Block is a prominent building on Wallace Street in Virginia City. Ed.

35. Leeson, *History of Montana*, 1,314, discusses Cornelius O'Keefe. Ed.

36. George A. Bruffey, *Eighty-One Years in the West* (Butte, Mont.: The Miner Co., 1925), 51–52, writes: "Early in the spring our flour was scarce, forcing the price to one hundred twenty-five or one hundred fifty dollars per hundred weight caused much alarm. A meeting was called at Jim Ryan's store in Nevada City; about five hundred people attended. Mr. Shinn was chosen chairman. [Undoubtedly Mr. Bruffey means Mr. Sheehan, as he claims to have known Mr. Sheehan well, but always pronounced it "Shin"] The merchants were charged with demanding exorbitant prices for their flour. He [Sheehan] told the people that the roads were impassable to Fort Benton, and that the roads to Salt Lake were snow- and mud-bound, while several freighters had lost their oxen in trying to force the snow-bound passages of the mountains; the owners lay in their teamless wagons waiting for help that was not likely to come." See Dorothy M. Johnson, "Flour Famine in Alder Gulch, 1864," *Montana The Magazine of Western History*, 7 (winter 1957), 18–27. Ed.

37. Granville Stuart and his brother James were among the first white prospectors and miners in Montana. They prospected along Gold Creek between 1858 and 1862. Mary here mentions Granville's first wife, Aubony (Awbonny), a member of the Snake Indian tribe. The couple married on May 2, 1862, and together they had nine children. Aubony died in 1887. Ed.

38. Harriet Sanders herself tells of this in W. F. Sanders and Taylor, *Biscuits and Badmen*, 27. W. F. Sanders was prosecutor of George Ives and a founder of the vigilantes. Their charming home still stands on Idaho Street in Virginia City. Ed.

39. In January 1865, the two fighters went 185 rounds, the longest recorded bare-knuckle fight. See W. J. Brier, *The Frightful Punishment* (Missoula: University of Montana Press, 1969). Ed.

40. Martha Plassman writes about the Fourth of July in 1865 in *Rocky Mountain Husbandman*, July 28, 1928.

41. The discovery date was actually July 14, 1864. Ed.

42. There are different versions of this story. See Vivian Paladin, "Naming Helena," in *More from the Quarries of Last Chance Gulch*, 3 vols. (Helena, Mont.: Independent Record, 1996), 2:122–27. Ed.

43. A. K. McClure, *3,000 Miles Through the Rocky Mountains* (Philadelphia: J. B. Lippincott and Co., 1869), 285.

44. See Peter Ronan's humorous telling of the incident in *Sunday Oregonian*, October 7, 1928. For the history of camels in the gold camps, see Ellen Baumler, "When Camels Came Back to Montana," *Montana The Magazine of Western History*, 50 (autumn 1999), 64–71. Ed.

45. Mary Ronan presumably means Professor T. F. Campbell, who taught Helena's first public school on the corner of Broadway and Rodney. See Sallie Davenport's memoirs (Mrs. A. J. Davidson) and her recollection of the school and Professor Campbell in Small Collection 606, Sallie Davenport Davidson Reminiscence, 1865–1928, Montana Historical Society Archives, Helena, Montana (hereafter SC 606, MHSA). Ed.

46. On Helena's hanging tree, see Jon Axline, "A Monument of Terror to Desperadoes," in *More from the Quarries of Last Chance Gulch*, 3:92–96. Ed.

47. *Rocky Mountain Gazette*, July 27, 1867. Ed.

48. SC 606, MHSA. Ed.

49. See Merrill G. Burlingame and K. Ross Toole, eds., *A History of Montana*, 2 vols. (New York: Lewis Historical Publishing Co., 1957), 2:189–299 on Couldock and 2:191–314 on theater in general. Ed.

50. Civil War hero and popular lecturer, Meagher was appointed secretary of Montana Territory in 1865 and became acting governor in 1866. His actions in Montana were highly controversial and his death mysterious. Meagher disappeared off a steamboat docked at Fort Benton, July 1, 1866. The *Rocky Mountain Gazette*, February 9, 1867, reports $1,600 was taken in during this lecture at the People's Theater. Ed.

51. Superstition held that a child born with a "veil" or "cowl" like Mary Ronan describes possessed psychic abilities. James Francis Sheehan left Missoula in 1898 and was not heard from again. He does not appear in the 1900 Montana census. The reason for his disappearance was unknown to his family. Ed.

52. Dolly Varden, a character in Dickens's *Barnaby Rudge* (1841), inspired this lavishly embellished style. Ed.

53. Massena Bullard became a prominent Helena attorney.

54. Neil Howie single-handedly arrested road agent Dutch John Wagner, January 2, 1864, as Dimsdale described in his *Vigilantes*, 136–46. See the *Rocky Mountain Gazette*, January 12, 1867, for a description of winter sledding in Helena.

55. The popular hot springs was two miles west of Helena along Ten Mile Creek, near the later site of the renowned Broadwater Hotel and Natatorium. Ed.

56. James Whitlatch was the discoverer of the Whitlatch-Union Mine at Unionville. Ed.

57. L. B. Palladino, S.J., *Indian and White in the Northwest* (Baltimore: John Murphy and Co., 1894), 287–92, describes the arrival of the Sisters of Charity in Helena.

58. Palladino, *Indian and White*, 279 ff.

59. These are all well-known, early-day Helena residents. On future copper king W. A. Clark's Helena business, see Helen F. Sanders, *History of Montana*, 2:855. Ed.

60. Bill and Ellen Tiernan had three daughters. A son died in 1871. Bill died in 1887 of pneumonia, and Ellen lived in Sheridan, Montana, until her death after 1900. Ed.

BOOK TWO: YOUTH AND ROMANCE

1. According to a clipping in Mary Ronan's scrapbook, Martin Maginnis made this statement in a toast at the third annual meeting of the Montana Press Association in 1888. Maginnis and his wife, Louise, were close friends of the Ronans. He was a prominent and influential territorial figure who served six terms as territorial delegate to Congress (1872–84) and played key roles in drafting the legislation that brought the railroads to Montana and opened reservation lands to settlement. Maginnis was a delegate to the constitutional convention of 1889 and had a national reputation as an orator. His extensive obituary is in the *Butte Miner*, March 3, 1919. Ed.

2. It was this meeting that eventually helped bring the Sisters of Charity and, later, Mother Vincent herself to Montana. Ed.

3. In 1862, Idaho was part of the Territory of Washington. Congress created Idaho Territory with its capital in Lewiston in March 1863 just before the discovery at Alder Gulch. Montana Territory was created on May 26, 1864, on the first anniversary of the Alder Gulch discovery made by Henry Edgar and Bill Fairweather. Peter Ronan told his own account of the discovery and the resulting stampede in an address he delivered at the first meeting of the Society of Montana Pioneers on September 9, 1884, collected in *Contributions*, 3:143–54. Ed.

4. Virginia City property record files, housed as the Montana Historical Society Library, show that Peter Ronan disposed of his Madison County claims in May and October of 1865. Jim Ronan's name does not appear in the transactions. Ed.

5. The first newspaper of substance in Montana Territory was the *Montana Post*, first published on August 26, 1864. Ed.

6. See J. Beadle, *The Undeveloped West* (Philadelphia: National Publishing Co., 1873), 122, for this epithet. Other towns made the same claim. Fort Benton, Montana, dubbed the "Chicago of the Plains." Ed.

7. Owen Meredith, a pseudonym for Edward Robert, First Earl of Lytton, published *Lucile* in 1860. He was a prolific writer, once called "third among living poets." *Lucile* was a lengthy novel set to verse glorifying the heroine and women in general: ". . . born to nurse, /And to soothe, and to solace, to help and to heal / The sick world that leans on her. This was Lucile." Ed.

8. As late as 1875, J. A. Graves wrote, "The streets, nothing paved, were seas of vile-smelling mud in winter-time, and were full of suffocating dust in summer notwithstanding constant sprinkling." J. A. Graves, *My Seventy Years in California, 1857–1927* (Los Angeles: Times-Mirror Press), 114. Carey McWilliams wrote, "Southern California was as remote from the rest of the country, in 1869, as a foreign country or an island." Carey McWilliams, *Southern California Country* (New York: Duell, Sloan and Pearce, 1946), 115. C. D. Willard, *The Herald's History of Los Angeles* (Los Angeles: Kingsley-Barnes and Neuner Co., 1901), 270, reports the population at 5,614 according to the 1870 census. Ed.

9. An earthquake in 1812 destroyed the mission, but the beautiful ruins stand today. Ed.

10. Mexico ceded California to the United States in 1848 and California became a state in 1850. San Juan Capistrano was the site of one of the twenty-three missions set up under the leadership of Father Junipero Serra along the mission road, El Camino Real. San Juan Capistrano was established in spring 1776; legend persists that swallows leave San Juan Capistrano on St. John's Day, October 23, and return on St. Joseph's Day, March 19. Ed.

11. Although no documentation for this claim has come to light, it was not uncommon for California squatter's claims to be heard in the United States Supreme Court. Maginnis (see 229 n. 1) was indeed an eloquent speaker well known in Washington, D.C., and knowledgeable in the law. His close friendship with the Sheehans and the Ronans make Mary Ronan's assertion quite plausible. Ed.

12. "In the seasons of 1869–1870 and 1870–1871 there was little rainfall—a total of only ten inches for the whole period." Willard, *Herald's History of Los Angeles*, 304.

13. Annie Brown later entered the order of the Sisters of Charity of Leavenworth, Kansas.

14. Mary sent this clipping, preserved in the Ronan scrapbook, to Peter Ronan. It went on to say, "Among those present we noticed . . . the redoubtable Richard Egan, Señor Don Juan Avila, and the acknowledged belle of Capistrano, Miss Mollie Sheehan."

15. Don Juan (John) Forster acquired Pio Pico's rancho Santa Margarita y las Flores in 1864 for $14,000. Forster also agreed to assume his brother-in-law's extensive gambling debts in return for the deed. Thus Forster became the largest landowner in California. He eventually owned over 200,000 acres. The ranch house Mary visited began as a two-room house built before 1827. Forster remodeled it and added many rooms arranged around a beautiful, flower-filled courtyard. When Forster died in 1882 the ranch was sold to James Flood and Richard O'Neill. The two families retained ownership until 1942 when the United States government purchased a major part of it for use as a training facility. This became Camp Pendleton. The historic Forster home is today a high-ranking official's residence. Ed.

16. *Los Angeles Tidings*, June 19, 1931, reported that Cave J. Couts celebrated his seventy-fifth birthday at the house on the Cuajome (Guajome) ranch near Vista in San Diego County where he was born. His father, Colonel Cave Johnson Couts, settled there in 1851 and made a fortune in cattle ranching. Rancho Guajome, the twenty-room adobe ranch house, where author Helen Hunt Jackson (1830–1885) gathered material for her 1884 novel *Ramona*, is a National Historic Landmark. See Willard, *Herald's History of Los Angeles*, 222, for a story about how Señora Bandini made the first American flag in California. Ed.

17. E. M. Herstory, "The Alcalde of San Juan Capistrano," *Los Angeles Times Illustrated Magazine*, June 10, 1923.

18. Robert Field Stockton commanded the Pacific squadron in the Mexican War and aided in the taking of California.

19. Willard, *Herald's History of Los Angeles*, 278–88, discusses the culmination of a long era of violence and lawlessness among warring Chinese societies on October 24, 1871. A mob of five hundred looted Chinatown and slaughtered nineteen Chinese.

20. According to Willard, *Herald's History of Los Angeles*, 306, St. Vincent's College at Broadway and Sixth was established in 1866.

21. Palladino, *Indian and White*, 288, wrote that Rose Kelly, "a young lady of rare musical talents," was the lay teacher who had come with the first Sisters of Charity of Leavenworth, Kansas, to Helena to found St. John's Hospital in 1869. Sometime after Downey's Spanish wife died, Mary Ronan asserts that Rose Kelly became his second wife. However, others report that Downey never recovered from the shock of losing his first wife, who was killed along with numerous others in a horrific train wreck in 1883. He died in Los Angeles in 1893. Ed.

22. This is the same picnic described in the previous chapter and 230 n. 14. Ed.

23. The pressed bouquet, just as Peter had it framed, was still in Mary's possession in 1932.

24. Margaret Ronan included her mother's lengthy graduation address. It is here omitted but may be found in the *Los Angeles Star*, June 15, 1872. Ed.

25. *Anaconda Standard*, November 13, 1891. Between 1869 and 1874, nine disastrous fires destroyed much of the early business district. Ed.

26. *Rocky Mountain Gazette*, December 16, 1872. The reference to orange blossoms, the well-known symbol of brides and weddings, made Peter's intent to marry obvious. Ed.

27. Peter was thirty at the time of his marriage; Mary was twenty.

28. "I carried this money all the way to San Francisco for him. Why it was entrusted to my husband and me I do not know. It would seem from my journal that my responsibility did not rest heavily upon me." Mary C. Ronan.

29. Here the diary breaks off. "I remember that I kept it throughout the journey to Helena and for some time after we had made our home there. It is not strange that the rest of it was lost, but it is strange that these few pages have been preserved through the vicissitudes of these many years since those penciled words were scribbled." Mary C. Ronan.

30. James Whitlatch made a fortune with the discovery of the Whitlatch-Union Mine at Unionville in 1865, the first gold-bearing quartz discovered in southwestern Montana. Impoverished in 1890, he committed suicide in San Francisco. Ed.

31. The *polonaise*, revived from an earlier period, was a coat-like combination of bodice and cutaway overskirt popular in 1871–72; a *basque* was a fitted bodice, often with an extension over a skirt. Ed.

32. As early as 1864, the *Montana Post* advertised a run of four days by

stagecoach from Virginia City, Montana, to Salt Lake City, Utah. According to Thomas J. Schlereth, *Victorian America: Transformations in Everyday Life, 1876–1915* (New York: HarperCollins Publishers, 1991), 21, "the epizootic of 1872 claimed almost a quarter of the nation's horses (over 4 million) and brought the country to a virtual standstill." The epidemic was somewhat milder in the West, and Mary Ronan's experience with the epizootic came in January 1873 at the end of the epidemic when cold weather eradicated the mosquito-borne virus. Ed.

33. Carrie Adell Strahorn, *Fifteen Thousand Miles by Stage* (New York: G. P. Putnam's Sons, 1915), vividly describes the conditions of traveling through Montana during the 1870s. Ed.

34. John Caplice was Peter Ronan's partner in Alder Gulch and good friend. Pioneer attorney Joseph K. Toole was territorial governor when Montana achieved statehood in 1889 and was elected governor again twice, serving from 1900 until his resignation in 1908. Ed.

35. I remember well that I wore the brown silk poplin with the little gold stripe. Mary C. Ronan.

36. L. F. LaCroix was an accountant for the *Gazette*.

37. Lawrence Benedict Palladino, professor of Latin and Greek, writer, and Jesuit priest, came to the Bitterroot Valley in 1867 to work among the Flathead Indians. He was long associated with St. Ignatius Mission, with parishes in Helena and Missoula, and well known to Montana's early Catholic community. He died in Missoula, Montana, on August 19, 1927, at the age of ninety. Mary Ronan notes: "The crucifix carried for seventy-five years by my beloved Father Palladino is now in my possession." Father Anthony Ravalli came to the Bitterroot Valley in 1845 and helped build St. Mary's Mission. Father Pierre-Jean De Smet and the other Jesuits sold the mission to John Owen in 1850, but Father Ravalli returned in 1866 and remained among the Flathead until 1884. Ravalli County was named to honor this man of many talents. Ed.

38. Daniel S. Tuttle came to Virginia City in 1867 as the bishop of a large diocese that included Idaho, Montana, and Utah. He conducted the first Episcopal services in the territory at Virginia City, traveling twelve thousand miles by horseback, stage, and on foot during his first diocesan visit. The well-loved Reverend Tuttle remained a prominent religious figure throughout his tenure in Montana. In 1880 the huge diocese was divided, and Tuttle went to the western half; he became bishop of Missouri in 1886. Ed.

39. Leeson, *History of Montana*, 717, corroborates this information.

40. The Little Blackfoot River country is east of the Continental Divide and thirty miles west of Helena, Montana. Mines opened there in 1865. Ed.

41. Dr. William Steele, known as Montana's "grand old man of medicine," practiced in Helena from 1864 until well after the turn of the twentieth century. He was very active in the community, serving as county sheriff and

county treasurer, ten years as county coroner, and three terms as mayor. He was also elected to the state legislature. Dr. J. S. Glick came to Bannack in 1862 and practiced medicine in Helena from the mid-1860s. Ed.

42. John Owen was the first agent appointed to the Flathead Indians in 1856. The agent's role was to represent the government in its dealings with American Indians. Owen was an honest man who advocated for his charges, but agents were often ill prepared and consequently did a poor job. The government did not make relations easy. Owen resigned in bitter frustration in 1862. After a succession of agents, Charles S. Medary was appointed in 1875 after the suspension of agent Peter Whaley. Medary was so hated by the Indians that an armed guard under Lieutenants Scofield and Fuller was sent to the agency for his protection. Lieutenant Fuller found a sad state of affairs, reported his findings, and Agent Medary was removed. Peter Ronan was appointed to fill the unexpired term. The Flathead Indian Reservation, formerly known as the Jocko Reservation, today includes the Jocko and Flathead valleys and the Camas Prairie country in northwestern Montana. Part of it was opened to white settlement in 1910. The town of Spring Creek, in present-day Lake County, was renamed Ronan for Peter Ronan. Ed.

43. H. A. Lambert, a pioneer founder of St. Paul, Minnesota, had come to Montana in 1871 as clerk of the United States Army. He had later been appointed agriculturalist or "head farmer" for the Flathead Indians.

BOOK THREE: LIFE AMONG THE FLATHEAD

1. The Pend d'Oreille River on this stretch is now the Flathead River. Ed.

2. The mission school at St. Ignatius was founded in 1864 and maintained by free-will offerings until it became a contract school in 1876. Palladino, *Indian and White*, 271. Ed.

3. Mary Ronan did not provide the source of this quotation. Duncan McDonald was the son of Angus McDonald, an early Northwest trader who operated in the Flathead and Clark Fork valleys. Angus was factor at nearby Fort Connah, established by the British Hudson's Bay Company in 1846. The fort operated in the twilight of the fur trade era, escaping scrutiny when the 1846 Oregon Treaty established United States ownership of land below the forty-ninth parallel. It was allowed to operate because it dealt in items difficult to acquire such as hair cordage, buffalo blankets, and rawhide. Duncan was its last factor when the fort finally closed in 1871. Angus McDonald eventually bought Fort Connah and died there in 1889. The single building that remains at Fort Connah is Montana's oldest standing log structure. For a fascinating history of the McDonald family, see James Hunter, *Scottish Highlanders, Indian Peoples: Thirty Generations of a Montana Family* (Helena: Montana Historical Society Press, 1998). Ed.

4. Throughout Mary Ronan's memoirs, Indian words and names are spelled phonetically as the Ronans learned from the Indians to pronounce them. Ed.

5. The six commissions were signed by presidents and secretaries of the interior Rutherford B. Hayes and Carl Schurz, Chester A. Arthur and L. I. Kukiny, Grover Cleveland and S. Q. C. Lamar (twice), and Benjamin Harrison and J. W. Noble.

6. The appointee was required to post a bond to show his honorable intentions. The twenty thousand dollar bond Peter Ronan posted as agent was signed on February 18, 1878, by Peter Ronan and John Caplice in the presence of John Sheehan and by Christopher P. Higgins and Francis L. Worden in the presence of Alfred J. Urlin. Franklin H. Woody's name is signed as the notary public. The latter four men were all early Missoula pioneers.

7. The Missoula River was the same as the Clark Fork River. Ed.

8. Mollie married Kenneth Ross, general manager of the Anaconda Copper Mining plant at Bonner.

9. "The person responsible for the name of the Jocko was Jim Finn. He established himself on its banks before the year 1840, and the stream came to be known as Jim's Fork. Then the Jesuit priest, Father De Smet, settled in the neighborhood and, following his own language, he called it Jacques' Fort, which was finally contracted to Jocko." *New York Daily Sun*, August 15, 1883.

10. Mount Ronan was the name given to this peak by the Transcontinental Survey Commission, but Peter Ronan always called it Finnerty's Wart after J. T. Finnerty, editor of the *Irish Citizen* and special correspondent to the *Chicago Times* who visited the agency.

11. Ovando Hoyt later left the agency and took up a farm near the town of Ovando, Montana, named for him.

12. Peter Ronan's scheme for educating and making useful citizens of the Indians was to use all the government facilities in giving practical demonstrations in building, farming, dairying, stock raising, and various handicrafts.

13. This was the Nez Perce War of 1877. Ed.

14. For the Nez Perce War from the Indian point of view, see Allen P. Slickapoo, *Noon Ne-Me-Poo (We, the Nez Perces) Culture and History of the Nez Perces* (Lapwai, Idaho: Nez Perce Tribe, 1973); for a general study of the war, see Jerome A. Greene, *Nez Perce Summer, 1877: The U.S. Army and the Nee-Me-Poo Crisis* (Helena: Montana Historical Society Press, 2000). See also Helena Addison Howard's thorough account in the chapter on Charlot in *Northwest Blazers* (Caldwell, Idaho: Caxton Printers, Ltd., 1963). Ed.

15. Spiritualism, belief that the spirits of the dead survive after life to communicate with the living, was in vogue in some circles during the late nineteenth century. Ed.

16. This was later called Fort Fizzle. Ed.

17. The Kootenai Trail, according to David Thompson's early maps, started where the Thompson River flows into the Clark Fork River, followed it downstream to its merging with the Kootenai River, then went along that river into Canada. Thompson marked this trail "Kootenae Road." Indians certainly did not always follow the same routes, although likely the routes were approximate. M. Catherine White, *David Thompson's Journals Relating to Montana and Adjacent Regions* (Missoula: Montana State University Press, 1950), 22 n, 120 n, 121 n. Mary Ronan has the trail ascending the Clark Fork to the Jocko River thence into Canada. Ed.

18. Leeson, *History of Montana*, 138.

19. Peter Ronan, *The History of the Flatheads* (Helena, Mont.: Journal Publishing Co., 1890), 5; Helen F. Sanders, *History of Montana*, 265.

20. Looking Glass was killed during the battle with General Nelson Miles in the Bears Paw Mountains, October 1–5, 1877.

21. "Joseph moved his entire possessions of effects and families between the forces of Rawn and those at Missoula, within gunshot of the former, crossed his line of communication, camped almost upon the trail, and with unparalleled intrepidity on open ground in the face of superior numbers and in the enemy's country." Leeson, *History of Montana*, 141.

22. The Northwest Territory was a British possession in 1877, hence the term "British Miles" refers to the land north of the present-day Canadian border. The Bears Paw Mountains are near the Canadian border, south of present-day Havre. Ed.

23. Chief Joseph died there September 22, 1904.

24. This is a distance of about twenty-five miles. Ed.

25. Cadotte Pass leads over the main range of the Rockies southeast of the Elk Fork of the North Fork of the Sun River.

26. Spokane Carez was also called Spokane Carry. He was sent by Hudson's Bay Company to Red River to be educated. He spoke English and French and acted as interpreter for the Protestant missions. He died in Spokane in 1892. Governor Stevens said he was "a man of judgment, foresight and great reliability."

27. Lieutenant Tom Wallace, nicknamed "Handsome Tom," drowned a short time later while attempting to cross the Missoula River on horseback a few miles below the Fort. *Anaconda Standard*, March 6, 1892.

28. Peter Ronan reported to Governor Potts on July 14, 1878. The report is printed in full in *The Frontier*, 10 (November 1929), 79. Ed.

29. Fort Ellis was near present-day Bozeman, Montana. Ed.

30. Mrs. Lambert was the wife of the agency agriculturalist, H. A. Lambert. See 233 n. 43. Dr. L. H. Choquette was a graduate of Victoria College in Coburg, Ontario. He and his wife, Hermine, were natives of Montreal. They arrived in Missoula on July 4, 1877, and he was appointed agency physician in August. The Choquettes remained at the agency until

1882 when the family returned to Missoula. There Dr. Choquette opened a successful drugstore and private medical practice. Leeson, *History of Montana*, 1,302. Ed.

31. Dave Polson was an old Hudson's Bay Company man who resigned to conduct a store at the foot of the Flathead Lake. The present town of Polson is named for him.

32. F. L. Worden and A. B. Hammond were prominent Missoulians. Ed.

33. The title "Major" was entirely complimentary. Ed.

34. The building was later used as an officers' club. Fort Missoula was a place of pleasant assignment for the soldiers stationed there. The Battle of the Big Hole in August 1877 and a skirmish in 1878, in which soldiers killed six Indians involved in stealing stock, were the soldiers' only serious encounters. Ed.

35. The Sisters of Providence of Montreal established the school at St. Ignatius in 1864.

36. Arlee was the Indian attempt at the French pronunciation of Henri, the name by which the Jesuits had christened him. Ed.

37. In *Montana Adventure, the Recollections of Frank B. Linderman* (Lincoln: University of Nebraska Press, 1968), 42 n. 3, Linderman writes that Aeneas was a full-blooded Iroquois, likely named by the missionaries after Aeneas of the *Iliad* because the old chief was also a man without a country. Linderman states that "of all the Indians I have known, he was the only one with whom I had trouble." Ed.

38. See 233 n. 3 on Angus MacDonald.

39. In summer 1878 Sam Walking Coyote, a Pend d'Oreille chief, drove six buffalo calves from Milk River country over Cadotte Pass of the Continental Divide to the Flathead region. Here he built a herd of twenty buffalo, which he sold in 1884 to Charles Allard and Michel Pablo. From this herd came the buffalo on the American National Bison Preserve near Moiese, Montana. The preserve was established, in part, through the efforts of M. J. Elrod of the University of Montana. See Burlingame and Toole, *History of Montana*, 2:21–22. According to trader Charles Aubrey, Walking Coyote was married to a Pend d'Oreille woman but had an affair with a Blackfoot woman. He tamed several buffalo calves to make amends, and these were the beginnings of the herd. See Robert Bigart, ed., *"I Will Be Meat for My Salish": The Montana Writers Project and the Buffalo of the Flathead Indian Reservation* (Helena: Montana Historical Society Press, 2001), 265. Ed.

40. General Thomas James, *Three Years among the Indians and Mexicans* (St. Louis: Missouri Historical Society, 1916), 53. "The Flatheads are a noble race of men, brave, generous and hospitable." Flathead, however, is a misnomer. Salish means "the People" and is the Indian name for the tribe whose ancestral home was in the Bitterroot, Mission, and Jocko valleys.

41. Lewis and Clark likened the uniquely guttural Salish language to a "brogue," and thought perhaps the Salish were descendants of the Welsh king Madoc who, according to persistent legends, settled in North America in 1170 A.D. See Clark's journal entry for September 5, 1805, and Bernard De Voto, *The Course of Empire* (Boston: Houghton Mifflin Company, 1952), 68–73. The Gaelic songs Mary learned at her father's knee likely prepared her to acquire the Salish language more easily than she might have otherwise. Ed.

42. Peter Ronan gave this account to his kinsman, Bernard Corr, a Boston newspaperman, for publication in the *Boston Pilot*. Ed.

43. This is from an article by Peter Ronan that appeared in the *Deer Lodge New North-West*, August 8, 1879.

44. The church, however, was not built for several years and was dedicated under the name of St. John Berchmans, August 4, 1889.

45. Archbishop Seghers resigned the Archiepiscopal See of Oregon in 1884 to return to his former diocese on Vancouver Island. After an extended tour of Europe, he was returning home on November 28, 1886, when his attendant shot him dead. His remains were transported to Helena where he was interred in the burial vault at the Cathedral of the Sacred Heart. Palladino, *Indian and White*, 422–23. Ed.

46. I went to see Agnes in Polson in 1928. I was told that I might find her down on the bridge fishing. As we strolled back to her cottage, she told me how good her husband had been to her, of his sudden death, of her unutterable loneliness. She ended with a deep sigh, "I forget a little sometimes when I am down at the river fishing." Mary C. Ronan.

47. Mary Ronan's recollection of the date is not quite accurate. Notice of Baird's murder and his obituary actually appeared in the *Deer Lodge New North-West*, December 12, 1884, from a dispatch dated December 5. The crime occurred a few days previous. Ed.

48. Malcolm Clarke, longtime trader who in his youth was expelled from West Point and came west, was murdered and his son wounded by his wife's kinsmen in a dispute over horses in 1869. Clarke was buried at his ranch near Helena. The site of Clarke's grave and homestead are part of the present-day headquarters of the Sieben Ranch near Helena. Ed.

49. Mary Ronan's pages of correspondence with Father Ravalli are included in Margaret Ronan's original text. Only this brief excerpt is included here. Ed.

50. The driving of the golden spike took place at Gold Creek, Montana, on September 8, 1883. See Malone, Roeder, and Lang, *Montana: A History of Two Centuries*, 177. Ed.

51. In the summer of 1882, Koonsa (Kuntza) murdered Frank Marengo, a half Nez Perce interpreter at Fort Missoula. Agent Ronan had a posse arrest Koonsa, but the posse took the prisoner to Chief Arlee's home where he was tried and sentenced under Indian law to jail time and fined ten horses.

There was a dispute, however, over legal jurisdiction, and Ronan retrieved Koonsa and took him to jail in Missoula. The case was thrown out in court because the judge ruled that a man could not be tried twice. Koonsa went free. The Deer Lodge *New North-West*, January 12, 1883, recorded Chief Arlee's testimony. Arlee maintained, "When an Indian is drunk and kills another Indian we don't consider he did anything. The Indian never had whiskey before the white man came here, and we blame white people who gave him the liquor." Ed.

52. Joseph was not sent to the Lapwai Reservation in the Wallowa region of Oregon but to the Colville Indian Reservation in Washington in 1885. Ed.

53. Arlee and Adolf put their signatures on the Garfield Treaty of 1872, but Charlot refused to sign. His signature is not on the original document. The government, however, allowed reports to the contrary to be published. See Malone, Roeder, and Lang, *Montana: A History of Two Centuries*, 121–22. Ed.

54. This correspondence, not included here, is preserved in Margaret Ronan's original thesis. Ed.

55. François Saxa's father, Ignace, was leader of the delegation that went to St. Louis in 1835 to persuade the Jesuits to come among the Flathead. François accompanied his father. In an interesting aside, Mary Ronan related that months after Peter Ronan's death, François came to her and handed her eight dollars, which he said the White Chief had loaned him some time before. Ed.

56. The description is included in Palladino, *Indian and White*, 77; and in A. L. Stone, *Following Old Trails* (Missoula, Mont.: M. J. Elrod, 1913), 89.

57. Charlot died at Jocko Agency on January 10, 1910.

58. Both Mrs. Custer and Alice Palmer Henderson visited the agency in 1890. The article was in the *Northwest Magazine*, August 1890. Mary C. Ronan.

59. Vincent died in Los Angeles, October 20, 1930.

60. Joseph Carter died in Los Angeles, May 11, 1931.

61. The Sisters of Providence of Montreal at the Sacred Heart Academy were two blocks away; this Michel is not the same Michel as the interpreter Mary Ronan described previously. Ed.

Index